IF THESE OVARIES COULD TALK

THE THINGS WE'VE LEARNED ABOUT MAKING AN
LGBTQ FAMILY

IF THESE OVARIES COULD TALK

THE THINGS WE'VE LEARNED ABOUT MAKING AN LGBTQ FAMILY

Jaimie Kelton and Robin Hopkins

LIT RIOT PRESS
BROOKLYN, NY

Published by Lit Riot Press, LLC
Brooklyn, NY
www.litriotpress.com

Book and cover design by Lit Riot Press, LLC
If These Ovaries Could Talk logo design by Mary Littell

Library of Congress Control Number: 2020931935

Publisher's Cataloging-in-Publication Data

Names: Kelton, Jaimie. Hopkins, Robin.
Title: If These Ovaries Could Talk: The Things We've Learned About Making An LGBTQ Family / Jaimie Kelton and Robin Hopkins.
Identifiers: LCCN 2020931935 | ISBN 978-0-9992943-9-0 (pbk.) | ISBN 978-0-9992943-7-6 (hardcover) | ISBN 978-0-9992943-6-9 (Kindle ebook).
Subjects: LCSH: Lesbian-parent families. | Lesbian couples as parents. | Lesbian mothers. | Gay parents. | Children of gay parents. | Same-sex parents. | Children of same-sex parents. | BISAC: FAMILY & RELATIONSHIPS / LGBT. | FAMILY & RELATIONSHIPS / Alternative Family. | FAMILY & RELATIONSHIPS / Parenting / Motherhood. | HUMOR / Topic / LGBT. | HUMOR / Topic / Marriage & Family.
Classification: LCC HQ759.915.K45 2020 (print) | LCC HQ759.915 (ebook) | DDC 305.85--dc23.
LC record available at https://lccn.loc.gov/2020931935.

To our wives, Mary, and Anne, for their never-ending love and support, and also for handling all the dinner making, bath taking, and homework checking while we were off creating.

And to our kids, Maxine, Henry, Rose, and Orion. You're the reason all of this exists.

ACKNOWLEDGEMENTS

Thanks to our publisher, Ben Taylor, for taking a chance on our ovaries and trusting us to make sense in book form. While we're at it, we'd like to thank all the good folks at Lit Riot Press who painstakingly added comas, removed commas, and never once lectured us on where the period goes when using quotes.

The word "thanks" will never be enough for Barbara Volterra, Brett Henne, and Erin Kelly, otherwise known as Writer's Group. We're forever indebted to them for their encouragement, creative development notes, polite suggestions, and for being available to us 24/7 for tweaks and twerks.

Love and gratitude to all our loyal listeners who helped transform our little idea into a much larger project that just keeps on growing.

Thank you to all the guests who appeared on the *If These Ovaries Could Talk* podcast. You shared your journeys with us and made this book possible. But more importantly, you shared your stories with the world. They were funny, heartwarming, engaging, sometimes sad, always uplifting, and downright inspiring.

And while we're thanking folks involved in the podcast (who started this whole thing), we have to thank our fearless editor, Steph Colbourn, from EDITAUDIO. Each week, she helps us create a cohesive story, highlighting and shining a spotlight on our guests while cutting the parts where we ramble on.

Thanks to Tom Calderone for his guidance, love, support, and for being the very first industry exec to believe in us. Oh, and for letting us glom onto all his hard-earned business smarts.

A huge thanks to Jaimie's mom, Mama Sue. This book wouldn't be complete without one more mention of her.

And last, but not least, we have to thank Jaimie's bout of infertility for leading us to the idea of creating a podcast about our families. That led to Robin's 5,000 Google docs, which led to a book, which led to a community and, dare we say it, a movement.

TABLE OF CONTENTS

FOREWORD   11

AUTHORS' NOTE   13

WELCOME TO OUR BOOK   15

PART ONE: MAKING A BABY WHEN YOU ARE
            AN L, G, B, T, OR Q   21

Chapter 1: Deciding You Want to Make an LGBTQ
            Family   23

Chapter 2: Your Path: How Do You Make Your
            Family?   44

Chapter 3: Choosing an Egg Donor, Sperm
            Donor or Surrogate   61

Chapter 4: The Scientific Route: Paths and Pitfalls   97

Chapter 5: Adoption and Foster Care   120

Chapter 6: Trans and Fertility   151

Chapter 7: Money and Your LGBTQ Family   163

PART TWO: YOUR LGBTQ FAMILY HAS A BABY:
NOW WHAT?   180

Chapter 8: Being Out as a Family   181

Chapter 9: Talking to Your Kids About Their Family   201

Chapter 10: All Types of Families   219

Chapter 11: Non-bio, Adoptive, and Step Parents   240

Chapter 12: Intersectionality: Race, Religion and
            Gender Fluidity   258

Chapter 13: The Legalese of LGBTQ Families   280

Chapter 14: Growing Up with Gay Parents   304

Chapter 15: Our Families Are Just Like Yours   322

GLOSSARY OF TERMS   327

GUEST APPEARANCES   331

IF THESE OVARIES COULD TALK PODCAST   333

JAIMIE KELTON   344

ROBIN HOPKINS   345

CONNECT WITH IF THESE OVARIES COULD TALK   346

FOREWORD

Judy Gold

The great Harvey Milk said, "We will not win our rights by staying quietly in our closets." But the truth is that even when we storm out of the closet and slam the door shut, we still have to come out every single day. Why? Because people constantly make assumptions, and then voice them. Loudly. Whenever my partner Elysa and I check into a hotel, the person at the front desk asks if we'd like to change our king deluxe room for one with two queen beds. When we decline the offer, the next question is, "Are you sisters?" Yes! Really close sisters! I'm 6'2" and Elysa is 5'5". I have quite a large schnoz and Elysa has a perfectly shaped nose because of rhinoplasty. We look nothing alike. Yet we're sisters who travel and sleep together in a king-size bed. Sisters of Sappho.

When you are LGBTQ and you add children to the equation, the comments and assumptions get even worse. One afternoon when my sons were young, I brought them to one playground in Riverside Park. A parent who was there asked me if I was planning on raising my boys as homosexuals. Absolutely! The only music we allow them to listen to is show tunes, and since we live in a one-bedroom apartment, they'll be spending the first 18 years of their lives in the closet. And this happened in New York City! How does that even make any sense? Did my straight parents raise me to be a lesbian?

Since I'm a very tall stand-up comic, I'm used to people making stupid comments to me like, "Wow! You ARE tall." Did they think I was lying about my height when I was on stage? Often, when I'm with my younger son who happens to be six foot eight inches tall (yes, he plays basketball), someone will, without a doubt, ask the seemingly innocuous question, "How tall is his father?"Simple, right? Nope. Nothing is simple when you are a member of an LGBTQ family. "Normal" questions can open up a can of sperm. I mean worms.

He doesn't have a father. He has 2 mothers.

He doesn't have a father. He has a sperm donor who is 6'3".

Father? What's that?

Please don't ask me if his father plays basketball.

So how can we avoid these awkward situations? Do yourself a favor and learn all you can about how LGBTQ families are created. Become knowledgeable about people whose families look different from yours, and maybe you'll figure out we're not so different after all. Look, none of our kids are mistakes— it's not like we got drunk one night and started dialing up the sperm bank. We had families because we wanted to. We jumped through hoops to make something that comes so easily to so many others. And as for our children? You can bet that they have to "come out" to every new person they meet who asks about their parents.

Robin and Jaimie have put together a masterpiece. It's funny. It's informative. It's brutally honest.

And as for my kids? Despite all of my efforts, they turned out to be heterosexual. Barbra Streisand has a gay son. Why does she get everything? Talent. Success. Money. And a gay son who tells her she looks fabulous and that her voice sounds exactly the way it did in 1975. I'm lucky if I get a reciprocated hug. But that's okay. I raised them to be straight. Fingers crossed for the grandchildren.

Judy Gold

AUTHORS' NOTE
How to Read This Book

This is a book. Reading it should be intuitive, and in one sense it is, because you can read it cover-to-cover. But for folks who want to veer off the beaten path, there are a few alternative ways to read this book.

You can read by guest. We've added a reference section in the back of the book that lists each guest and the chapters in which they appear. So if you become enamored with Staceyann Chin, and we know you will, you can follow her journey throughout the book, story-by-story.

You can read by author. Your lovable authors kick off each chapter with our personal stories as they relate to the topic at hand. You can use that same reference section to read each of our stories in linear fashion.

You can read by topic. We want you to know that if you're frantically flipping pages because you need to get to the chapter that tells you your son will grow up to love you and not be resentful that he has two dads, then the Table of Contents allows you to skip directly to Chapter 14. There you will hear how it all shakes out from a cool group of queerspawn with LGBTQ parents who tell it like it is.

Last, if you just read the previous paragraph and said to yourself, "Um. What's a queerspawn?" Then you'll be happy to hear we have a glossary of terms at the end of the book. Because we would never leave you hanging.

Now, let's get into this.

WELCOME TO OUR BOOK

Hello, and welcome to our book. We know it's a bit nontraditional to welcome readers to a book they've just bought, but as you'll soon see, your authors are all kinds of nontraditional.

Now we've got you here, we're making the assumption that you likely fall into one of two main categories.

First, you saw our catchy book title that shouts out, "This is going to be a book about how an LGBTQ couple makes a baby." And you thought to yourself, "Hmm, I'm an L, G, B, T, or a Q, and I always wanted to have a baby. But I have no idea how to do that. Maybe I'll buy this book."

Second, you've always been curious about how that lovely gay couple from down the block with the very nice-looking lawn, got their adorable daughter. But you've been too afraid to ask. Well, we're excited to report that this book is for you. After reading it, you'll each get the answers you're looking for. You'll also learn the etiquette around asking about your neighbor's situation, whether you've had wine or not.

We cover some serious ground in this book. We talk about the decision to make a nontraditional family, all the different ways LGBTQ folks can make a family, from the medical process to adoption or foster care. We cover how much it costs, and hold on to your hats, it costs *a lot*. And we dip our toes into the legal protections that nontraditional families need to consider and put in place.

But this isn't just a how-to or a why-to book. We also talk about what life is like for nontraditional families once that baby arrives. What it's like to navigate parenting roles with two moms or two dads or a trans parent? What it's like to navigate insensitive questions like, "Who's the *real* dad?" We tackle being out as a family, teaching your kids about their nontraditional family, and what life is like as the nonbiological parent. And we touch on religion, intersectionality and gender fluidity.

Like we said, we cover a lot of ground.

We think the most exciting part of this book is that you will not just hear from the authors. This isn't a biology textbook that you found at a garage sale. Those books are fine, but this one is a lot more, how do you say, unprofessional. We don't take positions and try to woo you toward a conclusion about what our families are like because there is no one-size-fits-all LGBTQ family. Pardon the cliché this early in the book, but our families are a veritable rainbow, made up of different experiences and different stories. You'll be hearing straight from the mouths of LGBTQ families about their journey, and we're here to guide you along in that process.

Now you're probably nodding your head as you turn the pages, sitting slightly forward, intrigued by what's coming in the next couple of hundred pages. But your eyes are slightly scrunched because you're wondering who the hell is the *we* who are talking here?

The *we* who will be with you throughout this book are Jaimie Kelton and Robin Hopkins. That's us. We're moms, we're both lesbians who are married to other ladies, and we each have two kids. We're also the hosts of a popular podcast called *If These Ovaries Could Talk*. And besides the two categories of readers we already described who we thought may be interested in this book, there may be a third category of reader, fans of our podcast who are dying to see how we've transformed the podcasts into a readable and informative book.

We started this journey back in the summer of 2017. Jaimie's wife Anne had their first baby several years before that, and when it was Jaimie's turn to have the second, she experienced years of unexplained infertility that took both a financial and emotional toll on Jaimie and her wife. To find comfort, Jaimie searched the Web for stories about other LGBTQ families experiencing infertility.

When Jaimie couldn't find more than an anecdote or two, she had the idea that she should put her entertainment background to good use and make a podcast talking with her friends about their journey to parenthood and the fertility process. But she didn't think she would actually make the podcast. To be honest, she has a lot of ideas and admittedly does none of them. That's kind of her thing.

So it was Pride Month and Jaimie met up with her friends at the LGBTQ Family Pride Picnic and Robin was there with her wife and two kids. Just like every year before, the group of friends headed off to a neighborhood bar that had a "kid-friendly" back room. And over margaritas, Jaimie said, "Oh hey, Robin. I have this idea for a podcast."

What Jaimie didn't know was that Robin had recently finished up an acting and writing project and had time to spare. Robin doesn't do well with spare time, and she needs to fill it. Also, Jaimie was unaware that Robin is an absolute maniac with zero ability to do a project as a hobby.

They met up at Robin's office and with a laptop placed between them, Jaimie looked on in horror as Robin created approximately 1000 Google documents. If you can't imagine the scene, picture Jaimie crouching next to Robin, back curled, silently mouthing the words, "What's a Master Production Template?"

And a podcast was born.

We went into production, and after recording just two episodes, we realized that the focus of the show was not quite right. We decided that the goal of the podcast should not be to teach LGBTQ people exactly how to make a baby, even though that type of information is an undercurrent of the show, and we get countless emails from listeners thanking us for helping them navigate the process. But our goal became to normalize (for lack of a better word) our nontraditional families. To show the world our struggles, our love, our joy, our thoughtfulness and our humanity.

We focus on what makes each couple or person special, what makes their journey unique. Our intention is to spread the word about our families to LGBTQ folks, straight allies and that dude who thinks he has never met a gay person. The more our stories are told, the more we are heard and seen.

Since the podcast first aired in January 2018, we've met some really beautiful people with fascinating stories. We talked to a family with five parents and two kids, and it all works, to a sperm donor from the UK, to some queerspawn who said it turned out okay (with some bumps along the way), to a couple whose first child was stillborn, to a doula who breastfed her adopted baby, and to a couple that found love *and* the Lord. We talked to everyday folks and to a few famous people like Judy Gold, Staceyann Chin, Iowa State Senator Zach Wahls, and *the* Rosie O'Donnell.

In this book we're sharing excerpts from these conversations organized into chapters by topic. You'll get a sense of the shared LGBTQ family experience, as well as all the differences that make us a spectacular, glittery rainbow of a community.

Oh, and you'll hear about our own journeys too. Both of us have had our own different paths to parenthood. Jaimie's included partially liquidating her wife's pension. Twice. We don't recommend that. Robin's included a trip to Bogota, Colombia where she was given a single vial of sperm in order to try to have a second kid by the same donor as the first. We don't recommend that either.

We've often compared the journey to parenthood for LGBTQ folks to a roller coaster ride. At first, you're really excited. You're sure that after the ride, you'll get off exhilarated and buy that picture of yourself screaming as you shoot down the big drop, hands raised high in the air. But the reality of roller coasters is that you wait on a really long line, squish yourself into one of those tiny seats, and then as the safety bar locks into place, you realize you can't fully exhale. The car chugs up the hill, clink-by-clink, and suddenly you're wondering when was the last time they tightened the bolts on the tracks? But there's no turning back now. You just have to hold on and try to enjoy the ride.

That's how it is when you're spending a lot of money trying to create a family in a world that's not set up for families like yours. That's how parenting is in general. And that's probably what it will be like with us as your guides in this book.

So strap in and enjoy the ride!

Jaimie and Robin

PART ONE

MAKING A BABY WHEN YOU ARE AN L, G, B, T, OR Q

CHAPTER 1

DECIDING YOU WANT TO MAKE AN LGBTQ FAMILY

"And I said, 'At the end of our lives, what are we going to wish we had, a family or a bigger apartment?'" - Gary

In our interviews we discovered that while growing up or in the early stages of relationships, many LGBTQ folks didn't think of having kids. That was mostly because they didn't see a path where they could create a family for themselves. They didn't know any gays raising kids. If they did, those families were often made up of kids from a previous heterosexual relationship. They didn't know of any famous LGBTQ parents until Rosie O'Donnell and Melissa Etheridge. And they definitely didn't see any nontraditional families in movies and TV. Some couples knew they wanted to be parents, but had no idea how to make that happen, since no matter how hard we try, we can't get pregnant the old-fashioned way.

But over the last two decades, both fertility treatments and LGBTQ rights grew by leaps and bounds, and a path to parenthood slowly emerged. As that happened, we began making our very intentional, nontraditional families.

But just because we *can* make a baby doesn't mean every

person *wants* to make a baby. In that sense, the LGBTQ world is no different than the straight one. Figuring out if you want to bring a child into the world can cause fights, leave two people stranded at an impasse, and even lead to breakups.

Here are excerpts from our podcast discussions with couples and single folks trying to answer the age-old question, "Do we want to bring a baby into this insane world? Or should we just continue on with a life filled with free time, money and spontaneity?"

Wait. We're kidding. Parenting is totally worth it. We really mean that.

ROBIN

Co-host of *If These Ovaries Could Talk*

I always wanted kids, even after I switched teams from unsuccessfully dating boys to unsuccessfully dating girls. The only difference in my mind was that now my future children would have two moms, instead of one mom and that strong black dad I envisioned back in college.

I always saw myself as a mom. My childhood wasn't an easy one. My mom showed me many more examples of what *not* to do rather than what to do, but it never deterred me. I was confident that I would know how to be a good parent, and I'd perhaps even right some of the wrongs that were done to me. I felt so strongly about parenting I was fond of telling people that being a mom was one of the reasons I was put on this earth. That's funny because now that I'm a parent, I'm constantly worried I'm breaking my kids in some subtle emotional way that will definitely require therapy.

That said, if I had I not met my wife, Mary, I would have gone forward on the "single mom by choice" path. Thankfully for both me and my kids, I found Mary because she's a way nicer mom than I am.

When we first started dating, we immediately talked about

whether or not we wanted to have kids. I recall asking Mary if she wanted to give birth. I thought this was a fairly basic question. I wasn't asking if she wanted to have a baby with me. It was only our third date, and that would have been too soon even by lesbian standards. But I was asking if she thought it would be a cool experience to, you know, pop a baby out of her vagina.

She responded to this question by immediately making an appointment with her gynecologist to see if she was still physically capable of having a child. I thought that was hilarious. Her lack of communication skills was cute in our early days, but I continued peppering her with questions until I understood what her issues were.

Mary was like many LGBTQ folks. She didn't think having a baby was a possibility, so she didn't allow herself to dream about it. She never pictured herself marrying a man because that didn't feel right, but she had a sense it was expected of her. So instead, she assumed she'd grow up to be a divorced woman, like Mary Tyler Moore, but without the marriage.

Once I convinced her we could make a baby, she was forced to think about changing our relationship dynamic and adding in a third party, in the form of a baby. She had this theory she called the "Upside-Down Triangle Theory", which stated that in any situation where there's me, her, and another person (like a kid), the focus of my attention would be on the other person, leaving her alone at the bottom of the triangle. She also had a very real and probably not misguided fear that the world was running out of peak oil, and all of us would die a slow death not dissimilar to *The Walking Dead*.

But I didn't watch that show, and I wanted kids, and so I would not be stopped. I told Mary that we'd figure things out if she didn't want kids. I am not sure I meant that, but I wasn't going to get bogged down in the weeds. I asked her to spend a couple of weeks considering her life both with and without kids before deciding. I believed it was important that she really think things through. Plus, I figured I could talk her into it. I had to because Mary was my person, and that was that.

So Mary thought about it. Luckily for me, she concluded that if we didn't have kids, our life would be a series of weekend trips to towns we'd already gone to, and shoulder shrugs about what to do with all our free time. Now that we're parents, the idea that we would be bored with all that free time is hilarious. So, we're a family with two kids, one cat, two moms, and at the time of this writing, two fish. And I've never regretted it, not once. Okay, that's a lie, but I'm going to stand by it because I think it makes me look better. I'm kidding, really. I love my little animals and can't imagine my life without them.

JAIMIE

Co-host of *If These Ovaries Could Talk*

I have always wanted to be a mom. Back in high school, I got that science assignment where they give you a bag of sugar and tell you to take care of it as if it were a real child. I took the assignment seriously. I'd been waiting for this my whole life. I went to the thrift store and bought outfits for her that I changed daily. I painted eyes, nose and lips on the flat part of the bag where her face would go, and I made sure my high school boyfriend knew that this baby was both of ours. Such a feminist I was, and such a fun girlfriend, obviously. I named her Angelina because she was an angel from the skies, and I wanted her to have Latin flare. She went everywhere with us. We were the perfect family. One day she got soaked from the rain, and I dried her out in front of the fireplace while my boyfriend and I hung out in his room. All the while, I was thinking I'm really nailing this mom thing. I just knew I was destined for motherhood.

I also assumed mom-ing ran in my blood. My mom is truly better than all the other moms. Wikipedia should use Sue Kelton's name as the definition of a mom. She's that good. She's a natural-born nurturer. I have always wanted to carry on the genuine mom-dom that runs in my veins. I learned from the best after all, and I owed it to society. I was also very modest, and I think I still am.

When I figured out that I liked the ladies more than the gentlemen, the need to be a mom didn't disappear. I might have to try harder to make it happen, but I was destined for this shit. Any partner of mine would surely see that and be on board.

Fast forward to my current reality. I just said to my 5-year-old, "If you don't stay in bed tonight, I will tell Nana to stop buying you presents. Like forever, little girl. So close your eyes and don't open them again until morning." And my son is currently asleep in his stroller, which we also use as his crib. This is due to the fact that I'm either too lazy or too much of a wuss to sleep-train him.

Perhaps my dad's blood runs stronger in my veins than my mom's. His mom smoked cigarettes and drank whiskey on the regular and called everybody "lady", even her grandkids. So maybe I'm carrying on a tradition, just not the one I hoped for.

The takeaway here is this. I'm a mom now, but I'm surely not the mom I thought I'd be. And though I joke about my parenting skills, deep down I'm extremely proud of my little family. We built it with intention and patience and tenacity, and we're doing our best with what we've got. I definitely lose my patience way more than just a little and rely a bit too heavily on the chardonnay, but my kids are turning out to be pretty good humans.

I'm a mom doing her best, and for that I'm proud.

DAVID

David, a self-described 50-year-old-millennial, never saw having kids as an option in his life. But when he met his husband, Billy, he knew he couldn't deny him kids.

DAVID: I'm not the model of a first-time gay dad who had a kid. I didn't want to have kids, mostly because I never thought that was an option. It didn't occur to me. Growing up, I was an Air Force brat, and we literally moved every two years to increasingly horrible places.

I was 28 when I came out, and that was pretty daring for me. So for what is half of my life, I was in the closet. The combination of always being in a new place where I didn't fit in, plus being gay, I had this other life which was in my head, and I didn't share it with anybody.

I think I'm still that guy. I had a lot of shame about my everyday feelings and thoughts and opinions, and to have a child is so public and so social. I wasn't ready for that. But my husband Billy was open and honest from day one and said, "I want kids. I've always wanted kids."

I thought, "Oh, I'll deal with that later."

Ultimately, I got there because, whether this was a good reason or not, there was no way I could let him down. I couldn't do that. I wouldn't do that. And so I said, "Sure."

RAE AND MARGIE

> Rae and Margie were pioneering lesbians, who conceived their daughter, Emma, in the 80s using an anonymous sperm donor. From the beginning, Margie wanted kids, but it took Rae longer to warm up to the idea.

RAE: We talked to every one of our friends about having a child, and we met all these women who were adopting children. Emma was born in '85, so we started talking about this maybe five or six years before. Our friends all said, "Do it already. You'll be good parents." We talked with everybody, though I didn't discuss it with my family or my brothers.

ROBIN: What were your concerns? Bringing a kid into the world as gay parents or just you two being parents? Or all of the above?

MARGIE: All the above, I think.

RAE: I was always fearful someone would come and take the baby away. I lived with great fear, and I didn't think my family would accept us having a baby, though it turns out that when we finally told my brother, he said he would have helped if I had asked. That idea had never occurred to us. Also, while it was not something that we had thought of doing, my nieces and nephews are really terrific, our daughter Emma is terrific, but it wouldn't have been a terrible thing.

MARGIE: She wouldn't have been blonde though.

RAE: Correct. So Margie wanted to have a child, and she wanted to birth a child. I don't think I loved myself enough to do that. Second, I was always concerned about my weight and I knew with pregnancy that would adjust. I thought my weight was in a manageable area, so I was really rooting for the adoption.

MARGIE: I wanted to actually try this pregnancy thing. I thought, "You know people have been doing it for thousands of years. It might be something I want to try." But I felt like it would be strange to have other people determining whether I could or couldn't have this baby, and then there was also the threat of somebody coming in and taking the baby away. And that was even more of a threat for Rae because she would not have a legal relationship to the baby. In New York there weren't second-parent adoptions yet. At the time there also wasn't legal same-sex marriage, so she would have had no legal relationship to the baby, which would have been true if we had adopted as well.

PATRICIA AND KELLEN

When this fiery couple started dating, the question of having kids was front and center. It turned out that the decision to have a baby was much more about their commitment to each other than whether or not they should have children.

PATRICIA: When we first started dating I said, "I have to tell you one thing. I am having a baby, and it's with or without you. I don't know if it's with you because I don't know if we're going to be together forever. But are you willing to date a woman who's going to start the process to have a baby?"

KELLEN: And I never wanted to have a baby. I didn't want to have a child. I wasn't into children. I didn't have the desire to give birth or anything.

PATRICIA: But what did you say?

KELLEN: Yes.

PATRICIA: She said yes! So you know what it's like when you meet the one and it's the first few months. You're in heaven. You're in bliss. So when she said, "Yes, I wanna have kids," and, "Yes, I wanna get married," in my mind, I had met the one, and I was letting my guard down. Then one night, she invited me over to her place, and we were making dinner, and she said, "I have something to say."

KELLEN: I told her I thought she should have a baby with a man because I didn't think I wanted to have a baby. In reality, I got scared.

PATRICIA: My beast came out. I was so mad. I was so hurt. I was like, "How dare you? You chased me, you pushed after me. What kind of a person, what kind of a human being are you? Don't you see what you've done? You've torn my heart out of my body." Oh my god, I let her have it.

KELLEN: I called my best friend and he said, "You did what? You broke up with Patricia? Are you out of your mind? I'm not talking to you."

I said, "Come on. You have to help me here. I'm devastated."

He said, "No. I'm not talking to you. You deserve this."

But I was scared shitless, and I couldn't lie. It wasn't in me.

PATRICIA: Well, we met up, and we tiptoed back into the conversation. We said, "Okay, let's slow the whole thing down. Let's not talk kids right now. Let's get back to, 'Are we good for each other?'"

KELLEN: And I said, "So marry me then. If you want to have a baby, I want to get married."

PATRICIA: I said, "I don't want to get married." And she's like, "Well, I'm not having a baby because then you're going to give all the energy to the baby, and I'm going to be left here."

KELLEN: Well, it's a big commitment, so if you want me to have a baby—

PATRICIA: I think that the marriage was probably the bigger deal than the kids.

KELLEN: For me, yes. I felt like, "I love you forever. And I'm going to be with you, so if you want to have a baby, I'm on board. But let's be together."

PATRICIA: Then we were on the same team.

MARK AND GREG

> Dr. Mark is a fertility doctor who helps make babies for a living, so he knew exactly where he stood on the kid question. It took Greg longer, but Mark's experience came in handy during their decision-making process.

GREG: Three years into our relationship we were headed up to visit friends for the weekend and on the drive up he said, "I'd like you to think about this over the weekend, and you don't have to answer until the way back, but I'd really like to have a family with you."

MARK: I said, "If you're not willing, we're wrapping this up."

GREG: I saw it coming, and it was a tantalizing moment. But I did wait till later in the weekend to tell him because I wanted to be thoughtful about my decision.

MARK: Greg's a very special person, and I met him, and it really changed my perspective on life, and I was thinking of moving forward with parentage by myself. But I met this person and fell in love and that's awesome, but I still wanted to be a dad, so that was important to me.

GREG: So we decided to move forward, and I was really coming at it blind in the sense of not knowing how, what, who, when, where, why. And it was overwhelming once we got into it. I was very thankful that this is what he does for a living.

TIQ

> As a transgender man, Tiq couldn't fully commit to the idea of becoming a parent until he transitioned.

TIQ: I always wanted kids. There was a point in my life where I thought, "I know I want to have children, but I don't want to be a mother." This was before I transitioned, and I didn't understand then that I was trans, so I put it in the back of my mind.

Then I transitioned, and when I met my wife, we were talking, and she wanted to have kids, and I wanted to have kids. So I was like, "Great. Because I finally met someone who wants to have children, and we were in the same place.

THE ABBYS

> Sam and her wife Laura, author of the book *2Brides 2Be: A Same-Sex Guide for the Modern Bride*, spent time on a reality TV show called *The Newlyweds*. They went on the show to have some fun, but the network had other ideas, pushing them toward parenting much earlier than they planned.

LAURA: The network wanted to take us to get our eggs tested and do some fertility testing. I knew nothing about any of it. I guess I thought, "Someday we'll have a baby." So we agreed to go get this testing done. We figured, "Sure. If they'll pay for it."

SAM: But listen, we were 28, living in New York City, pretty early in our careers, and we weren't looking to start a family, at all. But we went in and both did ultrasounds, blood work, whatever else they wanted us to do, but we made it very clear, do not expect a baby to happen during this season of the show.

LAURA: Weeks went by, and the next time the producers showed up they told us, "We're going to go back to the fertility clinic and get your test results." They were going to film us, and our doctor who we really liked, was out on maternity leave, so they put us with this older doctor.

SAM: He was the partner who had started the clinic.

LAURA: He was one of those doctors that doesn't really prepare you for news. He just dropped a bomb on us. He started telling me how some men can't have children, and then he went on this tangent about sperm. I knew he was going to lead that back to something like, "And some women don't have eggs."

SAM: It was his chance to be all, "I'm on TV."

LAURA: He talked so much. Then he slides this piece of paper in front of me and takes out the tip of his pen and he says, "This is a normal AMH level. And this is yours." And he points to the lowest possible number. And I was like, "Okay."

SAM: Your AMH is how many eggs you have left.

LAURA: He said, "You need to start trying to get pregnant right now."

SAM: And you still might not be able to have a baby.

LAURA: Of course, we then told our family and said, "Hey, before you watch the show, it's not that big of a deal, but I might have trouble getting pregnant."

SAM: And Laura's mom is a very emotional woman, so she cried.

LAURA: She's like, "I don't understand. I got pregnant no problem."

SAM: And we were like, "We know!"

LAURA: So then the producers take us outside to get the shot. We're in the middle of Brooklyn in a Hasidic community, and there are children everywhere. And the producers say, "We're going to film you walking down the street talking about how you feel about this." But they had to set up the shots, so we had to stand there and wait with the producers saying things like, "Don't talk to each other!"

We just stood there looking at each other. And Sam's one of those people that wants to make me feel better, and she's trying to rub my shoulders. And I don't want to be touched when I'm in a mood.

SAM: This was really hard because we're not very emotional people. And this was a bomb.

LAURA: That was probably the closest I came to really losing it on camera because I felt like, "I don't want to do this right now."

SAM: It was hard because I would say, "We're gonna figure this out." And she was like, "No."

It was rough.

ROBIN: You weren't even trying to have a baby. So all of a sudden someone just told you, you can't have something that you weren't even trying for.

LAURA: That was exactly it. I'm not there yet, so I can't emotionally connect with this loss, if I would even call it a loss at this point.

SAM: Laura's also someone who doesn't process things until they're happening to her. She has to be in the moment to be feeling what is going on.

LAURA: So we did nothing. The producers wanted us to do it now, and I was like, "Nope. Still not ready to have a baby." It was actually good though that we did this whole thing with that TV show because we realized I would have to carry first. But Sam still had to push me to move the baby thing forward.

EMMA BROCKES

> Emma is the author of *An Excellent Choice: Panic and Joy on My Solo Path to Motherhood* and is a single mom by choice. She spent loads of time waffling over whether or not to have kids.

EMMA: Well, I turned 37 and that was it, really. And it was early to panic. I mean, I've been upbraided by lots of women who tell me I shouldn't have started panicking until 44. But I was really worried about the money. I knew that it was going to be expensive because the pregnancy was going to have to be assisted. And every year after 40 was going to be another 15 grand.

Then it was basically getting my nerve up. I kept losing my nerve, and I kept thinking, "It's too weird. I don't think I can do it." And, "What will people say?" Which is so strange because it's not like I live my life like that. I knew one person who'd done it [single mom by choice], but no one in the generation above me. So I felt like I had no template. And I had trouble imagining what it would look like. I didn't know where we were going to live. I felt dislocated in a million different ways. Then I just had this relationship going on at the same time, which was unresolved. So I kept getting near to making the decision then retreating.

But I thought in terms of money, and I thought in terms of outcome. I realized I would be devastated if I couldn't do it, which was a shock to me because it's not like I sat there for five years hoping that I could have a kid. But suddenly the possibility that it wouldn't happen completely floored me.

LISA AND JENNIFER

> Lisa and Jennifer both knew that they wanted kids. They discussed it early in their relationship and were ready to go, but life got tricky for Lisa when she got cancer. That forced her to reconsider if she really wanted to be a parent.

LISA: I always wanted kids, and the closer I got to 40, something shifted in my brain, and I no longer was certain that I wanted to have children. And Jennifer's twin sister was pregnant at this time, and Jennifer was like, "Chop, chop. When are we having a baby?"

JENNIFER: We had to go to therapy. The way I said it to her at the time, and it's still what I think, is that it's one of life's great experiences. And I didn't mean great as in great versus terrible. I meant great as in awesome. And I felt like I didn't want to live my life without that experience being part of it.

LISA: And we had discussed it early on in our relationship.

JENNIFER: Yeah, we had cleared this up at the beginning.

LISA: It was a bit of a curveball when I said I don't know if I want kids.

JENNIFER: I thought, "Ahh. If you don't want to have kids, we might not be able to continue the relationship." And there was no question that we wanted to spend the rest of our lives together—she was my person. So we went to a couples therapist for a few months, and we talked through a lot of stuff, particularly around Lisa's mother's early death. Lisa's mom had cancer when she was a kid. And as we were getting closer to thinking about having kids, the idea of potentially having cancer and abandoning our children was unconsciously heavy for Lisa.

LISA: I think I've always been afraid of getting cancer, dying young and leaving a child behind. And lo and behold—literally, in our last appointment.

JENNIFER: Lisa had gone to the gynecologist for a checkup because of some bleeding, and given her family history, the gynecologist said, "Let me do a little biopsy."

LISA: Two weeks later—

JENNIFER: We found out that Lisa had endometrial cancer. And so that was what we talked about at our last appointment with the couples therapist.

LISA: Even the therapist was surprised.

JENNIFER: Because we had been talking so much about Lisa's fear that she would get cancer and die, and then she got cancer.

JAIMIE: That's when you just decided you wanted to have a kid?

LISA: Yeah, we were like, "Let's get online. Let's pick some sperm. Let's do this."

ROBIN: How did you make a right turn to saying, "Now seems like a really great time to bring a family into the world?"

JENNIFER: Well, it was just like, "Come on, can we get on with our lives?" You want to embrace life.

ACTOR DAVID BEACH

> David and his husband spent somewhere in the neighborhood of two decades deciding to have a baby. But eventually, they got there.

DAVID: We met when we were 23, and we kept on thinking,

"Oh, you know, we're definitely about ready to have kids. We had the names picked out, Benjamin, and Emily. So we had all that set aside. And for a long time, if I was home cooking and Russell would come home, I would say, "Hey, Benjamin, your father's home." And the people downstairs, I think really thought we had a kid who we never let out. It was awkward. They must have thought it was the strangest thing in the world. And when we finally brought home a baby, I think they were all, "Well, the first kid's still not around. Don't lose this one."

But I think that we would have definitely had more kids if we had started earlier. But everyone who was a parent who we talked to, it seemed like they must have hated having kids. They'd say to us, "Oh, you're about to have a kid? It's not easy."

People would say, "You guys are gay. You don't have to have kids. No one's forcing you. Really, you do not have to do this."

Or they'd say, "You will get into fights with your spouse that you have never had before. You're going to find things about each other that you have never known, and it's going to get so dark."

And I'd think, "Why are you telling me this?"

Of course, some of that is true, but that whole sense of people just really wanting you to know that it's going to be dark.

Also, I didn't want to make a baby if there were babies that needed homes. That's just the way I felt. And with adoption, I couldn't deal with the fact that in some states, you have this amount of time where a birth parent can change their mind. Or if the birth father is in the military, he can come back a year later, and then still get the baby. I couldn't do that. I couldn't put myself in that kind of vulnerability.

And I thought, "So what do you do? You withhold love for the first 30 days?" You're just like, "Oh, nice kid, but don't really cuddle them." So we finally had to embrace the fact that you have to be vulnerable to that. There's no way around it.

We were getting older and older and thinking we still might want to have a kid, and people would say, "So how's the kid thing coming?"

And we'd say, "Oh, we're still thinking about it."

They'd say, "Dudes, you're 41. You can't just be thinking about it. If you're thinking about it, then you're not doing it. And it's a passive no."

We had been talking about our future kids, and we knew where we were going to send them to school and where we were going to vacation and all that kind of stuff. I mean, we knew Benjamin Thomas would be doing all these great things. He just wasn't there. So then we finally we went to one of those introductory talks at an agency.

After that, we're like, "We're gonna have a kid."

TOM

Tom is a single, successful gay man who wasn't planning on having kids. It crossed his mind, but he had a full life. Then, without much thought, he volunteered to donate his sperm to a lesbian couple.

TOM: When I was younger, like prepubescent I thought, "Oh, I can't wait to have a boy." And at that point, my sisters had a friend whose son's name was Robert Michael, and I thought that was the best name, and I just couldn't wait to name my son Robert Michael.

As I got older, I became a gay man. Of course then I dated a Robert, a Michael, a Robert Michael, and a Michael Robert. Yeah, they really deterred me from any thought of having children.

By then, I'd been single basically longer in my life than I'd been in relationships, and I'd had a very full life with performing arts and work. I thought a little bit about kids, but I didn't think I really wanted a kid attached because I liked having my life.

But when the opportunity to donate my sperm presented itself, I thought, "I'm not doing anything with it. You want it?" It was not predetermined. It wasn't like I laid in bed and thought, "I want to donate my sperm to the birth moms." I suggested it very off the cuff.

And they said, "Are you serious?"

And I said, "Yeah, we can talk about it."

Shortly after that, we got together every couple of months and had dinner and talked about this idea. I heard what they wanted. They wanted somebody who the kids would know growing up, and I didn't really know what my level of expectation was going to be. How often am I going to see them? How much are they going to keep me informed on things?

As I continued with the process, even after the sperm banking, and through the legal process, I thought "Is this what I really want?" But ultimately, we figured it out. I realized I wanted to know who the kids were as well. I wasn't just going to write them off as a donation I made in the past. It was over the course of a year and a half that we figured it all out. And everything just sort of lined up.

GARY AND TONY

> Gary was raised by parents who said, "Waste not, want not." and he felt pretty strongly that applied to his extra sperm. So before he and Tony had any children of their own, they both offered sperm to several lesbian couples to help them create families.

TONY: We were at a wedding party event when we met our friends, Leslie and Alicia. We had been talking with a couple who wanted to have a baby with a known donor, but they were moving to Washington and we decided it probably wasn't the best situation. And then we started talking to Alicia and Leslie about it, and they were really interested.

GARY: Actually it was Karen and Francine who were the first, and there was an email I saw they sent to you, and I responded, "Are you looking for sperm?"

I said, "We have this stuff, and I know it can be expensive." They didn't really respond. But that's what started the conversation.

I looked at it like it saves money. My parents were depression era, which meant you use the things you got. I knew none of our friends had tons of money, and I know my grandparents lived to be 100, so there's health in my family. That's when I offered to the first couple. And then the second couple who thought about it, but then they were gonna move away.

TONY: Then Leslie and Alicia. And I donated.

ROBIN: How did you decide who donated?

TONY: Well, we were both kind of working with both partners at the same time, and Alicia got pregnant first.

JAIMIE: Whoa. So you donated to one of them, and you donated to the other, and whoever got it first was gonna be the one?

TONY: Yeah.

GARY: Yeah.

ROBIN: Wow. Talk about letting the Universe decide.

TONY: And we ended up with Piper who's now almost 13.

GARY: They live a block from us, and we all work together, and our kids go to the same school.

TONY: So it's a wonderful kind of family forest, as opposed to a family tree. But it changed the way we thought about parenting, and we kidded with one another that Piper was our test child.

GARY: Because we could babysit her and parent, and be fun, and help her study and then drop her off and still go see a show.

> Over time, it became clear they wanted a kid of their own, but they couldn't swing the cost of surrogacy. So they assumed that the nontraditional set up they currently had would be their only link to parentage. Then their neighbor passed away and left them a large chunk of money giving them the opportunity to have a child on their own.

GARY: I've always lived in walk ups. And there's always been that one old lady living in the building. And I've always said, "If you need my help, I'm here." So Tony and I helped a woman in our building for 10 to 15 years, even when she was on her deathbed.

TONY: Helpfulness is a deeply ingrained part of Gary. So many times, I got mad at him because we'd be walking on the street, and I'd turn around and he'd be gone. And I'd see him ushering a little old lady across the street or checking on someone who was by themselves. His parents taught him so well. So of course we took care of the woman in our building.

GARY: Every day, twice a day.

TONY: We would bring her the mail and help her with her bills. She lived this wildly rich life, and we were really fortunate to be able to get to know her. When she died, she left half her estate to Gary and me. We had no idea she came from this family fortune, and it was a very significant amount of money that she left us. We never, ever would have been able to do surrogacy and have our son if she hadn't left us that money. All of a sudden we had this opportunity to have a family the way that we really wanted to, though there was a moment where we did think, "Should we get a bigger apartment, or should we have a kid?"

GARY: And I said, "At the end of our lives, what are we going to wish we had, a family or a bigger apartment?"

TONY: We still have her ashes in our apartment.

CHAPTER 2

YOUR PATH: HOW DO YOU MAKE YOUR FAMILY?

"I don't care how, but I'm not leaving this earth without carrying a child." - Patricia

There are so many decisions that LGBTQ couples have to make when deciding to have a baby, because we have too much of one thing and not enough of the other. Two women have two uteruses, but they don't have any sperm. Two men have all the sperm in the world, but come up short in the eggs-and-hopper department. And with trans fertility, the questions are more specific to each individual or couple, but that doesn't mean there are fewer questions to be answered.

Lesbian, Gay, Transgender, Queer, Non-Binary, wherever you fall on the spectrum, if you want to have a kid, you'll have to figure out how to make that baby.

There are so many paths. You can embark on the scientific route. If so, you'll need to figure out who will carry the baby, whose egg will be used, who will donate the sperm, who will go first. Perhaps you'll consider using a surrogate, or doing IVF, IUI, or even trying at home with what we like to call the "turkey baster method". You may think about adopting, and if you do, then you'll need to figure out if you want to adopt internationally, or domestically, or if you want to use an adoption lawyer or private agency. And don't forget there's always the option of being foster parents.

All those choices can make nontraditional heads swirl.

Now, you'd think with all that choice and cost associated with these paths, we'd hear a lot of couples grumbling about how hard it is for us to make families. Well, we're here to tell you that hasn't been our experience. All of our guests shared stories about how they made thoughtful and personal decisions, how they were deliberate and intentional at every turn. And instead of the process feeling like a cross to bear, every choice these couples made, defined and illuminated their families in love.

And to quote Jaimie, that's beautiful.

JAIMIE HERE

As I told you earlier, I always knew I would be a mother. And when I switched over to the ladies, I also always knew I would be the one to carry too. I'm fairly sure I've talked about having babies with every partner I've had since high school. The night I first met my wife, I asked her if she wanted to have children, while in bed. She miraculously stayed with me past that first night. I am one lucky girl. I am also one helluva sexy girlfriend, obviously.

Sexiness aside, I have always wanted to experience pregnancy and childbirth. My mother glamorized my birth so much throughout my childhood that I *had* to try it out just to see what all the hype was about. The picture my mom painted of a glowing and euphoric childbirth felt like a real possibility that I was hell-bent on not missing out on. Turns out, that story really was just a bunch of hype. My baby didn't "slip out of me" like I "supposedly" did out of my mother. Quite the contrary. Talk about painting an unrealistic picture. Thanks, Mom. But I digress.

Considering my steadfast will to carry the fruit of my loins, imagine my shock and surprise when I was in a bar with my wife about a month after our wedding, and she said, "Ya know, I think I wanna have a baby."

"I'm sorry, what?" I asked as nonchalantly as possible, while trying not to choke on the sip of beer I was having trouble forcing down my throat. This was not the plan. She never wanted to carry. *I* was always the one having the baby. *I* was the one who would get to bask in the glow of pregnancy. *I* was the one who would be praised for my strength and determination after laboring through hours of excruciating natural childbirth. *Not* her!

"Yeah, I think I do," she replied. Anne is not one to elaborate on her reasons for things, which makes therapy fun for us, so I knew I wouldn't get much more in the way of an explanation. But it threw me for a loop. A big loop. Anne was older, which meant we would have to start right away, and this was *not* the plan. And if we both wanted to have a baby, this meant we had to have two babies, which also wasn't part of the plan. A month into our marriage and we were already negotiating whose bloodline would carry on in our offspring, and how many of said offspring we would bring into this world.

I got scared, which is pretty much what I'm known for. My anxiety kicked in, and I made Anne promise that if she had our first child, she would in no way, ever in a million years, no matter how hard it was, or how poor financially we got, suggest that we stop after the first. If we do this "you have a baby" thing, I still get to have mine too. I'm so mature, I know. She assured me she wouldn't back out of our agreement. We would have two children, no matter what. Being a person racked with fear most of the time, I forced her to reassure me of her promise over the next five years. That included throughout her pregnancy, our daughter being born, purchasing sperm for number two, during inseminations, after inseminations, and throughout the three years of infertility I went through to create child number two. I made her pinky swear her loyalty to the plan, right up until the moment that little boy was in our arms. Once again, I'm a real fun spouse.

So there you have it. We planned our family in a bar over beers like any self-respecting lesbian couple *should* plan it. I always knew I would carry a child, and I did. What I didn't know was that I would also get to experience watching my wife grow and give birth to our first-born. I never imagined how impressed I would be when I watched my wife bravely push a nine-pound baby out of her hoo-ha in less than an hour without even flinching. She's really one tough lady. I never imagined the plethora of emotions I would experience from mothering a child I didn't give birth to. My parenting experience is vastly richer than I ever could have dreamed of because my wife threw me for a loop in a bar and decided she wanted to carry too. Us lesbians never cease to amaze.

ROBIN HERE TOO

From the moment Mary and I learned about reciprocal IVF—the process of using one of my eggs that Mary would carry, we were all about it. The idea we could make a baby that would have the blueprint of my genetics, and literally be made from Mary's bones, seemed like the coolest, most amazing science experiment ever invented. This plan also solved the issue of Mary possibly having dusty eggs because of her age.

We knew that was how we would create our family.

The downside? My insurance only covered one IVF procedure and even with insurance, the money guy at our doctor's office said it would cost somewhere between $6,000 and $26,000. I remember staring at the printouts the guy gave us and saying, "Well that's a big discrepancy between those two numbers, huh?"

He nodded. No more information was forthcoming.

We only had enough money to try this route once. That didn't just mean no more IVFs, but it also meant no more savings account. But we were blinded by the idea that the baby would be made of the two of us, and we forged ahead. It wasn't until the day they handed us ten different prescription forms that we began to question our thinking. All we had to do was order the prescriptions and the cycling would begin. Yet neither of us was picking up the phone. Seeing all those forms laid out on the table stopped us in our tracks. And I couldn't help but think about the fact that the odds of us having a successful pregnancy in one round of IVF were not necessarily on our side.

That's when Mary said, "Are we going about this the hardest possible way?"

And the answer to that question was "Yes, we were." So we had a bunch of cocktails and talked through our plan. By the third margarita, we realized that we loved the idea of the baby coming from both of us, but if we were being honest, our motives were much more about trying to fix Mary's fears that she would have no connection to the baby and would feel left out.

In that very moment, we changed directions and decided to go forward doing an unmedicated IUI with me. Simply put, we bought some sperm, and the doctor put it in near my important parts, and I got pregnant fairly easily with both our kids.

The good news? Mary felt love for our babies the second they popped out. There was never a doubt that she is every bit the mother that I am, genetics or not. And now that my oldest is ten, I see so much of Mary in her.

There are so many ways that we can make our families. How Mary and I first planned to go about things is not at all how we ended up conceiving our kids. And it was a big lesson, not just about family creation, but also about parenting, to be open to what comes your way and to really listen to your instincts. Paths that seemed cemented, shift and change. Things that seemed right at the beginning of our journey, now seem funny. Ultimately, the family that we were meant to have showed up for us.

And I can't see us any other way.

SARA AND HILARY

Hilary is that rare kind of lesbian who knew exactly how she wanted to make a baby, long before she met her wife Sara.

HILARY: I did a lot of research online. I mean, I've been wanting to do this my whole life. I knew I was going to be with a woman, and I wanted to carry a baby. And I knew it was impossible any other way.

SARA: She's been buying baby clothes since she was about 17 years old.

HILARY: Yeah. I was never deterred by it. I had the fortunate experience growing up surrounded by a community of gay people, which was really lovely. Some of which had children.

SARA: Fortunately, it was really easy for us because we fill each other's gaps. It was an easy decision. I didn't want to be pregnant, Hilary felt a very strong desire to be pregnant. I wanted to pass along my genealogy, and Hilary did not have a desire to pass along her genealogy. Not that she didn't have desire, it just wasn't a strong desire.

It was an easy solution to harvest my eggs and plant them into Hilary's womb. That way, we would both have a physical connection to the child, which was very important to us. So who would be pregnant, and how do we get pregnant was a very easy decision. It took about five seconds.

HILARY: It's called reciprocal IVF, and it's expensive, but it was just the way we wanted to do it, so we went along that path.

AIMEE AND MYRIAM

To finalize a plan, Aimee and Myriam had to factor in lots of pesky little details like who had insurance and whose eggs were older. They knew though that genetics were important, so for their first child, Aimee carried Myriam's

egg.

MYRIAM: I wanted her to carry my egg just to have that experience. And I didn't want the bloodline to stop.

AIMEE: We are both only children.

MYRIAM: I always wanted to be a parent, but I didn't want to carry the child. I love children, but I'm a strong believer that not everyone is meant to carry the child. Well, let me just say it like this, I am not a carrier. And I'm proud. But I will love the kid to death.

AIMEE: And I think I was probably getting old. Well, you know, old for the fertility world. Once you get past 35, it's all "That's not going to happen."

I think what played a major role in our decisions was where we were job-wise, meaning who had the insurance. But ultimately, we went with Myriam's egg first because she's a little older than I am.

MICHELE THE DOULA

Michele is a doula who has helped bring many babies into this world. She knew it would take a lot to have her own baby. Ultimately, she realized she didn't necessarily need to go through all that to be a mom.

MICHELE: I realized that it was going to involve a lot more people, a lot more resources, a lot more science, and a lot more money. And if IVF was going to cost that much, and take that much time with that much uncertainty, I wasn't interested.

I'm not that attached to birthing a baby. I'm around birth all the time. But I realized that I was really into the breastfeeding part. That was the part that was emotional for me, that I really wanted.

Also I just really wanted to be a mom. And my wife said, "I don't really need to give birth either."

When I said, "What about adoption?"

She said, "Yeah, that sounds awesome."

It was really simple, actually.

> **Michele adopted but didn't have to give up her dream of breastfeeding. In preparation, she did a bunch of stuff that included science, herbs, and manipulation and was able to breastfeed her adopted baby. Us gays never cease to amaze.**

BETH AND JEN

> **Jen is a divorced mom who remarried Beth. That makes Beth the stepmom to their daughter, Mia whom Jen had in her previous marriage.**

JEN: My ex and I went to a fertility specialist because she wanted to carry. They told her, based on some medical stuff, it was going to be a tough journey. But the fertility specialist told me that it would be very easy for me to get pregnant, and I said, "No. No. We're not here for me."

Also, with my ex, it felt like, "If I can't carry, and you can, I'm going to resent you forever." So we started the process with her, knowing it was going to be a journey with a lot of obstacles.

I remember, the day after our first consultation, she said to me, "Wouldn't it be easy if somebody just gave us a baby, and we didn't have to wait the year?"

And I said, "Well yeah, that sounds awesome."

In the meantime, a family member out west knew somebody, who knew somebody, who called us and said, "I know you're looking to grow your family. I have a friend who is having a baby and can't keep it."

My ex and I talked about it. We knew opportunities like this don't just fall into your lap. So we got the birth mother's cell phone number, and we told her we'd like to take the baby, and she said, "Well, I have some people. You know, I have a couple of other candidates. Can I think about it?"

A week later, she called back and said, "Um, yeah, so I pick you."

But there was a language barrier—our birth mother is an Iraqi refugee. So we said, "You know, we're together *together* right?"

And she said, "Actually, that's why I'm choosing you."

She had some oppressive men in her life and so she wanted two women.

> To this day, Jen still reflects on how her daughter magically appeared in their life and how it all felt very "meant to be".

BETH: Sometimes Jen says, "It was just so awesome, someone handed me a baby."

JEN: It works out. I feel like the soul that is meant to be with me is going to make its way, and I'm fine with however it gets here. I believe the same thing with termination, miscarriage, stillborn. They come back.

When I was 22, I went to a psychic, and at the time, I thought, "This is some new-age bullshit." But I went anyway, and she said to me, "Oh, you're going to get a baby from the desert."

And I thought, "I don't even know what that sentence means. Why do I have to pay $25 to you?"

But sure enough, not only is Mia half Iraqi, but she was born in Phoenix. I got a baby from the desert.

STACEYANN CHIN

Poet, activist, and author of *The Other Side of Paradise:*

A Memoir and Crossfire: A Litany For Survival and all-around powerhouse, Staceyann Chin knew exactly how she wanted to make a baby. And she gives zero apologies for wanting her child to share the same genetics as herself.

STACEYANN: The question comes up all the time. "Why didn't you adopt?" Or all of those other blah blah questions. "Why did you decide to go and make a child?" As they say in Trinidad.

JAIMIE: Like it's a selfish thing to do?

STACEYANN: Well, it kind of is. But I think it's okay to be selfish. Men are selfish all the time and nobody gives them shit about it. I wanted to have a relationship with someone who had a biological connection with me that was a positive relationship. I wanted to have someone who looked like me, that I could look at them and not feel so much shit about where I was from and who loves me and who doesn't love me and who left me. So I knew that for my own sanity, that was the direction I wanted to at least attempt to go.

KAREN AND TOBI

Deciding who would carry their baby wasn't a hard decision for Karen and Tobi, but there were still some feelings that came up for Karen about not having any genetic ties to her child.

JAIMIE: Karen, how did you feel about Tobi carrying?

KAREN: I think I was sad about it a little during her pregnancy.

TOBI: I think that's also one of the reasons why I love Karen so much because when something bothers her, she vocalizes it and is open and very transparent about it. So she shared the fear, and we talked about it, and then she didn't talk about it again. So I sort of felt like it was resolved.

KAREN: I didn't think about it that much. I do remember thinking about it during the pregnancy and thinking, "Wow, that kind of stinks that she won't have the same DNA." But then I was like, it really doesn't matter. And I didn't think about it, especially after she was born, it was just not a big deal at all for me.

GARY AND TONY

> For Gary and Tony, choosing surrogacy over adoption was much more about their age and the amount of time each process would take.

GARY: I thought that we would probably adopt because I always felt there's enough food, money, love and water in the world. We just have to get it to where it needs to go.

TONY: We looked into adoption. You know, we went to meetings at the [Gay & Lesbian] center and all of that. But we were 45. And with surrogacy, the timing is a lot more defined. I think people don't understand that once you get in the track, and you're matched with your gestational carrier and your egg donor, depending on how lucky the transfer is, you could have a child in a year and a half.

CRYSTAL AND KELLY

> After being together for years, Crystal and Kelly decided they wanted to have a family, and foster parenting was the route they wanted to take. Since making that decision, some kids came to their home temporarily, and many more have stayed and been adopted.

JAIMIE: What made you guys decide to foster?

CRYSTAL: Well, we can't make a child. And back in 2010 we started talking about kids. We'd been together almost 14 years, and we both started saying we wanted a child, and something was pulling at our hearts to adopt someone with special needs, to give back. We knew how many kids were in the foster care system, and it opened our eyes to how many kids needed a home and how many kids were considered unadoptable.

But, we didn't know anything about being a foster parent. We thought we could just email and say, "Hey, we like this kid. Can we adopt him?" And when we did that, the woman who was handling the case said to us, "Do you have a caseworker?"

And we're like, "Um, no. We just saw a boy and thought he needed a home."

She laughed and said, "It's going to take about six months to get certified."

We thought, "No way." We weren't going to wait six months.

So I Googled how to become a foster parent. And there was a get together at a library here in Austin where you could go, and different people from different placement agencies would be speaking. We went that same week, and we met this lady named Jamie. She's actually a friend of ours now. But she was the head of this agency at the time, and we absolutely fell in love with her because we were really worried about being a same-sex couple and adopting. We worried about what people would say or what people would think. I remember thinking, "There's no way they're going to give us a kid, especially in Texas." And when we met Jamie she said, "No! Everyone's welcome. Let's get this started."

They told us it would take six months, and we were certified within a month and a half.

KELLY: Yup. Every Wednesday and Saturday, we were in a training to get everything done.

> **Once Crystal and Kelly opened their home, the decision to take in a child was never one they struggled with, in fact, they rarely consulted one another.**

KELLY: So I'm at a luncheon and I get a call from a case worker who we adore and I say, "Hey Ashley, how are you doing?"

She's says, "Good. And guess what? I have a 10-month-old who's in adoption placement. A little boy. Are you interested?"

I said, "Yeah we'll take him." I didn't even call Crystal.

CRYSTAL: Yeah, this is how we get our children, we don't talk it over, we just say, "Absolutely. We'll take in more."

THE TWO BARONS

> **Two millennials who are dating are named Baron and Barron. Baron with one "r" refers to his boyfriend as "Other Baron", so we will too. The Barons are young and trying to figure out how they will make a family. They're approaching the process with a youthful naiveté that while refreshing, is also nerve wracking for your hosts who desperately want to mother these two through the process.**

JAIMIE: In an ideal world, how would you make your baby?

OTHER BARON: We would use Baron's sperm and possibly my sister's egg, if she volunteered it, and then probably have a surrogate carry it.

BARON: But then you're saying we need to know the surrogate? What if I don't like them?

JAIMIE: There are agencies that help you find them. And they have to choose you too.

BARON: How fast do you have to make that decision?

OTHER BARON: We have to make more female friends.

JAIMIE: Well, if you could find a friend to do it that would be amazing.

BARON: I'm not asking any of my friends to carry my child.

JAIMIE: There are agencies who handle this whole surrogate, egg donor business and you go into the agency and then they help you through the process, but you need money.

ROBIN: You are showing how much thought has to go into it. I think if you were straight at your age, and had the same relationship, and knew you wanted to be together, I don't know that you would be having this conversation. You would just be like, "Let's start trying." You two are in this weird, interesting, fun space, bandying about all these ideas like, "Maybe I'll get a baby from Mexico or from my sister" because you have to, but at the same time because you can. I think those are two really interesting things.

OTHER BARON: Well and I think too, in addition to the financial stuff, emotionally preparing for the vastly different ways that we might have to, I'll say, acquire a child, because that's literally what we have to do. That emotional preparation is such a big part of it too. It's not just saving up $100,000 so that we can have a baby. But what if it goes wrong? What if it's hard? What if it happens too fast?

BARON: Yeah, it's a lot.

ROBIN: What's your trying number? When you would start trying?

OTHER BARON: I would love to be really serious in conversations at 37.

BARON: Oh, thank God. I was so scared he was going to be like 28. I was thinking 35, which is interesting.

DAVID

> For David, our self-proclaimed 50-year-old-millennial who also happens to be an introvert, the process of choosing how to have a child was all about which path would allow him the most anonymity. That path was surrogacy.

DAVID: So we considered what I think of as the big three—

adoption through an agency, adoption via a lawyer, and surrogacy.

We started with adoption, which was what I wanted to do. I thought adoption was the best, most noble and most compassionate thing to do. And so we went to an adoption fair, and I remember saying to Billy, "Okay, game face. Be really smiley and nice because we're two gay guys, and it's going to be mostly heterosexual couples. And we have to seem like we're adoption ready."

What I didn't realize was that for a lot of the heterosexual couples who were there, this was their last resort. Whereas for us, it was our first experience. In general, it was a sad vibe. It wasn't about being friends with other people because there are only "X" number of potential pregnant women who want to give their babies up for adoption. It felt like I was in competition with everyone in the room, and I don't want to be in competition, ever. I'm like, "If you really want it, take it."

The other reason that it didn't work out for us was because there was an open-ended time limit. You're waiting to get chosen. We have friends who had been waiting for three years. At the time I was 46 going on 47. I didn't have time to wait for three years.

Then another friend of Billy's said we should try a lawyer. And so we went to see this lawyer and it was the most harrowing experience of them all. Her office was covered, every space of the walls, with little wallet-sized photos of the kids that had been placed with families. But there were so many pictures that it didn't seem celebratory. And I remember it feeling like those detective movies, with the light swinging and someone smoking, and she's leaning in intensely. None of that happened, but that was the vibe.

Then she launched into her speech. "Here's what you have to know, 85% of the birth moms chain smoke, and the other 15%

are lying about smoking."

I said, "Okay."

"75% of them are on methadone."

I said, "Why?"

And she looked at me and said, "Are you serious?" Then she explained about the drug problem in our country. This was years ago, so I wasn't as aware of the tragedy of the opioid crisis that I am now.

And so I just said, "Oh."

Then she said, "I can get you a baby in six months."

Just like that.

"Here's what you need to do. Do you have a phone in your home?"

I said, "No. We got rid of our landline."

"Get a landline. Get a dedicated number. Someone needs to be manning it all the time. You're going to put out an ad in the Penny Saver and you're going to get calls and some of them are going to be people shaking you down for money. Some of them are going to be people just seeing if they can ingratiate themselves into your lives, and then one may be golden, but you take all those calls. I'll prep you on the conversation, and we'll go from there."

I remember thinking, "I am never going to work with you. Ever."

Again this was just my experience. I can't imagine that they're all like that. And in one way I do appreciate how frank she was, but she wasn't a good salesperson. It really was very scary.

So we settled on surrogacy. And really, the path we took goes back to a lot of what I was saying about my personality and being closeted, the shame of it all. To me the surrogacy route, ironically, was the least publicly intrusive.

CHAPTER 3

CHOOSING AN EGG DONOR, SPERM DONOR OR SURROGATE

Choice. Choice. And more choice. That's the world of nontraditional family fertility. On the surface, it's fabulous. Unburdened by the old "put the penis in the vagina to make a baby" requirement, LGBTQ couples get to intentionally choose the who, what, and even the where of fertility.

But once you delve into the options, you'll find there are nearly 1000 ways for an LGBTQ family to make a baby. Okay, it's more like eight, but that's still a lot of ground to cover in one chapter. And we really want to avoid a scenario where you're exhausted from a hellish day at work and you're lying in bed reading, but you're so tired you can barely hold our beautiful book up in the air. You're trying hard though and saying to yourself, "I just have 127 more pages to finish this chapter. Then I can go to sleep."

We want you to get your rest, so this chapter focuses solely on egg or sperm donors and surrogates.

How does one choose a donor? You can ask a friend to

donate. You can buy sperm from a sperm bank online. There you'll find search tools allowing you to filter everything from ethnicity to education to hair and eye color.

Sperm banks also have audio files of donors answering questions. There are baby photos. There are even details like what celebrity the donor looks like. And that's great. Except, how do you wade through all that information and pick a person whose genetics you'd like to use to make a baby?

The answer? For some, it was an easy, one-night decision, while others agonized. Their reasoning was as different as the couples interviewed. But we noticed a trend amongst many of the folks going through the process. We dubbed it the "Superman Phenomenon".

Superman Phenomenon
Noun
> When prospective parents get so intoxicated by the idea of choosing the perfect donor, they eliminate donors for minor health history infractions or slightly quirky personality traits.

It turns out it's no different when choosing a gestational carrier. In the beginning of our interviews, we mistakenly thought a carrier was nothing more than a hopper, and one only needed to find a healthy person to carry a baby to term. But we were corrected darn fast by a doctor who told us you need to be concerned with the emotional well-being of your carrier. If she is stressed out, that can affect the genes that are turned on or off in utero during the pregnancy.

We know there's a more scientific way of saying the above, but what we heard was choosing a gestational carrier is a hard decision too.

So let's dig into all the different ways folks made these decisions. But first, here's a cheat sheet defining some of the jargon related to donors and carriers.

Anonymous Donor (AKA Closed Donor)

Noun

> A person who donates sperm, generally to a sperm bank. The personal records of the donor are sealed, and the purchaser of the sperm agrees in writing that their children will not be able to determine the identity of the sperm donor when they are older.

Open Donor

Noun

> A person who donates sperm and who agrees in writing that when the child reaches age 18, the child has the right to learn who their donor was. The agreement may also allow one or more contacts between the child and the donor, and these agreements often vary from sperm bank to sperm bank.

Known Donor

Noun

> A person who you know and who is willing to donate sperm to make a baby for your LGBTQ family. How much this person will be involved in the child's life, and how much legal protection you want to set up around that relationship, is something you should clarify, preferably in writing, with the donor.

Egg Donor

Noun

> A person who donates her/their eggs so they can be used by another individual or couple to make a family by in vitro fertilization (IVF). Similar to sperm donors, egg donors can be anonymous or open.

Gestational Carrier

Noun

> A person who has someone else's fertilized egg

implanted in her/their womb. The objective is to carry and give birth to a child for another person or couple. A Gestational Carrier is also referred to as a "surrogate" in this book. Surrogacy is not currently legal in all states.

JAIMIE HERE

It's hard work choosing a donor. The options are endless. In the beginning Anne and I had a gay BFF that we contemplated using, but ultimately, we went the anonymous route. This was partly because we're selfish and didn't want to share our kids, and partly because the work surrounding a known donor scared the bejesus out of us. So much money, so much paperwork, so many details to hash out. Would we keep him in our lives? What would the kids call him? How involved would his family be? There were a lot more considerations involved in this decision. Imagine me and my scattered brain trying to hash out all the details of our new, utopian, three-parent family. It didn't take us long to realize that anonymity was best for us. We didn't want to know him and therefore our kids wouldn't want to know him either. This felt like the easiest path for all parties involved.

So off to the sperm bank website we went. We had some general criteria when we started out. We wanted someone who resembled us. Luckily, we look alike, so it was easy to narrow down which attributes to look for. We wanted someone with light hair, light eyes, and under 5'10". I'm on the short side and I didn't want my child to tower over me. I had always had this uncomfortable vision of myself as a tiny mother shaking a finger into the chin of my giant super-sized child. Screw moving the needle, I needed my kids to know who's boss. So we tried to find a shorter donor, but realized in our search that they don't really exist. Most people must want their kids to be tall, go figure.

Height wasn't the only decision we anguished over. This is where the search for Superman seriously reared its ugly head. I have to say, the power of the search is intoxicating. I can only liken it to a kid going to one of those Build-A-Bear factories. The options are endless and building the perfect, cuddliest bear gets overwhelming. To a similar degree, prospective gay parents become so befuddled by the possibility of configuring the perfect human specimen that our decision-making muscle can go a little haywire. None of the donors are good enough once we really start digging in. This one has a big nose. This one had acne. This one has beady eyes. This one has a grandmother who died. All really important stuff that totally matters, insert eye roll emoji here. Additionally, I wanted a musical guy and Anne wanted an athletic guy, two characteristics that rarely go hand in hand.

I didn't make a detailed binder like Robin and all the other organized lesbians we spoke to, but I did make a favorites folder in the sperm bank website that I would go over with Anne nightly. We toiled over this list that kept growing and shrinking for quite some time, and it started to seem like we would never be able to pull the trigger on a damn donor.

Until one day, we were out to dinner having a talk about our gay BFF whom we had considered asking to donate. He is a wonderful guy with good morals and a great personality, but he had none of the physical characteristics we were looking for at the sperm bank. And we realized it wouldn't matter. None of the silly stuff we'd been anguishing over for months mattered. Let the kid have acne. It would still be a child we would love and adore regardless of how oily their skin was. We went home that night and chose a donor.

Here's where we hit a little snag. We bought four vials of this guy's sperm and went forward with an insemination, which didn't work. Before our next insemination we went out with our good friends who had already had a child via a sperm donor. They started talking about why they had chosen an open donor versus a closed (anonymous) donor. They didn't know we were trying at this point, so they didn't know we had chosen a closed donor. They told us their reasoning for choosing an open donor.

They wanted to give their daughter the option of finding this guy if she had the desire. They felt that they were making all these other decisions in her life and that was one decision that they didn't want to make for her. You know, being all thoughtful about the future of their child and stuff, blah blah blah. Up to that point, Anne and I hadn't even been thinking about the possibility that our children might have opinions of their own and want to meet their donor someday. Children have opinions? But hearing these moms talk about this from the child's point of view suddenly made sense. Who were we to deny this right to our unborn babies? We were screwing them up before we even conceived them. Our eyes locked across the table, and we knew what we had to do.

We went home that night and picked a new donor who was open. Ultimately, we chose him not because of his physical attributes or his height, but because in his audio recording, he said he would be happy to meet his children in the future if they wanted to get to know him. Funny how you can start in one place and end up somewhere else entirely different.

So now, both of our children share the same donor, who was our second-choice guy. And they're perfect just the way they are.

And we wouldn't have it any other way.

ROBIN HERE TOO

Mary and I knew right from the get-go that we wanted to use a sperm bank. We also knew that we wanted to choose an open donor in case our kids had an interest in meeting their donor after they turned 18. We felt very confident with this decision. We figured by the time our kids are that age, we'll have nailed the whole parenting thing, and in that case, the donor's no threat to us. Or we will have failed miserably, and then maybe the donor will try to buy their love by paying for college. Win. Win.

Then one night we went out with all of Mary's gay

boyfriends. She has a lot of them. We shared our plans to make a baby over cocktails. It's so nostalgic to think about the time before kids when we spent an inordinate amount of time with friends, in bars, sitting on comfy couches, talking about nonsense. Anyway, within minutes of us sharing our plan, every guy we were out with offered his sperm. Mary and I didn't take any of them too seriously (because of the booze). The next day, I laughingly retold the story to my co-worker, Jeff, and he was ready to throw punches if I chose someone else's sperm over his.

All this was very flattering for a gal who was never asked to the prom. And it made us think about whether we should consider a known donor. After all, if we used a known donor, we wouldn't have to trust some report called "Staff Assessment" where a random sperm bank employee writes, "Donor #12345 is handsome, in a rugged way. He's soft-spoken, yet also hilarious. He has a twinkle in his eye that says he's up to something, but that something is his PhD in aeronautics!" If we used a known donor, we would see exactly what the donor looked like and how our child might turn out. This idea was momentarily appealing.

But I knew in my heart it wasn't the way I wanted to go forward. I wanted our family to be just me, Mary and our kids. I didn't want to bring in someone else as our kids' "Dad/Uncle" just because we needed his sperm to make the babies. In using a donor sperm bank there was a clear and delineated line stating that the donor was just that, a donor, and he was not part of our family. And it was a serious bonus that there was legal paperwork backing this up.

So we ended up with a transactional experience where I handed over our Amex card and someone sent a nitrogen tank of sperm straight to our doctor's office.

I would like to note that Mary and I were not above the whole Superman Phenomenon though. In our pursuit of perfection, we kicked a donor out because his Aunt had Eczema. Eczema! There was a reason we were being crazy though. There's a serious family history of alcoholism on my side, so the idea that we could weed out addiction was titillating.

But after the eczema incident, Mary reminded me that if we made a baby together, our kid would have all of my big girl, drunken German family genes, and also all of Mary's riddled with cancer, mom dying early from a blood clotting disorder genes too. Given the choice though, we would have jumped at the chance to make a baby together with both our faulty genes. That moment of clarity allowed us to take a breath and a giant step back, and consider medical history, but not be insane about it.

We ended up having to choose three different donors because the first one ran out of sperm, and then the second one left the program. But the choice got easier each time, and we ended up with two fabulous kids, if I do say so myself.

My advice with all this choice? Trust your gut.

CHOOSING A SPERM DONOR

"Probably the donor sperm thing was the biggest hurdle...I didn't know how you made that choice. And then all the things that I worried about, as it turned out, were meaningless...But isn't it terrifying how close you come to making huge decisions on the basis of nonsense?" – Emma Brockes

EMMA BROCKES

For Emma, deciding to have a baby on her own meant having to make very complicated decisions alone. She realized that not having a support system, whether it be a partner or the LGBTQ community, really slowed down the process.

EMMA: I feel like I was water circling down a drain. I just kept going around and around and around. I was trying to decide whether to use known sperm from a friend, which initially felt more natural to me. But then I came to the conclusion, like many of us do, that way was just too complicated.

And then the whole thing of even just picking donor sperm was so hard. I think if I'd have been embedded in the lesbian community slightly more, all of this would have been normalized and I would have known a million people, and the donor sperm stuff would have been something I was very familiar with, but I was in a very straight social group, so it all felt alien.

Probably the donor sperm thing was the biggest hurdle, actually. I was worried that it would be difficult for the kids. I didn't know how you made that choice. And then all the things that I worried about, as it turned out, were meaningless. Always right? But isn't it terrifying how close you come to making huge decisions on the basis of nonsense?

AIMEE AND MYRIAM

For Aimee and Myriam, religion is a very big deal, and as luck, or faith, would have it, God placed their sperm donor right in front of them at the exact moment they needed it, and we do mean literally, right in front of them.

AIMEE: We were at Brooklyn Pride, and we were at the point where we needed to find a sperm donor. It was so hard for us to decide. How do you choose? How do you pick these things? And our church tent was set up directly across the street from a lesbian owned sperm bank called Pacific Reproductive Services. And we were like, "Gosh, we need to find sperm. Maybe we should talk with them."

So we walked over to the table and told their representative that we wanted somebody that looked a little bit like me because we were using Myriam's egg first. And the lady was like, "Oh, you should go with donor 5696!"

"What, you have them all memorized. Really?"

And she said, "His smile looks like yours. Honestly, you should check it out."

We went home. We looked on the computer at that donor and we said, "That's him."

That was it. It was done. And it was exactly at the time when we needed him.

> **They also had some other considerations that were important in their choice of a donor.**

AIMEE: We really wanted to use the same donor for both our kids. And since we used both our eggs, it's cool that our kids are related to each other and also related to each of us. We wanted to have an open donor too, so if at age 18 the kids wanted to have that conversation, they could.

TIFFANY AND CARISSA

> **We talked to Tiffany and Carissa at various points during their process of trying to make a baby. They shared a lot about picking out a donor. It involved twists and turns like starting with a cryobank and shifting to a known donor they met on a Meetup type group.**

CARISSA: We have found a very different route to getting the donor samples that we need at the *not* cryobank price that we definitely do not need to continue to pay. We love the donor we found [from the sperm bank]. But it's just not feasible for us right now to continue paying that amount of money for something like sperm.

TIFFANY: So I was invited to this weird Midwestern chapter of Donor Illuminati. That's what I'm calling it. I found it via social media. It's like donor Tinder. It's a space that pairs donors who want to give anonymously, free of charge, to folks who are trying to get pregnant. We actually got paired with a person and went to meet up with him. And we had this very awkward -

CARISSA: Almost like an interview. We thought we were interviewing him, but it turned out, he was also interviewing us. Apparently, he says no to more people than he says yes to.

Because, to quote him, "He doesn't want to contribute to an already bad situation." So he's vetting folks that he wants to contribute sperm to.

TIFFANY: He seemed pretty conservative. No shade to the conservative folks, but I said, "Are you sure we're the ones? Because, you know we do bring some different stuff to the table here."

CARISSA: No, he was very impressed with us. It was weird that he was so impressed. I was surprised by that.

And he's kind of nerdy too, and awkward. We got an altogether good vibe from the situation. I mean, obviously, it's awkward. Even he started the meeting with, "So this is always awkward. We just have to push through the awkwardness."

Which we did. And it is funny looking back. Tiffany kind of took the route of, "Let me sit back, listen and watch this guy while he's talking to us and say certain things and see how he really acts." And I was the one with all of the questions. I asked all of the very direct, history related, legal, medical history questions. I was doing a little bit of sussing out the character too, but I was definitely trying to rack my brain for all of the questions that you're supposed to ask these people.

TIFFANY: And he was like, #wokebay. Because his ancestry seems to hail from the caucus.

CARISSA: He's white.

TIFFANY: Yes, but also like working class white guy from the Midwest, you know, the people that Trump is trying to reach, he's definitely one of them. But he was very honest, and very knowledgeable. He was definitely schooling us on how the law works here with regard to situations like the one we all were entering into in that moment, and helping us understand how contracts work, and how they can be used against us, and also used against him as well. Mainly how the laws can be.

> Tiffany and Carissa planned to use that donor until their
> doctor expressed some serious concerns because they
> had no way of testing his sperm prior to an insemination.
> So they switched directions, finding discounted sperm
> from a bank. Who knew that was even a possibility?

CARISSA: Then we had another change in our plan. We were going to go the route of the free donor.

TIFFANY: Yeah, but I had this really interesting trip to the doctor, and she kind of vetoed our plan, based on a number of things.

CARISSA: It was all mostly health related.

TIFFANY: And just in general being concerned about the lack of control on the science front.

CARISSA: Yeah, not knowing what would be in the specimen that would be going in Tiffany. I mean, we could have forced this dude to go and get tested for this, that, and the third, and show us the test results. But that didn't seem like something that was on his to do list. He said he got tested, but we don't know to what extent.

TIFFANY: I guess I still have trepidation about who, what, when, and where is the best way to go about doing things, and the best way to go about making babies. What's the safest thing to do? Some of this seems very slanted towards one specific nuclear way of making a family, cis-het nuclear.

But I think the real concern from my doctor's perspective was the more control we have, the better. Also, she suggested we go through a fertility clinic. So we have an appointment. That's one great thing about being a couple who can't actually just "baby dance" on our own, we have to rely on science. And so our doctor wants to take advantage of that just to make sure we have as much success as possible. Which is good. But the other side of that is money. So we selected a cryobank that will let us basically BOGO.

CARISSA: I love calling it BOGO [Buy One Get One] and I love seeing the expressions on the very select people that we've said the phrase BOGO to, specifically Tiffany's mom. Because BOGO is a hilarious way to talk about donor specimens.

TIFFANY: My mom is basically like, "What on God's green earth are you people doing?" Seriously though, it is helpful. It does limit the donor choice. But, financially, that's just the way we're going to have to do it, especially if we're going through a fertility clinic, where there's a little bit more intervention, a little bit more cost. At least this will be a little more affordable. Money is money.

I think we'd be remiss if we didn't talk about the fact that I have really had to tighten the circle of people that I'm even talking to about this in my life. I'm shocked at how aggressively shamed I've been by people. My circle has now gotten smaller because of people's responses to the route we chose to go with. People can't handle the fact that we didn't choose a cryobank or one of Carissa's family members. It's just very strange to me that that would be the case. It's very classist also. These are queer people with money. This is a privilege you have when you have money and jobs that will allow you to spend as much money as you want before the kid even gets here.

CARISSA: So we've decided to go this route, where we don't spend as much money, maybe don't have as much control over the donor selection. It's more about being able to spend less money on this whole getting pregnant process with the intention that we want the bulk of our money to go toward this kid or kids when they're here.

TIFFANY: It just doesn't matter, at least for me. Who cares who this person is? Our priorities have shifted. We just don't care about the baby batter anymore. We care about the baby.

MARK AND GREG

> It's always nice to get the perspective of a doctor. Here's Mark, our resident gay dad and Reproductive Endocrinologist, talking about choosing an open donor.

MARK: I think it's nice for the children to have access to their genetic gamete donor [egg or sperm donor]. We went through the process of making sure our donor knew that we had to put a legal agreement in place so we would have permission for children to contact her in the future.

Nowadays in my practice, 95% of our donors are open. We have adult videos. We have pictures. Donors are willing to meet the parents. The same thing has happened in the sperm donor world. So now there are adult photos, you can see videos, you can do a video Skype.

THE ABBYS

> Sam and Laura had a ticking clock because Laura had some fertility issues, but it still took them a really long time to find a donor. Laura felt strongly that she did not want to be pushed into making a hasty decision.

SAM: I think we knew deep down inside that we didn't want to use anyone we knew as a sperm donor. We'd heard some negative stories, and also we knew ourselves, were not good sharers, so we knew a sperm bank was the way to go for us.

Next thing you know we're listening to these audio recordings of guys saying things like, "I'm 23, and I like soccer. My favorite subject is American literature, and my hero is Steve Jobs."

LAURA: Everybody's hero is always Steve Jobs.

SAM: At this point, our fertility clinic had given us a folder with recommended clinics, and I made us a couple of profiles with some of the FDA approved sperm banks. And listen, I know how Laura works. I can't throw a spreadsheet of 100 donors at her, but I did know that if I showed her like three donors every night, and we really went through them—

LAURA: And she made me really go through them.

SAM: So every night for months we would narrow things down. Eventually, it got to the point where we had three left.

LAURA: It is a good thing we got started early because I don't think I realized how long it would take.

SAM: She's not easy in that sense. Things take time.

LAURA: I'm not emotional in my decision making.

SAM: And Laura doesn't believe in signs or things like that.

LAURA: I'm very pragmatic.

SAM: But then something happened when Laura was looking at the last three choices.

LAURA: This one donor had written a quote in his little essay that my father had given in his speech at our wedding. I knew I needed something to help me make this decision, and that sign was really clear, even for me.

SARA AND HILARY

Sometimes choosing between a donor from a bank or asking a friend is more about timing and circumstance. Sara and Hilary wanted to use a friend as their donor, but it just wasn't in the cards.

SARA: Initially, we wanted a known donor. We had a friend who had donated sperm to a lesbian couple that he knew from high school, and they have a lovely family dynamic. They live in separate states, but they're part of each other's lives. And we wanted something like that.

ROBIN: What appealed to you about that?

SARA: Just that our child would know his biological or her biological father, and those are sometimes hard questions as the child gets older. And I worried that the child not being able to know who helped create them would upset them in some way.

HILARY: Yeah, we never wanted our child to feel like they were missing out on some aspect of parenthood, I guess. Parental figures.

SARA: So we thought maybe that's the way to go. Then we have this person in our lives and in our child's life.

HILARY: And I had a long-time friend from graduate school, and we were super close, best friends. And he was also gay and wanted to parent a child, but not necessarily be one hundred percent involved. So we started kidding about it. We'd go out to the bar and I'd say, "Why don't you be my baby daddy?" It was kind of a joke, but then it evolved into, "What if we actually did this?"

So when Sara and I started talking about having children, we thought, "Who is on the shortlist?" And, he was at the top of it. I don't remember when we approached him about it, but I remember it was very casual.

SARA: I remember. You guys were out without me and you had the conversation. And you asked him to think about it, and he just said, "I think I want to do it, but obviously I want to think about it." He needed to talk to his boyfriend at the time.

HILARY: Yeah, he was partnered up at the time.

SARA: It didn't take that much time though for him to say yes. So we went back to our fertility clinic, and unfortunately when he went to donate his sperm our doctor said that his was probably not the right sperm.

HILARY: He had low counts in all four categories.

SARA: They said they wouldn't recommend using this sperm.

HILARY: And you don't want to spend all the money and go through the whole process. We had to just make a decision and say, "This isn't going to work out." And it was heartbreaking for all of us, I think more so for him at that point than for us because we were ready to just move on and do what it needed to take to make our family.

SARA: So then we started the process of looking for an anonymous donor. We went to a large bank. And Hilary was fantastic about doing all the research. She was the one because I was like, "Oh my god, this is so overwhelming."

She had this binder and worked down to her favorites. I was like, "Talk to me when you've narrowed it down to five or six." So she found her top five or six choices. And then I got into the picture.

KAREN AND TOBI

> Karen and Tobi were one of the few couples who made the sperm donor choice without a lot of agonizing.

TOBI: We knew of two sperm banks. One on the East Coast and one on the West Coast.

KAREN: And everybody we knew had used the one on the West Coast, so I didn't want to use it. I was like, "Let's use the one we've never heard of."

TOBI: And I do remember thinking that we're going to be raising this child on the East Coast, so if she wanted to follow up with him the chances of him being there are better.

JAIMIE: So you chose the bank and you chose an open donor and that was a conscious decision?

TOBI: Absolutely. We felt that we were making all these other decisions in this kid's life and that was one decision that we didn't want to make for them.

ROBIN: Did you have a hard time choosing the donor? Did you agonize?

KAREN: It took about three seconds.

TOBI: We're fast decision makers.

KAREN: We had a shortlist that we made in one night.

ROBIN: But did you get all the pictures and pay for all that other extra available information?

KAREN: We did pictures and voice recordings.

TOBI: Just for the one we picked. And we chose a lot of Karen's traits and features, and someone who was tall.

KAREN: And, we didn't pay for "Ivy League."

TOBI: Wasn't the program called "PhD?"

KAREN: Whatever it was, I was like, "Gimmie a break with that." We did actually pay for the pictures and audio of two donors though because I remember listening to the other guy—he was perfect on paper—but then we heard the interview and he sounded like a douche. He sounded like an egotistical jerk, and then the other guy, answered "What was your favorite child-hood memory?" with "I used to like to go out and play street hockey with my brothers."

TOBI: Karen was like, "Done!"

KAREN: That's the one.

JANA AND LINDA

Before Linda and Jana were together, Linda had kids with a previous partner. For Linda, ethnicity was very

important in her donor choice, but she also had some reproductive challenges and worried she was getting too old. This meant she needed a donor ASAP, and she would have to be a tad bit more flexible with her must-haves list.

LINDA: In the beginning, our fallback was the sperm bank. I had a very close relationship with my father, and I wanted to allow our children to have a man in their lives. And I wanted a black man. That was really important to me, so I started asking friends, even acquaintances after a while.

ROBIN: Hello, my mailman. You're a handsome black man.

LINDA: Just short of that. I asked my personal trainer. He said no. It was like asking people to the prom, over and over and getting rejected. Probably the most irritating one, though I'm not that bitter about it anymore, was my ex-boyfriend from college. When he said no I was like, "Well you were trying to hit that when we were in college. You didn't care then." Not that I wanted to hit that, I just wanted the juice. So he said, "Oh, but I don't want children out in the world" I was like, "Well I'm sure you have children out in the world, at our age." We had a little bit of a tiff.

And in between asks, we tried a sperm bank a couple of times, but I never got pregnant. My doctor said that I had one ovary that wasn't working very well, and she said at my age, with the bad ovary, I'd do better with fresh.

So I did ask a lot of people and by then it was turning into a fix up. There was one guy who was a friend. He was Peruvian and he kept saying, "I will have the child with you."

And I said, "No. You're not black."

But, he had some old crumbled up picture of his grandmother, and he said, "Look. She's black!"

I was just like, "She doesn't look black. And you don't look black, so no."

But then when the sperm bank didn't work out, and most of the guys said no—we had found one willing guy, but unfortunately, his sperm was not viable. So finally, I started thinking, "You know what? What happened to that Peruvian guy? Because this is ridiculous. I need to manage my expectations about how hot I am as a lesbian."

JANA: He's looking a little bit black right about now.

LINDA: Let's see that grandmother again.

STACEYANN CHIN

> **Staceyann was single and spent years trying to find the right known donor to help her make her family. But after looking high and low, her donor showed up. It was a person she already knew, and he was the last person she expected.**

STACEYANN: When I came to the US, I was undocumented for a couple of years, and I married a gay man and we were going to make a family together. He had the sperm and I had a uterus. I was married to him for many, many, many years. We were trying to do something radical and rewrite the whole narrative for family, and we were going to make babies together. He would jack off and give it to Dr. B. and mix it with my eggs, and then voila, omelet. But then he got cancer, and he died. He was diagnosed in May and he was dead in December.

And so then I had to be hunting for sperm after that because my sperm tap had crossed over into the netherworld. I knew for part of my healing process, to heal the tragedy that happened in my own childhood, I needed to make a family with whom I could have a relationship with. And so when Peter died, I spent a couple of years chasing sperm. I remember being on a flight to LA when I was checking my ovulation and looking down the aisle and thinking, "That guy has great teeth. I could go fuck him in the bathroom. I'm sure I could make all the sounds, and then he would come, and I would get pregnant." Because it's always that easy, you just throw some sperm and catch me in the forehead and I'm pregnant, right?

So, ten years after my ex died, I still hadn't found the sperm. But I was still very close to my brother-in-law, and one day I was talking to him and I said, "Oh my god, man, if Peter hadn't died, I would have fucking sperm coming out my ears right now."

And he said, "Yeah, I'm sorry about that. But, why not just use mine?"

And so my brother-in-law donated the sperm and is now my daughter's Baba. And my mother-in-law is my kid's grand-mother and all my sister and brothers-in-law are Zuri's aunts and uncles.

USING AN ANONYMOUS SPERM DONOR

"We started trying in '94 so everything was really new. They didn't have open donors at sperm banks then. And we looked at the sperm like 'It's just a body part or an excretion from a body.' We decided that this was our family and that was it." - Judy Gold.

We heard from other families who made the decision to choose an anonymous donor. Sometimes the reasoning had to do with family autonomy, and in other cases that was the only available choice at the time.

RAE AND MARGIE

It was the mid-80s when Rae and Margie were creating their family. They didn't have the option of an open donor at a sperm bank. Their choices were someone they knew or finding an anonymous donor through another route. They ended up using a doctor who sourced sperm

from medical students.

RAE: It was on the Upper East Side of Manhattan.

MARGIE: Our doctor used medical students, who would, at the appointed time, come to some place and donate. What he told us was that they had been screened for basic things. I mean, there wasn't any real genetic testing done at the time. But I think they were screened for major illnesses in the family or conditions. And interestingly enough, because this was 1985, after I became pregnant, we started to worry about AIDS. But this was an anonymous donor with no chance for anybody knowing anything.

RAE: After Emma was born, they were maybe two or three occasions where we tried to find out information. One was around the AIDS crisis and the second was when Emma was about 20 or 22. We tried to investigate and find out what happened to the doctor's file, but we weren't able to.

ROBIN: How did you guys feel when that came up that she wanted to find the donor?

MARGIE: Well I think I was fine with it. I was not surprised. It wasn't the first time she had expressed an interest in knowing. Even when she was very young, she expressed an interest in knowing.

I think I always felt a little badly that we made the decision to not have a known donor. It was the best thing for us because Rae would not have been able to handle a known donor. I think it was hard enough for her not having a legal attachment, so I think it was the right decision, but it was a decision and it had repercussions. Emma would never be able to know this part of her genetic background.

RAE: So we did regret not knowing the donor and that we had made a decision to deprive her of that knowledge. That didn't feel very good.

MARGIE: So we put another 50 cents in the therapy jar, and that made it all better.

EMMA T.

Emma is the daughter of Rae and Margie. When Emma was a young child, she had a tough time understanding the concept that her donor was anonymous.

EMMA: It was explained to me for about the millionth time, that it was anonymous both ways to protect the donor, and us. He didn't know who I was, and I didn't know him.

And what I remember is, we were in my room, and we drew this picture of what I thought the donor looked like. Margie and I drew this picture of this made-up guy, and what we thought he would look like. It didn't feel deep at the time. It just felt like hanging out.

I drew this blonde guy. He was pretty feminine, and he had jeans on, and he was tall, slim, and very blonde, with a bowl cut. And he had this Cowboys sweatshirt on. We didn't know anything about sports. But I think my mom had had a boyfriend or, perhaps her ex-husband from way back when who liked the Cowboys or something. It was the male shirt to put him in. I don't know anything about that team. I assume it's football. I'm not even sure.

So he had a Cowboys shirt on, and his name was Francis. And it was really nice. It worked to satisfy my curiosity from my imagination, and it highlighted what began this journey of, what actually matters is, "What do you think he is?"

MAKEDA AND SADIE

Makeda and Sadie, are the authors of *Spawning Generations: Rants and Reflections on Growing Up with LGBTQ+*

Parents. **They're both queerspawn, and both are married, but to different people. Their parents did not have the easiest time trying to find donors in Canada back in the 80s and early 90s.**

SADIE: I also have an anonymous sperm donor but it was through a sperm bank. The situation in Toronto was different. I have no way of ever knowing who my sperm donor is because this was before the days of ID release. I actually know of two donor's siblings that I have. And I found out when I was 18 or 19 that we actually were blood related.

MAKEDA: In the mid-80s, my moms decided to try to have a kid. They didn't really know any other people doing it at that time, so they created a sort of do-it-yourself community of other lesbians in Vancouver who also wanted to try to figure out how to have kids.

They got an anonymous sperm donor. It was actually a friend of a friend, and he wanted to remain anonymous, and my moms also wanted him to remain anonymous.

ROBIN: So you don't know who it is to this day?

MAKEDA: I actually do know who it is now, but that only happened in the last five to six years, so I didn't know who he was until my late 20s.

They didn't use a sperm bank because in Vancouver there was basically one fertility clinic. That fertility clinic was run by a very homophobic doctor, and he did not inseminate lesbian couples. He wouldn't do it. Even single women had a hard time.

ROBIN: What a turd.

MAKEDA: Yeah, I know, right? The other issue was that he wasn't testing sperm donations for HIV because again, he was very homophobic, and he said publicly, "Well, I know all of my donors, and none of my donors are *like that*."

So my moms had a really, really hard time finding sperm because it was expensive to get sperm from a bank in the States. And my moms didn't know a lot of men. That just wasn't who was in their world.

ROMAINE

Radio host Romaine Patterson answered the question of why she and her wife, Iris purposely chose an anonymous donor. And this lady doesn't pull any punches. She gets straight to the point.

ROMAINE: We decided we were going to go with an anonymous donor from a sperm bank. We played a lot of scenarios out in our mind. We originally thought if I was having the baby, maybe we should ask Iris' brother to be our donor. But then I was like, "That's just weird. We're not doing that."

Then we looked at donor situations. I didn't want to use any of my friends. I like my friends, but I don't want any of them involved in raising my child. It's weird and it's awkward. And you know what? Raising a kid is hard enough with two people who may or may not agree on everything when it comes to child rearing. I do not need to add in a third person.

Then we thought, "Well, okay, we're going to go the sperm bank route. Do we want to have a donor that eventually our child could meet or not meet?" And I thought, "No." And I did it for purely selfish reasons. I just didn't want to complicate my life. Down the road, if she wants to go and meet a sibling, she could do the sibling registry thing. If she wants to, but I don't need any of that crap. I just don't. I don't need that extra stress of wondering if one day, is she going to grow up and think we weren't sufficient? Then she's going to want to meet her biological donor. I don't need that shit, and my wife agreed.

When I think about the types of people who are making these donations. A lot of these guys are college kids. They're getting their money to go party. Let's be honest about why these guys are doing this. And the thing is, here's the reality, I'm thankful that they exist. I'm thankful that they made the donations, or I wouldn't have the family that I do, but I don't know this person. I don't know anything about this person. If my child someday wants to meet this person, I don't want them to be disappointed by whoever the hell they're gonna meet. So I'm just not gonna make this complicated.

CHOOSING EGG DONORS AND SURROGATES

"When we looked for egg donors, there was not the Match. com selection choice that happens with sperm. Our donor egg nurse coordinator, who I love, said, 'You know, I think we found your donor!' I recently saw the coordinator and I just gave her a big hug because we love our kids so much, and she made that happen." – Dr. Mark

As lesbians, we're more than ready to stop talking about sperm. Let's shift the conversation to how one finds an egg donor and/or a gestational carrier AKA, surrogate.

MARK AND GREG

> Many folks (like your authors) thought that a surrogate is nothing more than a hopper. Dr. Mark, our fertility doctor extraordinaire, explained why a surrogate is so much more than a vessel. The health and well-being of the carrier is more than important, it defines your future baby.

ROBIN: If all the genetics are coming from the egg donor and from you guys, do you feel like she's a part of the children?

MARK: There's this whole field called epigenetics, and I think most people think of our genetic code as a hard code, but it's not. It's a flexible code and what genes are on and what genes are off are determined by the environment. And the most powerful epigenetic effect on who you are, is in utero. The second most powerful epigenetic effect is birth to five. So the woman who carries the pregnancy is basically in command and control of some of the genes that are either turned on or off in pregnancy.

Her hormones, her lifestyle, her mood, her behaviors are determining factors. There are extreme examples of identical twins, where one twin had a very difficult pregnancy, maybe they were getting less supply or maybe they were in one particular part of the uterus or they were sharing blood supply and one twin was getting more than the other. Those twins don't look identical. And they carried the same genes, but the expression of the genes changed because of the environment in utero.

Epigenetics is a hot thing in medicine right now. It's everywhere about how environment affects gene expression. Think about it, we're all using BPA free bottles for our kids because we think that the plastics in the bottle affects gene expression, which may affect the health and well-being of our children or their cancer risk and things like that.

For my patients who have to use an egg donor, they are biologically linked to that child because they're the person who carries that pregnancy. They're the person who's doing everything they can to take care of that child in utero and that affects gene expression.

I have patients using surrogates, and they worry about what she's eating, how happy she is, and all those other things because those things do translate potentially down to not only the health of the pregnancy or potentially the health and well-being of the child. I usually say, your carrier's not a vase that's growing a potted plant. They're actually taking an embryo from 150 cells to a seven-pound baby and that baby is interacting with your carrier's environment the whole time and that goes for women who are receiving donated eggs and women are receiving donated embryos.

So your child may have been slightly different personality wise if a different person carried them. We don't know for sure because we don't have that experiment. But it's possible.

Even though Mark is a fertility doctor who is incredibly knowledgeable in this field, when it came down to choosing the surrogate, he and his husband, Greg were just as nervous as any other prospective parents.

MARK: We worked with a surrogacy agency. They are the ones that present you with a match. Basically, you contract with the agency, and then they do a search and it usually takes three to six months for them to tell you you're at the top of the list. And when the next surrogate comes through the door that passes the preliminary screening, they present them to you. Then they coordinate a phone call.

GREG: That call is nerve wracking because you want her to like you.

MARK: And you want to like her.

GREG: I remember when we had our conversation with our surrogate. We were in our bedroom and we were very nervous to start the phone call.

MARK: When you connect with your surrogate initially, for a dad to be, you've already been waiting four to six months. So you're kind of incentivized to like her even if you don't love her because if you say no, you might have to wait another two or three months. And you already have embryos and you just want to have a baby.

GREG: Yeah, I also wanted her to like me because to me, this woman is giving us such a gift. And I can't thank her enough. She was wonderful throughout it. I mean, she was just so cool. And I was so appreciative of what she was doing every step of the way.

In addition to choosing a surrogate, Mark and Greg had

to also choose an egg donor. And even though Dr. Mark counsels people to be practical and logical in their donor choices, both he and his husband got caught up in the search for Superman, or, in their case, Superwoman.

MARK: Then we had to pick an egg donor, and Greg was really interested in height.

GREG: Initially, I wanted taller rather than shorter and there were a couple things that this process made me rethink and one was physical characteristics. It made me dive deeper into the questions, "Who is this person that's donating their egg and genetic material to our future child? And what are they like today?"

It was really interesting to read the questionnaire from the possible donors. How these women described their families and the activities they were involved in. And I realized that I was thinking more of superficial stats, which I think are important too, but I realized there was so much more to this. It occurred to me that this choice was a really, really big deal.

MARK: It is a really big deal. I've been wearing glasses since I was in second grade and I always hated them. So I didn't want anybody who was nearsighted. I don't want my kids to suffer like I did. You might as well move the needle, right? Greg was interested in someone that was tall. But, during the process, there were a few people, my professional friends, who know the process, and one of these women was over at our house. And she's not that tall. We talked about this and she was wearing four-inch heels. And she got on our tiptoes and looked Greg in the eye and she said, "What's wrong with being 5'4"?" That made me dive a little deeper.

DAVID

Finding a surrogate was a difficult journey for David and his husband. They went through two different unsuccessful surrogates before an unexpected volunteer stepped

forward to help them make their family.

DAVID: For us, the agency that we joined was a little—well, the town was a little dry, and they didn't have a lot of surrogates for us, so we we're waiting. We ended up "liking"—I'm doing air quotes—the first one we interviewed. I had reservations, such as the lack of eye contact, but she seemed fine, and she came well recommended. So I didn't have huge reservations about her, but I wasn't like, "This is the Dream Team!" And Billy felt the same way. But we had lost so much time, and I was approaching 50, which is obviously a thing for me, since I keep saying it.

Long story short, as it turns out, this first surrogate was actually looking for a revenue stream so she could have money to leave her husband. We did three or four transfers with her. All failed, and then she disappeared. She left her husband and left us.

So we got the second surrogate, who seemed lovely. Again they were a military family. You could tell they were happily married, and she had a passion for and a connection to France, which I also do, so I felt more connected to her than the first surrogate. And she was like, "Let's go, go, go! We're gonna do this for you."

I thought, "This is great."

We had a transfer with her. We put two eggs in, and she got pregnant, and it was very exciting. She was pregnant for 14 days before she lost them. And what happened was she lost one of them, and the other egg went ectopic. That was a disaster, and in the 14 days from when she lost one to when we found out about the ectopic pregnancy, she cut off all communication with everybody and was very aggressive with the nurses.

I feel, though I'll never know for sure because we never heard from her again, but I feel that she was so positive because she had been a surrogate once before, and she was so sure of her ability to get pregnant. When it turned out to be worse than not getting pregnant, but also the pain of the ectopic, I think she was really disappointed and angry. So we broke things off with her and that was harrowing, and it was sad.

But, the amazing thing that happened was someone who worked at our surrogacy agency stepped forward and said, "I'm going to do this for you. I'm going to be your carrier."

I mean, wow. It's sort of like if your coworker says, "I know that you're heartbroken. I'll marry you."

And I have to tell you, it was really crazy. And people think it's crazy when I tell them that, but it was the one time all this made sense.

GARY AND TONY

> During the process of trying to find their egg donor, Gary And Tony drove all the way to Florida to meet the candidate. The couple wanted so much to connect with this woman, but had to remind themselves to take a breath and make sure she was the right choice.

TONY: The hardest thing that we had to agree on was that we had to sleep on these major decisions. We couldn't just get caught up in the moment and go "We love you!"

GARY: Which is, of course, what happened.

TONY: So we went down to meet our egg donor. Holly is on active duty in the military. She's a single mom, and she was stationed in Jacksonville at the time. We went down and we got this hotel room.

GARY: But wait! We'd been together longer than online dating profiles have been around, so when we started looking at egg donor profiles online, we had never done anything like that before, and it was just crazy. I read the first one and I thought, "Oh my god, this woman sounds amazing!"

Then I looked at another one, and I said, "Oh, this woman uses capital letters, maybe that's important to factor in."

How do we judge this?

TONY: I knew from Holly's profile that I liked her, but what sealed the deal was she came to visit us at our hotel room, and she brought her son and a handful of family photo albums. One of my favorite memories was sitting with her at the table going through her family photo albums while Gary and her son, Noah bounced back and forth on the beds behind us. I told you he was the fun one.

And we just knew.

LET'S HEAR FROM THE DONORS

What compels someone to donate sperm or an egg or their womb to help other folks make a family? It's not an easy process. It's time consuming. There's not a lot of compensation for the time or effort, so that makes the stories of folks who donate even more interesting. Whatever the reason they chose to donate, we're thankful to all the folks who donate a piece of themselves so families like ours can be made.

TOM

Tom met the mom that he donated sperm to way back when they were kids. In fact, they have Sunday School to thank for their connection. Thank you, Jesus!

TOM: The birth mom and I actually have known each other for many, many years. We went to junior high and high school together, and before that we actually were in the same Sunday school class.

Though we didn't socialize a lot together, years later, we were all at a mutual friend's 30th birthday party. And as we we're catching up, they were talking about how they wanted to start a family. And I literally just came right out and said, "Oh, do you need a sperm donor?"

So now, my biggest joke with her is, "Did you ever think, back when you were sitting in Sister Bernadette's Sunday school class that the future father of your children was sitting right across the aisle?"

NATE

Nate is a single, gay man living in the UK, and he decided to become a sperm donor after listening to our podcast. That's right, our little podcast is making babies.

NATE: I listen to your podcast, and I obviously got to know a lot more about the US system of sperm donation than the UK system, and I thought I'll give it a look up in the UK. And I found out that we actually have a massive shortage of sperm donors here, so I decided to research it all.

ROBIN: The Great Sperm Donor Shortage of 2018.

NATE: Yeah, and since then, I started going through the process of donating sperm. It's a long process here.

ROBIN: Are you saying because of this little idea that Jaimie had that I turned into 47 Google documents, that now became a podcast, you decided to donate sperm?

NATE: I did.

ROBIN: Jaimie, we made babies.

JAIMIE: Our podcast made babies.

NATE: We've got a lot of regulations here around sperm donation. We've got a specific body called HEFA [Human Fertilization and Embryo Authority] that regulates everything having to do with sperm donation and embryos. But I think the biggest problem is that since 2005, here in the UK, donors have to be known no matter what.

Since 2005, if you donate sperm, you have to be willing that when that child turns 16, they can find out non-identifying information about you, your hair color, height and things like that. Then when they turn 18, they can find out your full name, your latest address, your email address and things like that. HEFA holds a database of everyone who's ever donated sperm since 2005, and the children contact HEFA directly. Then HEFA will contact you and say, "Oh, by the way, somebody has requested your details, so be aware that you may be contacted soon."

ROBIN: You may have baby knocking on your door soon.

NATE: Yeah, exactly. It's very difficult to be a donor. It's like one in 100 men or something are accepted to be donors, because we also have very strict laws about the quality of your sperm, how it can survive freezing, and you have to know quite a lot about your background and things like that to be eligible to donate.

ROBIN: How do they know if you lie?

NATE: I guess they just take you at your word. They have quite stringent medical testing. Just about a week ago, I gave six vials of blood to be shipped off and tested.

ROBIN: Have you actually donated the sperm yet or are you just in the process of gearing up?

NATE: I've donated sperm to be tested, and that's all been accepted as high quality enough.

ROBIN: Did you pat yourself on the back a little bit when you got the results?

NATE: Well, I didn't find out until after that it was so stringent. And then I was sitting in the lobby waiting for my blood tests, and I read the information they gave, and it said "About one in 100 men have what it takes. Do you have what it takes?"

JAIMIE: Wow, talk about pressure, huh?

NATE: Yeah, so I suppose it's a bit of an ego boost.

KELLY THE SURROGATE

Kelly has a bunch of kids of her own, but she always knew she wanted to be a surrogate and help someone else bring a child into the world. Once she started looking into that process, she insisted that she carry for LGBTQ families.

KELLY: When I was in high school, "Days of our Lives" was on TV. I guess it's still on, I haven't watched it in like 30 years. But Dr. Marlena Evans in real life had a surrogate, and I remember seeing the story on "Current Affair" and thinking, "Oh my gosh, how awesome is that?" That woman had a baby for her. A little seed was put in my head and I thought, "One day, I'm going to do that."

Fast forward to after I had my own kids. I thought, "Yes, I still want to do this." It was something that I had brought up to my ex, even before we had kids. This is a goal that I had for myself just like getting my masters and everything else. I said, "I want to do this before I die."

When the time came, it was 2007 and I Googled "surrogacy for gay dads" because I realized there was a population that I could help. Up came two or three different agencies, Growing Generations being one of them. And I clicked around, I kind of looked at the websites and Growing Generations had been around for a long time. Their website seemed very legit. They had lots of information. Even to this day, 12 years later, as a surrogate, some agencies don't tell you the information that you should be able to find out before you apply.

So I decided that Growing Generations was where I was going. And I feel like I lucked out there because now that I work at the agency, I have calls all the time with women who are just going with us blindly. And I think, "Thank God you're with us." If they were going blindly with somebody else they could really get screwed in the process. I feel like it's my job to protect women. That's the other reason why I have a blog about my surrogacy journey and everything I do. If other women are going to be doing this, they need to be smart about it, and make good decisions for you and your family. The only way that you can do that is if you have all the information.

KIM BERGMAN

Kim is the founder of the surrogacy agency Growing Generations, and the author of *Your Future Family: The Essential Guide to Assisted Reproduction*. Kim knows that it takes a very special type of person to carry someone else's baby.

KIM: Surrogates are just the most loving, altruistic people around. It's not about the money. It's a type of person. They want to help. They are so giving. They're the kind of people who would sign up for a bone marrow registry.

It's hard in the abstract to really understand who they are, but the minute you talk to a real life surrogate, you know. We sort of joke about them being like unicorns, this mythical figure. But when you're sitting with someone who's going to be or has been a surrogate, it instantly makes sense. You talk to them and think, "Oh, now I really understand."

CHAPTER 4

THE SCIENTIFIC ROUTE: PATHS AND PITFALLS

The scientific route can be overwhelming. It's like gambling. You've been at the roulette table for a while. You're far into the money you budgeted to spend, possibly even into that extra money from your back pocket that you told yourself you would not use to gamble. Now you're exhausted, and very aware oxygen is being pumped into the room. You have a decision to make. You've been betting on 33 black for a while, but you keep losing. You don't want to switch to 23 red though because you know, the moment you do, 33 will hit. Do you quit or keep going?

The scientific route can feel an awful lot like that.

Also, it comes with the extra added pressure of charging your credit card every time you walk into a doctor's office, meet with an egg or surrogate agency, order sperm from the internet, or get screened by a social worker or therapist—because a doctor made you do that, not because you wanted to check in on your mental health. You're fine, thank you very much.

But you believe this path greatly increases your odds of pregnancy because of the doctors. So you're optimistic. You know this will work because science. And also, why wouldn't it?

The short answer is you're right, it will totally work. But also, it might not. Some couples we talked to got pregnant right away, others had a journey in front of them with a capital JOURNEY.

And as you can imagine, every couple had a different story to share.

ROBIN HERE

Mary and I never considered the turkey baster route. Mostly because our original plan was to put my egg in Mary's hopper. Once we changed routes to IUI with me carrying the baby using my own eggs, we were already in the medical pipeline, so we didn't consider switching courses.

Also, I felt in my bones, not through any kind of actual research, that our odds would be better with a doctor and science. We needed two vials of sperm per month with either method, because at the time, the recommendation was to do two inseminations per cycle, and for that cost, we wanted the best odds we could get. Even if I made those odds up in my head.

We did our first IUI in the spring of 2007. After the insemination, we went to a playground to sit down for a moment and take in what just happened. I remember sitting on the bench that day thinking A. it's creepy that sperm is swimming around inside me and B. I might be pregnant. That second thought seemed both naive and completely possible.

Turned out, I was pregnant from that very first IUI. I was astounded and shocked and very much like WTF, as the kids today say. I remember being in tears trying to process the gravity of the situation, as Mary sang and made brunch. We didn't have kids, so we still brunched. Mary was very matter of fact about the whole affair, "Why wouldn't it work? He put the sperm right next to the egg." Her lack of excitement was a bit of a bummer, but I figured I'd deal with Mary's nonchalance later because I was pregnant!

Seven weeks later, we had our weekly appointment, and we

heard the baby's heartbeat. We cried, held hands and then went to work, like you do. But later that day, the doctor called to say that my numbers weren't doubling like they should be, and it was likely I would miscarry. It was a punch in the gut, and we were both devastated.

After an excruciating week of waiting, I miscarried, and we both had all kinds of complicated feels come up. I know this miscarriage stuff is a bit off topic, but I feel strongly that it's important we talk about miscarriages. They're common, emotional, sad, upsetting, stressful, and on and on. But the worst part is so many women suffer them in silence. Open up. Share. You'll feel better.

Anyway, we took a month off and recovered. We tried again. Ran out of sperm. Found out our donor retired out of the program. Chose a new donor, much quicker than the first time. Had a month where my follicles didn't get big enough. To which the doctor said, "Oh, that happens sometimes." The scientific route may come with increased odds, but it also comes with so much information, often more than you ever needed or wanted.

Then on the fourth IUI, when we were wondering if we might have to consider some kind of escalation to IVF, I got pregnant. And nine months later, give or take some days, our daughter was born.

During the process, we went from thinking science was solid, the only way to go and could never be wrong, to realizing that no matter how you make that kid of yours, it's always a miracle. And nothing is guaranteed.

JAIMIE HERE TOO

"Everything will be okay in the end. If it's not okay, it's not the end." – John Lennon

That quote holds a special place in my heart. Don't get it twisted though, I'm not one of those dreamy people who tape inspirational sayings around my apartment. Although I admire those people, I've never gone out of my way to surround myself with the "warm thoughts" I might need to make it through the day. I'd rather watch my favorite TV show and hope some inspirational words hit me from the mouths of my favorite characters. I learned everything I need to know from *Game of Thrones.*

But this quote helped me through a rough patch a few years back. I don't know if you listen to our podcast, but if you do you know that a big reason this podcast came about is because I suffered through two-and-a-half years of unexplained infertility before finally getting pregnant with my son. As you also know, Anne had our daughter first because her eggs were a little longer in the tooth, so to speak. Being seven years younger than Anne, we figured I had plenty of time to get started with the whole "put the syringe in the hoo-ha to make a baby" game. Turns out, despite my youthful glow, my eggs may have been more disadvantaged than Anne's from the get-go. "Hindsight's a bitch." That's another one of my favorite quotes.

So when our daughter Rose was 18 months old, we decided to start trying for number two. We wanted them to be close in age for some dumb reason that I can't remember. Seriously, let's have two babies in diapers at the same time and see what happens! Moms are silly like that sometimes. We started trying in secret, and I couldn't wait to surprise everyone with our news. "Look how awesome I am at being pregnant, you had no idea!" I would really knock everyone's socks off with my covert baby making skills. Fast forward to two years later, over ten IUIs, three IVFs, and more than $30,000 spent, I still wasn't pregnant.

By this time everyone was well aware of our secret "get pregnant" plan. The cat was seriously out of the bag. We had to confide in all of our friends, mainly because I had to cut back on my drinking and exercising to nurture my swollen, drug induced ovaries, and I never cut back on those things. They're the pillars of my very healthy life. So what was supposed to be a quiet, happy thing quickly turned into a very public, depressing, failure.

The thing with unexplained infertility is doctors don't

know why it's not working. The lady parts are all in working order and functioning fine, but the magic just isn't happening when push comes to shove. And when I'm pushing and shoving there should be magic happening, dammit. After a while, it became embarrassing to walk into the fertility clinic waiting room. I couldn't stand the receptionists' sympathetic looks or the nurses' gentle pats on the shoulder. I didn't want anyone's sympathy. I wanted my body to do what it was supposed to fucking do, thank you very much.

Every failed attempt made me more determined to make it work. I knew deep down that I would carry a child to term, and it kept me moving forward. "If it's not ok, it's not the end, if it's not ok, it's not the end," ran through my head like a broken record. I was not going to take failure for an answer.

Two years into the process, on our third and last try with IVF, I finally broke. It didn't work, and it devastated me. I didn't want to get out of bed. The doubt and fear and hopelessness I'd been holding at bay flooded in. I lost my hope. I got scared. We took an indefinite break. Our doctor wanted to use a different uterus or a different egg. That was not my dream. I was stuck with no clear path in sight.

During this break (bear with me here, this is where the San Francisco hippy child comes out in me), I had a dream (yup, I'm going there) I dreamt that my shoulders birthed rainbow wings. Yes, rainbow wings sprouted from my shoulder bones. When those rainbows burst forth, the fear and negativity I'd been harboring literally washed away with them. The bad feelings completely took flight on my newly sprouted vibrant gay wings. I woke up crying, a feeling of surrender washing through me. I got out of bed and continued to see rainbows everywhere for the rest of the day. It was Pride month, so that's not really that hard to do. But to this day, rainbows hold a very significant meaning for me, and not just a gay one. I would have dyed my hair rainbow if well-meaning friends hadn't advised me against it. I still might do that someday, maybe when I'm 80.

But the rainbows saved me from helplessness, and I could move forward. Thank you, rainbows.

We switched doctors. I read a bunch of books and started a hefty herbal regimen. I added acupuncture to my routine. After six months and two lightly medicated IUIs, I was pregnant. It was a rainbow miracle. Who knows why it worked, maybe it was the herbs, maybe it was the acupuncture, maybe it was the new doctor, maybe it was my mindset? It's unexplained, that's the point.

But everything turned out okay in the end.

Actually, it turned out even better than I could have imagined. I got my baby *and* a podcast from my struggle. My isolation during the infertility set me on a search to hear from others like me who struggled to get pregnant. Turns out, there aren't that many venues for gays to discuss their baby making experiences—go figure. A quick discussion with Robin over margaritas in a bar and our new gay baby-making podcast was born. Now I have three babies where there once were none. I have two beautiful children and a feisty podcast that keeps on giving. Like John Lennon said, "Everything will be okay in the end. If it's not okay, it's not the end."

MARK AND GREG

> You'd think using science to make a baby would be easy for Dr. Mark given that's how he makes a living. But he found it jarring to be on the other side of the table as they waded into the world of using a surrogate to carry their baby.

MARK: I knew the steps because this is what I've done for other people. But it was still overwhelming for me because it was personal. We had to identify the IVF clinic that we were going to work with, and then find an egg donor.

ROBIN: Did you use your clinic?

MARK: I did not use my clinic. You really want a degree of separation because if things don't go well, you don't want your people to feel bad about it. And not everything goes well. As a doctor, we're trained to separate the person from the problem, so when you operate on somebody, they just show you that little portion of the body. I wanted the people taking care of us to be able to treat us like everybody else. Also because when people have a connection sometimes they don't make the best decision for you.

So we used an outside clinic, but that's where it got interesting because all of a sudden, I was the patient. The process of assisted reproduction for gay men is pretty straightforward. You need sperm. You need eggs. And you need a uterus. You just need to put those things together.

But for gay men, where your eggs come from involves looking for a donor, talking to the social worker or the psychologist, talking to the egg donor coordinator, looking at pictures if they're available. When we did this, there were very few open donations for egg donors, so pictures were not always available. And then we had to negotiate a little bit together and we secretly shared our story with some people. But ultimately, we had to say, "Okay, this is our decision."

SARA AND HILARY

Sara and Hilary were "team reciprocal IVF". Meaning Hilary would carry Sara's eggs. As you can imagine, there are many jokes about what it must be like when two women in the same house are both on fertility hormones at the same time. But Sara and Hilary took it all in stride.

SARA: So we came back from our honeymoon, and we started a cycle harvesting my eggs.

ROBIN: Did you both cycle together?

HILARY: Sort of. What they do for the receiving partner is they completely shut your hormones down.

SARA: It's called medical menopause.

HILARY: Yes. So they basically put me through menopause. It was fun. Hot flashes and all that.

SARA: Essentially, it's day one. They shut down her cycle so they could control it manually by medicine because obviously they didn't want her tubes and ovaries and eggs getting in the way of the process. And I started shots in the belly every day.

ROBIN: I bet it was super fun in your house at that time.

SARA: It was so great!

HILARY: It was actually not traumatic at all because we were very on board for this.

SARA: We were very excited.

HILARY: And we knew what we were getting into.

SARA: I remember distinctly going back for the second cycle appointment and the doctor did the ultrasound and said, "Wow. Did you grow some eggs!" On the second cycle, I got 27 eggs. That felt amazing.

> **For this next set of podcast excerpts, there're all kinds of terminology that might be confusing, so here's a little breakdown.**

Turkey Baster Method (AKA Intracervical Insemination, or ICI)
Noun

> The not at all scientific name for when a syringe of some kind is used to inject sperm (either from a sperm bank or collected just before injection) into the vagina as close to the cervix as possible, in order to get pregnant. It's got about the same chances of success as straight sex.

Intrauterine Insemination (IUI)
Noun

> This procedure happens at a doctor's office. They separate the semen from the seminal fluid (it's called washing). Around the time of ovulation, they put that sperm inside the uterus, and if you remember from your 10th grade health class, the uterus is next to the fallopian tubes. This increases the odds of conception over ICI.

In Vitro Fertilization (IVF)
Noun

> A medical procedure whereby an egg is fertilized by sperm outside the body. The fertilized egg is then implanted in the womb.

AIMEE AND MYRIAM

These two ladies started off trying at home with the turkey baster method. They bought sperm, and pretty much put it in there to see what happened. Well, not much happened, so they moved things along to the world of doctors.

ROBIN: One technical question. When you buy sperm from a sperm bank, don't you have to have it spun? Because I thought that you couldn't do an at home insemination with purchased sperm?

AIMEE: You can buy the sperm washed or unwashed.

ROBIN: So you didn't do an IUI? You were doing more of a turkey baster method at home?

AIMEE: Yeah, and at first it was very romantic. Then the next few times were much more like, "Is this going to work or what?"

MYRIAM: It's stressful and there's an emotional toll. Now we recognize, thank God for doctors.

JAIMIE: So for all intents and purposes, you were trying at home like every heterosexual couple?

MYRIAM: Yeah, we tried to do it at home. We wanted to make it more cozy, but it just wasn't working.

JAIMIE: How many times did you try at home?

AIMEE: Oh, gosh, like six months, maybe? We had the little testers and waited for the little blinking light. But even that route was expensive.

MYRIAM: It's expensive either way.

AIMEE: Every month you had to buy the sperm. It's just money, money, money.

PATRICIA AND KELLEN

This story involves sperm hanging out a window, a turkey baster and two lesbians on a Vespa. It's not how Patricia and Kellen ended up making their babies, but it's a great part of their family creation story.

PATRICIA: We started the process, and first we went into turkey baster land.

KELLEN: Oh, yeah, at least seven tries.

PATRICIA: It was a disaster. We didn't know how to do the turkey baster part. So Kellen literally has a turkey baster, and it's not coming out. It's stuck! So she takes the edge off—

KELLEN: And I blow, and it goes—well, everything went in my mouth.

PATRICIA: I'm yelling, "Spit it back in! Oh, dear God." Yeah. It was just a big crazy mess. But it was funny. It was very funny.

Then we picked a friend as our donor. And we would go to his house. He'd leave it out the window. And then we'd get on the vespa and we'd store it under the seat and think, "Is this going to kill the sperm?" We did that how many times?

KELLEN: At least five.

PATRICIA: At least. That all went nowhere.

> **Later, after not being successful with at-home insemination, they changed their path to IVF using Kellen's eggs with Patricia carrying.**

PATRICIA: Turned out, my eggs didn't come to the game, and Kellen did not want to carry. So I carried her eggs. And the first round we did, she had so many eggs that we said, "Let's put some in you and put some in me and see who gets pregnant."

I actually got pregnant and she didn't. But then I miscarried that one. I was devastated, and I was sharing our process along the way with my class and they were devastated. I thought, "Okay. No more sharing because I have to handle my disappointment and their disappointment, and that was all, no."

It's devastating. Especially when you're trying so hard and you're older and you're scared. All of those things are really, really tough.

KELLEN: We went through this four or five times.

PATRICIA: Yeah, but what was interesting was after the miscarriage, I made a deal with myself. I said, "Okay, this is how it is right? You're either in the game, or you're not in the game." I literally said, "I'm not going to give up until I'm 50."

That was seven years away, and I figured when I turned 50, I would renegotiate. It gave me the ability to say, "This is a long-term situation. I'm gonna have to not freak out every time it doesn't work. Otherwise I don't get to play this game."

So I got pregnant.

And then we were talking about how I'm one of 11 kids, and my family's in California, and her family's in Brazil, and we're older parents. We knew we couldn't leave this child without a sibling. And I was a heavenly pregnant mother. I was in love with being pregnant. Everything about my life was beautiful and magical.

KELLEN: She made it seem so easy that when the conversation came up of let's have another baby, I was like, "I'm gonna try."

PATRICIA: I was a little sad because I kind of wanted to carry the second one too, but she said, "I'll try" And I had to say, "Okay."

KELLEN: So I did three more cycles to get pregnant. And then we had twins. And she said, "Do you have to be an overachiever?"

PATRICIA: I was a bit jealous because I loved to be pregnant.

KELLEN: I didn't mind it.

PATRICIA: She said "You did false advertising because you made it look so easy." I loved it so much. I really did. But she did great though.

NEE NEE

> Nee Nee, her best friend and his boyfriend, decided to create a nontraditional family together. Their plan was to have a baby and share the responsibilities. How did they go about that you ask? At first, they tried the low-tech route, at-home insemination.

NEE NEE: When I was ovulating they would take turns coming to my apartment. I would step out, they would do what they needed to do and leave a sample for me. I would come back to my apartment after they left. I used a syringe, like what you use to give medicine to a cat or a dog. Not a turkey baster, those are too big. I actually did try that, and that fell apart rather quickly. Literally. It was like the most disgusting stuff I've ever had to deal with. So I revised that area of the project.

JAIMIE: I need to back up a second. You said they would take turns? So you weren't sure who was going to be the bio dad?

NEE NEE: Not until after the child was born.

JAIMIE: And you didn't care which one it was, and they seemed like they didn't care either?

NEE NEE: At the time, it seemed like we were all okay with whoever.

JANA AND LINDA

When Linda and her ex were trying to get pregnant at home, she was very focused on increasing her odds of success. Naturally, Linda turned to the internet to learn everything she needed to know about how to be successful with at-home insemination.

LINDA: I looked at it like, "You know what? This is a science project." I went on the internet, on my little AOL account, and found out exactly how to do it. I had to create the sample. So the donor went and did that. Put it in a glass jar—not plastic, because you don't want it to stick to the sides. Then, let it sit, covered for half an hour. Then I used a syringe that would suck it in, put it up there. Throw your legs up in the air and have an orgasm.

JANA: Because that does create a suction.

LINDA: And at the beginning it was kind of romantic. Then, after a few times, because each time in my cycle I would do it more than once, but skip a day, so by the end it felt like, "Okay, let's just go. Come on."

JAIMIE: Did the donor stick around and wait for you to put your legs up and then come back out of the room?

LINDA: Yeah, in the beginning, we hung out and had dinner.

EMMA BROCKES

Emma was born and raised in England, so she experienced culture shock when she decided to try and have a baby on her own via IVF in the US. The number of decisions to be made overwhelmed her, because there is not a lot of choice in the UK healthcare system. Full stop.

EMMA: It's very unnerving for British people to be presented with choice of any kind, generally, but particularly with medicine. It was baffling and terrifying. It felt to me like the equivalent of being asked by your airline to choose a pilot. I don't know how to make that choice.

Actually, the first clinic I went to was a recommendation from a lesbian couple who had hit the jackpot. They had tons of kids. It is so weird that you start judging on such unscientific criteria. But I found when I met the OBGYN, she was just so drippy, and she had big sad eyes. She practically stroked my arms like I was grieved, and I thought, "I cannot spend months with this woman."

TOM

Tom was a sperm donor to a lesbian couple who were friends. That meant he wasn't in the day-to-day of their fertility process, and that ended up as a fairly surreal experience for him.

TOM: I remember walking into my Monday morning staff meeting, and my cell phone rang, and the moms said, "Oh, we were talking a lot about you this morning."

And I said, "Oh, why is that?"

"Oh, we're on our way to get inseminated."

I said, "Okay, good luck."

And I hung up the phone, and I sat at my meeting with my heart racing for like an hour. And I thought, "Holy fuck. This is happening."

I don't think the first one took, but then the second time it took. And my daughter's due date was July 4th.

DAVID

The fact that David, our 50-year-old millennial, was having a baby was hard for him to wrap his head around because his surrogate was carrying the baby on the other side of the country.

DAVID: It remained incredibly abstract the entire time because I don't go to California every week. So it was texts here and there. And it was all very strange. It was like, "Oh, I'm having a kid." But there was no evidence of it around me, other than all the bills, and I didn't really curl up with all of those bills.

MARK AND GREG

Dr. Mark and Greg cleared up the misconception that two gay men merely mix up their sperm and put both in with the egg to let the universe decide who is the bio dad.

ROBIN: How did you decide who was going to be the sperm donor?

MARK: You just split the pool.

JAIMIE: That's beautiful you guys get to do that. Did you already know you wanted two?

MARK: Yeah.

ROBIN: So did you say, "This one's mine, and then the next one is yours?"

JAIMIE: They pooled them.

ROBIN: But what does that mean?

MARK: Normally women release one egg per month. It's a really exquisite system, and 99% of the time, females have one baby at a time. What fertility doctors do is, at the start of a menstrual cycle, they pour in fertility medicines that lead to superovulation, so instead of one egg developing within a follicle, there might be 20.

Then they say which eggs are mature, and they fertilize these eggs with sperm from father A. and B. And then they run them down in parallel in the lab. Then they report the quality of the embryos. And you have a pool.

ROBIN: How did you decide who would go first?

MARK: Do you mean whose embryo to transfer first? Well, at that point we didn't have a surrogate yet, we were just focused on making embryos. And you need to know you have the embryos first before you can decide who's gonna go first because what if one of you doesn't do well. What if he doesn't make good embryos? So I don't think we ever really talked about who would go first.

> **Mark and Greg kept it close to the vest which embryo they implanted from which father for each of their kids, but that's fine because it's not really our business. They did share more about the rest of their process though.**

JAIMIE: You said you had to see a psychologist. Is that you speaking with a psychologist or the egg donor speaking with a psychologist?

MARK: We spoke with a psychologist and the egg donors also screen with a psychologist.

JAIMIE: Is that mandated?

MARK: Fertility medicine is not regulated by the federal government. So our parent organization, the American Society for Reproductive Medicine has guidelines and within those guidelines it's recommended that intended parents using donor gametes (whether sperm or egg) meet with a mental health professional to educate them on what's important.

ROBIN: I thought it was mandated. We used your clinic, and it was a requirement.

MARK: Well it's the policy, procedure of that practice, which I would agree with because who has any knowledge about how to pick an egg donor? Why not get education on that? And this is the same social worker or mental health department that screens the egg donors too. So it's a way of them getting to know you and kind of peeling the onion on what's important and not important. And in going through this process, as a patient, I really have a much greater respect for the mental health professionals that do this because they're very passionate about doing it well and protecting everybody in the process. The intended parents as well as the donors.

ROBIN: The only thing I would say, on the other side of it, is Mary and I were in the same family, and I was offended by having to talk to a therapist. I felt like, "This is my wife. If we could make a baby together, no one would need to screen us. I don't need to meet you to tell me anything because I'm a grown-ass woman, and I'm paying you, so just do what I asked." That was my feeling. I mean, she was nice and it was fine, but it felt like I was being mandated to do something that I didn't want to do. But that doesn't mean I can't see your point.

MARK: A lot of programs don't require it, and lesbian couples kind of come through the process from so many different angles. It depends on the doctor.

JAIMIE: Nobody talked to us about it. We came and they said, "So are you using a sperm donor?"

We said, "Yes."

They said, "Where are you getting it from?"

We told them, and they said, "Okay, so have it shipped here."

MARK: We basically require lesbian intended mothers to meet with a mental health professional to help them make that decision. How are you making your choice? What's important? Do you want an anonymous donor? Do you want a known donor? How are you going to talk to your child? What are you going to reveal to your family? Are you going to create a box or a book for this child, so when they start asking questions? Are you guys both on the same page and so on. Those are the things that doctors don't necessarily talk about.

JAIMIE: Robin and I always talk about this thing called "LGBTQ Drafting" where you get all your information from the other lesbian or gay couples who have done it before, but it doesn't hurt to go talk to somebody who can lay it out for you and say, "These are the things you need to think about."

SCIENCE DOESN'T ALWAYS MEAN SUCCESS

Even with the advances in medicine, and the use of science, there are still so many variables to fertility. You might get lots of eggs when harvesting or you might not. You might implant two eggs and end up with twins or end up with *nada*. You might be 27 with the insides of a grandma. The doctors can ballpark success rates, but Mother Nature still has some inexplicable role that she's playing, and the fact of the matter is, timelines and cost estimates are just guesstimates. Here's where we talk about the rollercoaster part of the medical fertility journey.

SARA AND HILARY

In the middle of their reciprocal IVF process, Sara was thrilled to hear she had the ovaries of a 20-something. But that didn't mean this couple would have an easy go at making a baby.

HILARY: When we finally picked a donor, we went back to our clinic, and we inseminated. We did the egg harvest and got eggs from Sara.

SARA: I had a bad cycle, so we had to harvest twice. When we did the initial consultation, the doctor looked at my ovaries and said I had the ovaries of a 25-year-old, and I was 37 at the time. And so I thought, "Woo hoo" because I was expecting to not have a high egg count. But my egg count was actually better than Hilary's who was five years younger. But when we went through the process and harvested the eggs, we only got 15, which sounded like a lot at the time. But it wasn't what they were expecting.

HILARY: And they weren't very good quality.

SARA: When we fertilized them, only three made it to day three, and the embryos were not quality. So we did a three day implantation instead of a five day. At that point, we were feeling hopeful. "We've got three. One of them's got to take." But none of them took. And that was heartbreaking. After that cycle, the doctors told us the sperm was not as healthy as they wanted from the sperm bank.

HILARY: Actually, the bank we use had a threshold level that they talked about on the website.

SARA: We went back to the bank and they refunded us for that vial. And we said, "Okay, his quality isn't as good we need, so let's find a new donor." And the doctor said in the event that the new donor has bad quality like the first one, we should have a backup. So we had choice A and choice B.

HILARY: So not only did we have to go back to the drawing board again and start searching through donor profiles a third time, we had to do it a fourth time to get the backup.

PATRICIA AND KELLEN

Sometimes folks that work in the medical industry can be cold and unsympathetic. Patricia and Kellen learned that the hard way on their IVF journey. But when that happened, they refused to be treated badly.

PATRICIA: We decided to go IVF, and we bought sperm. And it just wasn't working. After I did my first IVF and it didn't work, I was so upset. You know what the nurse said to me?

"What do you expect? Your eggs are old."

Can you imagine? That was so bad. But, it was one of those things that pushed me out of that place to find the doctor that we found. And get this, I walked into the new place that a friend of mine had told me about, and he had all the books that I read. He had affirmations on his doors. I'm like, "Okay."

We said, "I want to get pregnant."

And he said, "You know what? Let's do it. Let's get you pregnant."

That was it. It was like, "Oh, we're gonna do it, however we're gonna do it."

THE ABBYS

Sam and Laura spent a while trying IUI but were unsuccessful. They took a break in the process, and while they were on hiatus, decided to switch doctors. A decision like that is sometimes because of a gut feeling, and sometimes it's about how close the doctor's office is to the subway.

SAM: So we picked our donor in July. But we knew we wanted to enjoy the summer.

LAURA: So we went on vacation to Napa.

SAM: No, we had started IUI.

LAURA: Yeah, that's right. You made me get inseminated before we went.

SAM: I did.

LAURA: I was like, "I'm not taking anything. I'm not doing anything. I'm just drinking like all the straight women out there who get to say, 'I was so drunk, I had no idea I was pregnant yet.' That's what I'm gonna do."

We did an insemination on New Year's Day. And that felt like, "This has to work. It's the first day of the year." And then it didn't.

SAM: Then we felt defeated for a while. Then [as we switched to IVF] we came to the conclusion that the fertility clinic we were at was too inconvenient for us for IVF. And my sister-in-law had recommended a doctor, and it was a lot closer to our apartment.

LAURA: So we went, and we met with this doctor. And we left the office, and I was like, "This bitch is going to put a baby in me."

SAM: We just knew she was no joke.

LAURA: I just wasn't going to be emotional about this. I thought, "If we're laying down this type of cash, this is happening. And I'm going to do what she tells me to do." So we did three IUIs and then we went straight to IVF because we bought out all the sperm from that donor and it was only six vials, and we used up three for IUI.

ROBIN: So you did IVF, and you got pregnant the first time?

SAM AND LAURA: First time!

LAURA: And I only had a few eggs.

SAM: Three. They extracted seven, but only three were viable.

LAURA: I feel like you're just making that number up.

SAM: No, I'm not.

DAVID

> David and his husband really went *through* it on their surrogacy journey. They used multiple carriers, had multiple egg retrievals, and the process ended up costing them close to $200,000. The worst part? No one could tell them why.

DAVID: We had to do three or four retrievals. I'm telling you right now, we had a really bad time. Everyone from the doctor, and our doctor was one of the pioneers in IVF in Southern California, to the second doctor we used, was befuddled.

The agency said, "When you test and test and test and you're putting in A++ sperm and eggs, it usually works right away. We don't know what's going on with you. It's just that every so often it's bad luck."

I was like, "Wait a second. I'm paying for all of the science and your explanation is bad luck? Which is not an explanation."

I don't want anybody to go through what we went through. I don't want to meet anyone, and I say, "Here's my story." And they say, "Me too."

Yes, there are far worse experiences. We closed the deal, and we have our daughter. There are a lot of people who don't get to the finish line and that's terrible. But it was really Hell. It was really hard on our relationship.

> David was on his third surrogate, and he was at the end of his rope. But he hung in there, and at the end, he saw a little bit of magic in the fertility process.

DAVID: So we did a transfer with our last surrogate, and it didn't work, and she said, "Listen, I'm not feeling this doctor. I don't like his protocols for the medication. I've used this other doctor twice before, and I'm recommending you start all over with this new person."

And all I'm thinking is dollar signs because the doctor we were using was so desperate to help us and also to keep his success numbers up—because that's reported—that he was giving us super, duper discounts on the transfer. It became, "Okay, do we do another transfer in the situation that has yielded nothing, but we can afford, or do we start from scratch with money we sort of don't have?"

Obviously, we did the most prudent thing and that was to start with the money we don't have.

We did a transfer with the new doctor. And this is going to sound so corny, and perhaps earnest, but it really happened. We were in the room with the carrier, the representative from the agency, and the doctor. I watched the transfer on the screen because I stayed by her head and not anywhere near the thick of things, and I remember looking at the screen and I saw a little flash of light when he pulled back the instrument, whatever that is.

I remember thinking, "It's done. It happened."

And I'm not doing that thing where you sort of retroactively fall in love with someone and then say, "It was always meant to be." I'm not doing that. I swear. I saw it, and I could sense it.

It was very quiet and still in the room. And I remember leaving there saying, "I'm going to have a baby."

We ended up having a singleton and terrific pregnancy, and the surrogate felt great through it all.

CHAPTER 5

ADOPTION AND FOSTER CARE

"I don't want to exceptionalize people who build their family through adoption. I don't have some special soul. You have to be brave to have a baby any old way. You have to be on top of your own fears, and you gotta be brave, and you gotta be on that horse and going into battle." - Michele the Doula

You do not have to go to a doctor or follow the scientific path in order to have a family. We repeat, there need not be any talk about eggs or sperm because both adoption and foster care are viable paths to parenthood for LGBTQ families.

There are a few different types of adoptions. You can adopt internationally from another country or domestically using an agency or a lawyer. There's also the option to become a foster parent. There's no guarantee that fostering will lead to a permanent placement, but there are many cases where fostering ends in an adoption.

There have been a lot of changes with adoption over the last few decades. Adoption is no longer something to hide. These days, closed adoptions, where the birth mother signs off all rights to the baby and disappears forever, are rare in the United States. Although some international adoptions may still be closed, the conversation surrounding an adopted child's origins are trending in a much more open direction.

Now, as we talk about adoptions and foster care, we know you might be thinking, "I'm a gay, they won't let me adopt. Will they?" Or, "Doesn't it take a long time?" Or, you might even have some thoughts you feel bad saying out loud like, "I'm not heading down that road because I've heard a lot of adopted babies come from drug-addicted birth mothers, and I don't think I can handle that."

Kudos to you for being honest, but what we learned from our guests is there are loads and loads of misconceptions about adoption and being a foster parent, and the above are just a few.

So let's dig in and hear the truth about adoption and foster care and the LGBTQs.

ROBIN HERE

Mary and I initially planned to adopt. My personal life philosophy has always been to reduce, reuse and recycle, so adoption seemed like the "greenest" baby choice we could make. If we were going to create a family chock-full of kids who use up the planet's precious natural resources, there is no need for us to add to the problem by making more kids. Instead we can adopt a baby who's already here or on the way.

Then I went to an adoption seminar at my day job, and I learned that at that time, there were very few countries that would allow us to adopt as a gay couple. That meant one of us would have to go forward as the adoptive parent, and then we'd have to do second parent adoption to create parental rights for the other partner. That didn't sit well with me. I hated the idea of going back into the closet and pretending to be a single parent. And I liked the idea of paying a fee to a country that thinks my lifestyle ain't ok with the Lord even less. When we looked at all the factors—the cost, the lack of control around how long it could take to get a baby, well, we gave up.

We told ourselves, "We'll have one baby the regular good old 'buy some sperm on the internet to make a baby' way, then we'll adopt our second kid." I felt so strongly about this new path that when I was 7 months pregnant, I sold back the extra vials of sperm we had from our donor. Though, if I'm being honest, selling the sperm had more to do with the fact that I hated being pregnant. That also helped nudge us toward the idea of adopting our second kid.

But then a funny thing happened. I gave birth fairly easily, as far as pushing a bowling ball out of one's vagina goes. And then I did what millions of moms have done before me, I said, "Maybe that whole pregnancy thing wasn't so bad." How could I remember the horrors of pregnancy when I was holding a beautiful, fresh-out-of-the-oven, cherub-like baby in my arms?

When we decided it was time to have another baby, the idea of starting new binders filled with lists comparing and contrasting adoption agencies, learning the ropes of the adoption process, worrying about what kind of kid we'd be adding to the mix (though having a baby yourself guarantees nothing about what kind of kid you get), and wondering how long it would take to get our second kid, had us once again giving up on adoption. The fact was that I got pregnant and gave birth easily, and had a one-year-old at home who needed a lot of attention. It was too tempting to lather, rinse, and repeat.

And that's just what we did.

That said, though, I still believe in adoption, and I think it's a really viable path to parenting. If we had a difficult time making babies, I know we would have switched our path in a heartbeat because parenting was what was important to us, not genetics.

JAIMIE HERE TOO

When I was 10, I came upon an alarming document in my mom's closet. It was hidden in the back under a stack of papers, where most people keep really important papers. On the top of the page I saw the words "Adoption Certificate", and a little further down I saw my name, Jaimie Kelton. They had adopted me! Holy shit. My whole life was a lie. My ten-year-old self's world was rocked.

When my mom came home that evening I confronted her. The secret was out. I knew everything. It was time she came clean to me. She was going to tell me where I came from. At least this is how I remember the scene going. My mom doesn't even remember the incident which tells me it probably wasn't quite so dramatic. Nevertheless, I deserved answers, and I was going to get them.

It turns out though that the adoption certificate actually belonged to a stuffed monkey I had "adopted" at the county fair, and my name was on the certificate not as the adoptee but as the adopter. My mom and I hugged and had a nice laugh (obviously not that nice, because she doesn't even remember it), and we went back to our normal routine of being a biologically related mother and daughter. But I'll never forget the way I felt the moment I realized my whole life had been a lie. I developed so much empathy for adopted kids that day.

Turns out adoption has come a long way since the days of *Annie*, which I clearly watched too much of as a kid. I'm telling you I've really evolved in a good way since starting our podcast.

Honestly though, when planning our family, adoption was never on the table. And it wasn't because I was afraid I'd end up with a rabble rouser like Annie. It was because I wanted more than anything to give birth to a baby myself. Having a genetic tie really mattered to me. I wanted to see myself mirrored in a little person of my own creation, and I wanted my parents and extended family to see themselves in my baby as well. I wanted that deep connection that I mistakenly believed could only be found through a genetic connection.

It took me two children born to two different mothers— my wife and myself—to see how little the continuation of a bloodline matters when it comes to making a loving family. I love both of my children equally, regardless of the fact that I don't share a genetic tie with one of them. They are both very much my babies.

Every time we talk to an adoptive or foster parent about their journey to parenthood I think, "Wow, there really are good people out there in the world." I don't think they're exemplary because they want to raise a complete stranger's baby—we all end up with strangers in the end, don't we? Every child who comes into our lives, whether they come from our bodies or through adoption or fostering, is a fully formed stranger that we have to get to know and be terrorized by for the rest of our lives. I admire folks who are selfless enough from the get-go to not care about the genetics of their children, as I so adamantly did. They figured out, much easier than I did, that a family is not made through blood or DNA, but through love and commitment and understanding and acceptance. Most LGBTQ families come to that realization soon enough because of the creativity required when making our babies. But some parents take a little longer than others. Call me a slow poke if you will, I'm just super proud I got to this enlightened parenting state at all.

BRIAN ESSER

Brian is a lawyer who helps LGBTQ families, but he also happens to be a gay dad who adopted two boys. Jaimie and Robin knew very little about adoption, but thankfully Brian was there to walk them through the basics.

BRIAN: One of the ways to adopt in the United States is international adoption, which is a child that's available for adoption, but living in another country. International adoptions have dropped off considerably in the last few years.

There's an international convention, The Hague Convention, that the US signed, and it generally put a lot more bureaucracy around international adoption. And then a lot of countries have either closed their programs or scaled them back dramatically. For example, Vietnam, Ethiopia, Guatemala, some of them closed down because there were a lot of irregularities, fraud and abuse in the program, or at least allegations of things like that. Russia closed its program to the United States, mostly because of diplomatic issues. Even China is scaling back its program, particularly as pollution has gotten so bad in China and infertility has become a problem. So now there's actually more demand now.

Many countries still don't knowingly place children with same-sex couples. There's a handful now that are starting to. South Africa has a small program, Columbia will place with same-sex couples, and also Brazil and Mexico. I think that's about it. But there are options now, as opposed to a few years ago, where there were frankly, none.

When we adopted our two boys, we went with open adoptions with their birth families, which is pretty great. We went with an agency that's based in Pennsylvania.

The open adoption route is almost exclusively newborn placements, where a woman who has an unplanned pregnancy is deciding to voluntarily -

ROBIN: Couple of cocktails at the prom?

BRIAN: Something like that. You know, as much as the "Juno" situation is a popular stereotype, it's actually mostly not true. The biggest cohort of women who are making adoption plans are in their 20s, already have one child that they're parenting, know how difficult it is, know how expensive it is, are living paycheck to paycheck, and are not feeling like they have the resources to have a second child, and they're making a plan for that child.

ROBIN: Is there an issue with these women possibly having an addiction to drugs? Because that is a stereotype as well.

BRIAN: There are some women who are dealing with addiction issues, or are generally going about their lives and they drink, they smoke marijuana, they do whatever it is that they're doing because they're not planning on getting pregnant. They're not avoiding alcohol or other substances. It definitely is an issue that potential adoptive parents need to think about in terms of how they feel about that.

I can tell you that with most of the placements that I've done in the last couple of years, there has not been a lot of issues like that present. I think the reason that there is that perception is that when you sit down with a lawyer or adoption agency to start the process, that is one of the things that they talk to you about is how do you feel about a child that comes from this kind of background and because it is part of the initial conversation, I think it creates the perception that 100% of children available for adoption have that experience.

> **For Brian and his husband, they ended up going the agency route because at that time, he wasn't as educated on the ins and outs of the adoption process. So he did what most of us nontraditional families have done, he used LGBTQ drafting.**

LGBTQ Drafting
Verb

> The act of getting all your information from LGBTQ friends who have successfully forged a path before you. This applies to, but is not limited to, having babies, legal advice, and places to travel that are LGBTQ friendly.

BRIAN: We had a really wonderful experience working with a great agency. In New York, you can either work with an agency or do an independent adoption where you work with a lawyer who helps you connect with a potential birth parent.

We opted to go the agency route because at that time, I hadn't started my law practice, and everybody that we knew who adopted had gone the agency route, so we didn't even know that this independent lawyer route was an option for us. Even though we used a different agency than our friends, we thought that was just the way it was done.

MICHELE THE DOULA

As a doula, Michele's seen lots of babies born, so she didn't feel the need to give birth to a baby, and neither did her wife. Instead, they headed straight to adoption. But she wasn't quite ready for all the paperwork and self-promotion that can come along with that path.

MICHELE: We joined a really big agency. Then we got all of our stuff together. We got the FBI checks and the home study and the blah blah blah. We had a little, I guess you'd say, a pamphlet, or an advertising brochure about us. Man, we looked like we were running for Republican office. Looking at that thing, I was like, "Am I in an episode of 'The Good Wife?' What happened?"

We both are wearing blue gingham and holding each other, and I thought, "Oh man, this is not us." But every time we asked the agency, "Can we make it funky?"

They said, "Honestly? Everybody wants to make it their own, and then those people never get picked."

So it's a lot of work, and then it's a waiting game because somebody has to pick you. And that's going to vary on how much you're advertising yourself and how much you're putting your voice out there and everything, but it's also going to vary based on who you are.

For instance, we were sitting around one of the orientations for the adoption agency and they said, "How long is it gonna take?" Everyone wants to know that answer, of course. And there were two men of color who were also at the table—there was a lot of diversity at the event—and the person leading the seminar said, "Okay, we have a stat that's generally how long you have to wait, except for you two gentlemen." And she pointed to the two men of color and said, "That's going to be a quick turnaround."

There's some speculation from experts in the adoption field that children are placed faster with gay men in open adoptions because, either consciously or unconsciously, the birth mother may want to remain the only mother in the child's life. But that's way more speculation than your narrators feel comfortable standing by, so we'll just shrug our shoulders and say, "Apparently, it happens sometimes."

MICHELE: And then we went live—that's what it's called—which was an accomplishment all of its own. It was this feeling of, "The baby is coming. I have no idea when, but there is a baby coming."

We went about our lives, and we'd think about it all the time, then we'd forget about it. We thought of it as our gestational period, but we could do whatever we wanted, and nobody was tired going up stairs and nobody was sweating.

Then we went to Greece. I volunteered with an organization called "The Nurture Project" to help refugee women breast-feed their babies because in emergency situations, bottle fed babies are 1,000% more likely to die than breastfed babies. And that was really healing and inspiring and everything it should have been, and when our plane landed, we got an email from Cassandra, the birth mom. My wife was getting the bags, and I was in the bathroom, looking at my email, as you do, and then I just stood up and started screaming. "We got picked!" Apparently, while we were out of the country, Cassandra was pressing refresh, refresh, refresh, on her email account, waiting for us to respond.

Before this, we flirted with a few other people, but nothing ever came of it. They would text and then ghost out. But Cassandra said, "Hi, I want you."

And we said, "Great."

Then we talked to her, and we looked her up on Facebook, while we were talking to her, and we said, "We're Facebook stalking you, and you have the most amazing eyebrows."

And she said, "That's the nicest thing anyone has ever said to me."

So with open adoption, there are no secrets, and everybody is as connected as they feel is groovy for their family. And our family is super, super, super connected.

> **But their adoption was not without a few bumps in the road though. Actually, it was bumps, an adoption agency closure, and lots and lots of calls to their lawyer.**

MICHELE: In the first year, our agreement with the adoption agency was that we would see each other four times in the first year and at least once every year until the child was 18. But the adoption agency went bankrupt in the middle of our adoption. And so for a little while Cassandra had relinquished her rights as the parent and the baby was in our house and with us. Usually in that interim moment, the adoption agency is the legal guardian of the baby, but our adoption agency disappeared overnight because they went bankrupt.

The agency contacted Cassandra first. She had chosen that agency because they offered unlimited, lifetime counseling or something like that. But then they were like, "Sorry, birth moms. We're going out of business."

Cassandra called us and said, "What the hell is this letter?"

We said, "I don't know."

They sent a letter to our friends who hadn't been placed with babies yet, basically saying, "Sorry, you're out of luck. There goes your money and everything." And a lot of these people, this was their last chance to have babies.

There was just a handful of us who had babies who weren't adopted, and we didn't hear from the agency for weeks. I don't think they knew what to say to us. And so Brian Esser, our lawyer, represented us in court, and thankfully everything ended out nice and smooth in the end. Our daughter didn't get adopted until she was about 11 months old, but who cares? She was with us the whole time.

Open adoption really worked for Michele and her wife. Michele talks passionately about how to advocate for adoption, but she doesn't give folks the impression that adoption is perfect. No path to parenting is perfect or easy.

MICHELE: This is the thing. I don't want to exceptionalize people who build their family through adoption because I want more people to consider it. I don't have some special soul, so I don't want to promote that exceptionalism. I see people birthing babies all the time. I've seen babies come out the door, the window, come from somebody else. And what I'm saying is you have to be brave to have a baby any old way.

You have to be on top of your own fears and you got to be brave, you gotta be on that horse and going into battle.

Yes. There is uncertainty with adoption, but I've also seen a lot of births, and a lot of situations with babies that—there is no safe way out of this. To love somebody that much you can't protect yourself. And that's what I see when people are birthing. Like you can't have this baby come out of your body and hold back anything at the same time. You can't love somebody so fiercely and think that you're going to be protected from it.

CASSANDRA

Cassandra is the birth mom to Michele the Doula's baby. Together, with their open adoption, they have created a new kind of family.

CASSANDRA: I am Michele's birth mom or her "baby mama". I came to the point of adoption. It wasn't my first option, abortion was, and I was too late. I don't want to say that adoption was the easier choice for me. But parenting was never a choice for me. I already parent two other children, and a third was just not in the cards at the moment. My life was not together at all, and I didn't want to bring another child into that.

I called our adoption agency and they sent me like this ten-pound box with thousands upon thousands of fliers in it. And I was going through them all with my best friend, and I saw Michele and Ashling's flyer, and I knew. I knew automatically that these were my people. And I emailed them, and two or three days went by, and I didn't hear anything from them. I thought, "Oh, I guess they don't want my baby."

And then finally Michele saw my email and they got in contact with me. They emailed me back and the 20 weeks that we spent getting to know each other were probably some of the best weeks of my life. They were my sole support system because I chose to keep my pregnancy a secret from everyone I knew. And they were in the room when our daughter was born.

We completely defied the odds of what adoption is.

JEN AND BETH

Sometimes you go through an agency to adopt and sometimes, if you're very lucky, a friend of a friend calls you, out of the blue, and says she knows someone who is pregnant who needs to give the baby up for adoption. That's how Jen made her family. Jen and Beth refer to a home study in this podcast excerpt. Here's what that means.

Home Study
Noun

A required process for anyone adopting in the US whereby a case worker visits your home to meet you and check out your readiness to parent. They'll interview you and write a report about your day-to-day habits, parenting philosophies, the state of your home, and reasons for wanting to adopt. Before the home study, you will panic, complain that you have to do a home study and clean your house to a level that it's never been cleaned before. Then you will bite your fingernails until the report arrives.

JEN: So we didn't have a home study, we didn't have anything. We were like, "Uh, how do we put a rush on this stuff?" We got in touch with child youth services, and we got our home studies done, and our essays, and all that. It's amazing what you have to go through to adopt a baby, which should be the case, so that they know that they're going somewhere safe.

The birth mom was in Arizona, and so we didn't see her a lot, but about a week before my birthday she called us and said, "Oh, I'm cramping today." And after she shared a few more details I said, "Um, no, you're in labor."

One of us had to be in Pennsylvania for paperwork and legal purposes, and one had to go to Phoenix. My partner at the time had family in Phoenix, so she flew out. She got there just in time. So the baby came, and I was on the speakerphone. My partner at the time, cut the cord, and everything. And then she flew back to Pennsylvania with our daughter.

She was nine days old when they got back to Pennsylvania. And then we went through the adoption process.

CAMILLA

Camilla is a psychotherapist and social worker, who also does home studies. When she figured out she wanted to have a baby, it didn't matter to her that she was older, but it did mean that a biological kid wasn't in the cards. So Camilla and her wife pursued an international adoption from China.

CAMILLA: We started thinking about becoming parents a little bit late. I was in my 40s, and my wife was almost 40. We briefly entertained the idea of a biological child, but that really became kind of a non-issue.

ROBIN: Dusty eggs?

CAMILLA: [Laughs] Yeah, yeah.

JAIMIE: When you adopted, did you disclose that you were a lesbian couple?

CAMILLA: We did not. I went forward as a single parent. We said, "We want to be parents, and this seems like a good option for us." I was more of the driving force. Sometimes that happens, but it's very important that the other member of the couple be comfortable with that. And that's something I also explore with people when we're talking about adoption, you know, that sometimes there's somebody who is really the one in the driver's seat.

JAIMIE: How long had you guys been together?

CAMILLA: About ten years when we started the process. As with any adoption process, there's a lot of paperwork. With international adoption it's even more. So we actually started the paperwork in January 1997, and we completed our paperwork in July. And then I traveled to China a year later. There was a bit of a slowdown then. Though, now it takes years.

> The moment you pee on a stick, see two pink lines, and learn you're pregnant is exhilarating. It's a different experience finding out you're a parent with adoption, but it's no less exciting. Camilla's story even involved the FedEx guy.

CAMILLA: When there is a child who is identified, you get incredibly excited. My wife got the FedEx package and talks about hugging the FedEx guy. She still sees him, and they wave. It's not the same as carrying a child, but we were waiting, and that was intense.

JAIMIE: What's in the FedEx package?

CAMILLA: "A child has been identified and you've been matched." That kind of thing. The agency called us also, and we were over the moon.

ROBIN: How long was it from the FedEx package to picking up the kid?

CAMILLA: I think it was about six weeks to two months. Our daughter was in a child welfare institute, which is like an orphanage. At that point, and I think it's still the case, you're not allowed to travel to the institute. It was about two or three hours from the hotel where we received our daughter. It was me and two other people that were getting children that day.

Our daughter was very different from the other kids. She was very sensitive. She was very attached to one particular caregiver. I think it was a good thing, but it was also very hard because she was very, very upset because she was attached to that caregiver. Also, I looked different, you know, I have curly blonde hair.

JAIMIE: She was 15 months old and probably has never seen anyone who looked like you.

CAMILLA: Exactly. And there's a conference table and you're filling out tons of paperwork. And, there's an interpreter. Our daughter had a few words. She had one thing that she was able to say—"Bùxiang yào"—which means "don't want". She said that a lot. It was a hard transition. But I travelled with a young woman who had actually spent the previous year in China and spoke Chinese. And I was very grateful for her because she could speak to my daughter.

We found these red bean wafers, and she liked those. So we had a stack of them. I held her and then she finally fell asleep on the floor for a little while.

Then we got to New York, and it was a culture shock. My wife, then partner, was there. She said the doors to the international section of the airport opened, and they could see us, and she was waving madly. But we didn't see them until we walked out.

I remember a moment when I was holding her in the hotel, and she was crying, and I was crying, and I was on a phone call with my partner. It was a hard transition. But you know what? I have to say, she was, in many ways, resilient. I mean, you think about all the ways that a 15-month-old has traveled on this journey. She was amazing.

It does get better.

ROBIN: How long do you think it was before she felt at home with you as parents?

CAMILLA: It's really hard to say because it was up and down. There were moments when it was like, "Wow. She's doing great." And there were moments when it was an adjustment. She had night terrors. I don't know if you guys have experienced that, but it's crying and yelling, hysterically, and they're not awake, but they're arching back. We found that having ice chips would sort of wake her up, and then she would go back to sleep.

But I think one of the things in any adoption, there is a piece of loss, and there is a first family or a first environment where that child was held, and that's a loss that they have in their systems.

You just have to be aware.

> One thing that comes along with international adoption is that it's often closed. Camilla's daughter might have a very difficult time finding her birth mom, though they do know the town where she was born.

CAMILLA: We didn't do a return trip. But my daughter has said, "You know, I might want to do that when I'm older." And I think that makes sense for her. But also, it's important that she feels that this is her life. This is where she is. This is where she lives. These are her friends and family and—

JAIMIE: You gave her a good life.

CAMILLA: I would want her to speak to that.

ROBIN: Oh my god, you're so modest. I'd be like, "I nailed it."

ACTOR DAVID BEACH

> David and his husband found an adoption agency that spoke their language. They also found comfort in a group of other hopeful parents who went through the adoption journey at the same time.

DAVID: I think people who make babies are cool and all, but the adoption route was more our mindset at that point. We went to this agency, and I understood the way everyone talked. Then I wasn't scared about the process. They weren't saying, "We're going to get you a baby soon. You want a boy, or you want a girl?"

They were very thoughtful about the whole thing. They talked about how there's a real need for people to step up. And we have all these high needs babies, but if you're not people who think that you can handle a high needs baby, then that is not a good baby for you. So don't say, "We'll take any baby because that's not fair to the baby."

ROBIN: Do you think you just found the right agency?

DAVID: Yeah. I mean, we did research. And we went through the process with a group of people who were also adopting. We all had to do reading. We all had to do writing. We had to talk to each other. It was a home-study group.

ROBIN: Did you feel competitive with those people? I feel like I might.

DAVID: I was so competitive. You want to be picked. We were like, "You guys all seem really nice, but we're two guys so we might get picked first." That kind of thing.

JAIMIE: Were there any other gay couples?

DAVID: No. Everyone was heterosexual but us. And I thought that would differentiate us. If someone wanted to look through the books they'd see, "Straight. Straight. Straight. Oh, there's a gay couple."

ROBIN: Sort of like Instagram. "Selfie. Selfie. Selfie. Ooh, food shot."

DAVID: Yes, exactly. But it was great. We're still really good friends with those people. And we all have kids. And in the end our waiting process was not very long. We put our books out in May and we got a call July 4th weekend. And she was born August 19.

> David acknowledged that he got a bit obsessive when putting his family profile books together. But his creativity turned out to be the reason the birth parents picked them.

DAVID: Once we decided to adopt it was like, "We gotta have the kid now!" I would be up all night doing triplicate books. Russell decided he should sleep while I do pen and watercolor drawings in all our books, in triplicate.

ROBIN: You didn't have access to a copier?

DAVID: No, no. We had photos, but around the photos there were these pen and watercolor drawings. I was up all night doing these because I wanted to get them in. Because we needed a baby as soon as possible. And at the time I was watching these Barefoot Contessa marathons.

JAIMIE: Sure, like you do.

DAVID: But then when we met the birth parents, the birth mom, Caitlin said, "Who did those drawings? Those were really great." And Russell was like, "I told you."

I'm like, "I know, but I was the one who did them and you were sleeping."

> **David and his husband were picked by their birth parents relatively quickly. David chalks it up to the fact that they are a two-dad couple.**

DAVID: I think one of the reasons we got picked so quickly had something to do with the fact that we were a different family. And I don't want to psychoanalyze, but I think there's something about a young woman feeling like she's not being displaced by another woman. Our birth mom is so funny, though. She said to me, "You looked a little gay." Because I was trying to put pictures of me doing sports in the books.

ROBIN: Here's me doing badminton.

DAVID: It was more like croquet. And here's me doing *Words with Friends*. Oh no, it was the *Broadway Softball League*. I was just trying to make it seem like we were "outdoorsy." And she was like, "That looked a little bit gay."

But, I think she and the birth father were very comfortable with the fact that we were a different family setup. That we looked like we would be people they would like to hang out with.

The adoption agency also said, "Don't have any pictures of you drinking in this book." So I edited everything. Because so many times you're at a wedding, and of course you always have a drink in hand. There are all these like, Venus de Milo pictures. And I'm thinking that they're going to think that we don't have arms. "They're a really cool couple, but I don't know whether they'll be able to hold my baby." There was so much editing going on.

But it all worked. And we have one of those books now. The

agency kept one, and the birth mom kept another one. And when Sadie looks through it, sometimes she asks, "Why aren't I in this book?" I'm like, "That's the point of the book."

As this was an open adoption, David and his husband made an effort to make sure their daughter knew her birth parents. But it was their daughter, Sadie, who helped make all the parents feel comfortable on their first few visits together.

DAVID: The birth couple are not still together, but they're really good friends. We see them once or twice a year. The first couple times, when Sadie was old enough to really get who they were, we would go to the Queens Zoo or something like that. And what I thought was so fascinating was Sadie immediately thought there might be some discomfort. And so she was actually like, "Let me show you these animals. See this animal? This is a such and such." She would make it all up because she knew nothing about animals. But there was a little bit of awkwardness for the first five minutes of seeing each other so she would take care of it.

She was actually trying to protect them, like she wanted them to feel comfortable. She was so happy to see them, but she knew that we were the parents. But she wanted to say, "Oh, you're my birth parents. Here, let me show you this South American bear."

FOSTER CARE

"They say love this baby like she's yours, but know that she isn't." – Jessica

Outside of international and domestic adoption, there's also the option of becoming a foster care family. There are loads of good things that can be said about fostering. For example, there are kids in need of a home right now, so once you get through the training, it's likely a child will be placed with you fairly quickly.

Additionally, there's support from the state and the agencies in the form of cash to help raise the kids and in the form of classes and community to help you be the best foster parent you can be.

An extra bonus, from our chat with folks who work at foster care agencies, some agencies are very open to the LGBTQs as foster parents, which was a big surprise to us. But we would be remiss if we didn't say that while the representatives from the agencies we spoke with said it was all systems go for LGBTQ families to foster, we got reports from some of our listeners that they experienced discrimination by foster care agencies. Clearly, there's still progress that needs to be made on this front.

Also remember that just like any other path to parenting, don't forget to read the fine print. Fostering can lead to adoption, but if the birth parents or petitioning family members can get the help they need, the child can be placed back with the birth parents or their family members. That can be heartbreaking if you've bonded with a kid and thought they would be staying with you for the long haul.

What we learned is that it's important to really think through if foster care is for you.

SHEILA

Shelia works at the Graham foster care agency and is an LGBTQ ally. At that agency, it's A-Okay for LGBTQ couples and single folks to foster.

ROBIN: I was under the impression that LGBTQ people wouldn't qualify to be foster parents. Is that not true?

SHEILA: That's not the case at Graham. We believe family is made up of people who love each other. Family can be LGBTQ. Family can be black and white. Family can be siblings raising siblings. Family has no boundaries. We want single dads, single moms, we have grandmoms, we have empty nesters. Any and everyone is welcome at Graham because when we open the door, then everybody has a voice, and we learn from one another.

The other day a single gentleman came in and he said, "I want to be a foster parent, but does it sound weird that I want to do that?"

I said, "Why? Do you have a heart? Do you have love?"

He said, "Yes."

I said, "Do you have income? Do you have a separate bedroom?"

He said "Yes."

So I said, "Then you can be a foster parent. You're just another human being who is willing to open your heart and home to children in need. And Graham is open to accepting you because that's what we want."

> **Shelia is also clear that it's important for people to remember that sometimes it's the job of a foster parent to provide a stable home for a child, for a short period.**

SHEILA: ACS [Administration for Children's Services] and the state have changed the acronym from foster parents to resource parents. Because if you say you're a resource parent, it helps you to be able to mentally and psychologically begin to disconnect in case that permanent placement may not work. So if I say, "We're looking to you as a resource parent" then your understanding is, "I am opening my heart and my home to a child and it may not be a forever home, but I'm helping."

JAIMIE: If you go into it with that perspective in mind, maybe it's easier if things don't go the way you had hoped.

SHEILA: Correct because our goal at the Graham agency is always permanency, however that may look. It may be reunification—children going back to their home because the parents have done what was required of them or adoption. We're concurrently planning both, supporting everybody. Our goal is to make sure this child knows that they're supported, and they do have a forever home.

JESSICA AND HOLLY

Holly and Jess always knew they wanted to create a family through foster care. They opened their home to a beautiful 8-month-old baby who had been removed from a home because of addiction issues and neglect. They were at the stage where parental rights were about to be terminated and the adoption process would begin. That's when a clerical error was discovered which caused the then two-year-old to be returned to the birth mother.

HOLLY: We got a call from the agency about an 8-month-old baby, and we said yes right away.

JESS: We didn't even know her name. We just said yes. When they call you, they don't tell you very much. All we knew was her age and her gender. Often you don't know the ethnicity. You don't know the religious background. You don't know anything unless you ask. But we just said "Yes, we can." And then as we were about to hang up, we said, "Wait, what's her name? Who should we be accepting with open arms?"

HOLLY: She came to us the next day. All I remember is a minivan arriving and them pulling this beautiful, beautiful baby out of the car and just literally falling in love with her in that exact moment. Seriously, the amount of love that came into my body and my heart in that moment was just—I can't describe it.

JESS: She was a feather. She was eight months old but she was swimming in a onesie that was for zero to three months. She was only 13 pounds. Huge eyes, and she was so welcoming. And the two of us started tearing up because she came right to us. She was so willing, you know? And that was our first moment.

HOLLY: It was such a beautiful spring day and she was such a sweet baby, but she really had a hard time.

JESS: It was so sad. She didn't know how to respond to her name or anything.

HOLLY: She couldn't sit up. She needed occupational therapy and physical therapy, and we had to push really hard for that.

JESS: We came to find out that she was held very rarely in her previous foster home, and we started watching her and noticed that she had a weakness on the right side of her body. So we told the pediatrician, and she said, "I'm kind of concerned. I'm wondering if she had a stroke while in utero."

After like six months of sending back and forth questionnaires and surveys trying to get her some therapy, I called up and said, "Hey, the doctor thinks the baby may have cerebral palsy caused from a stroke while in utero."

They came immediately after that, but it took a lot of pushing. I think that's the thing too about having gays as foster parents, we're used to fighting. Fighting for the things that we need and fighting for our families and fighting for recognition and visibility and all of those things to move out from the margins. I think that's a reason why it's really important for the gays to foster.

And she was thriving. She was walking, she was jumping. I mean, I know those sound like little things, but when you hit those early intervention goals it's amazing.

HOLLY: She ended up staying with us for just shy of two years. Throughout the time that she was with us, the goal changed from "return to parent" to "adoption." We ended up going to a permanency hearing and the caseworker and attorney made a case that the mom wasn't making as much progress as she needed to, and so they started the process of terminating her rights.

ROBIN: And the mom knew this?

JESS: Yeah, we always tried to make sure to say, "Look, we want to maintain this relationship. This is not about us keeping Bella for ourselves. It's so important that she knows the full scope of everyone in her family."

ROBIN: But you wanted to adopt her?

JESS: Yeah, we think it's the safest place for her to be, and we just adore her. We love her. She's our baby.

HOLLY: Then we got a call that said basically ACS failed to prove neglect on the initial charge when Bella entered the system. Not saying there was no neglect. They just failed to prove it, and therefore every single thing that happened after that day didn't matter. And they said Bella would probably be leaving the next day to go back to her mom.

Bella's attorney wanted her to be adopted, so they filed a petition to stay, which basically would mean that she could stay with us until they had a chance to retry the initial charges. They said no, and so the day after, Bella left us in the morning.

The thing is, we have our feelings and our trauma and our sadness and our grief. But really, the thing that really gets us is thinking about her trauma, and the loss that she suffers.

And we spoke to her one time on the phone about two days later, but we haven't seen or spoken to her other than that because her mom doesn't want us there, for whatever reason.

JESS: In a usual case, since reunification is the goal, it would be a kind of weaning off process, so they spend one day with a parent, then two days and a whole weekend, Friday to Monday, and on and on. But because the charge was overturned, everything was immediate, and it was as if it didn't happen.

The agency was amazing though because they offered every kind of transitional service that they normally offer parents after unification to support that process, so that the kiddo doesn't end up back in care. But Bella's mom refused every-thing. She went to a facility. We weren't expecting that.

HOLLY: She went to a rehab. It's like a mama and me rehab.

ROBIN: Is there a possibility you could be reunited? Let's say, God forbid, they have to take her out. How do you know ACS would place her with you?

HOLLY: We don't even know ACS will place her with the same agency. But the chances are if they see that she was with Graham, they will ask Graham if they would take her again. Bella's attor-ney is absolutely phenomenal, and if Bella comes back into the system, she would represent her again, and so that would be the key. I think that Bella's attorney is the key to all of this.

JAIMIE: How do you move forward?

JESS: Unless people go through it, they really don't understand. So many people say, "You'll foster again."

Or "Don't ever do that again."

Or, "Come on. One of you should just have a baby."

Or "Why don't you guys just adopt?"

None of that's helpful to me. People really don't know how expensive adoption is. People just want to help so much and say the right thing and take away our pain. But really, it's such a painful process. You have to be aware that unification is the goal, primarily. We didn't go into it, thinking that a miracle would happen. We weren't expecting them to say, "You get a baby and you get a baby!" We knew that there could come a time, and they were right. They say love this baby like she's yours, but know that she isn't.

Just being able to get through a day without crying was a huge deal. We literally told ourselves, "If we have not received a call from Graham, then that means she's okay." The truth of the matter is when we get a call, that's when we know something bad happened. We don't ever want to wish for something bad to happen to her. It's such a weird place to be in. We just have to say, "You know what, we didn't get any calls today, so that means that Bella is okay." That means her mom is really trying, her mom is doing the best that she can do.

> **Jessica and Holly went through a very difficult period after they placed Bella back with her birth mother. But they supported each other, and they still believe in foster care and the importance of being foster parents.**

HOLLY: We make each other laugh a lot. You never know how much love you can be filled with just by having a kid literally pop into your life out of nowhere. The amount of love that I have for Bella, I can't even explain it, I will always love her. If we never get to see her again, I want her to always know that she's loved.

Foster care really is full of love. You get to see kids who have challenges that I could never even dream of having, and they overcome them. They're so resilient. That is such an incredibly profound thing to see.

People would always say that Bella was lucky to have us, and that would really make us crazy because we were the lucky ones. We got to be blessed by her energy and her love and her giggles even her hair pulls, whatever she felt like doing.

JESS: Yeah, it's really true. And I feel like that's true of any kid who comes into your home. Even if the kid was not the right fit for your family, you learn so much about yourself as a parent and as a human being. To see that this little person has gone through so much more than you could probably even imagine, and that they're still walking and talking and willing to love someone is incredible. I mean, it's incredible.

CRYSTAL AND KELLY

Crystal and Kelly are foster parents to approximately one bajillion kids. We're exaggerating of course. Hearing how and when they got their kids was a dizzying experience. But the essence of the story is this. When a social worker called with a child in need, Crystal and Kelly said, "Yes, we'll take them."

CRYSTAL: After Kelly got that call about getting Jace, our son who's now six, I got a call from a family member of Weston's who was fostering a little girl who was three years old. She had a tracheotomy and she was going into adoption placement. She called us and said, "Would y'all be interested in taking Lexi?"

I said, "Yeah, absolutely." Because we had met her when we went up to visit Weston one time, and she just came straight to me and sat in my lap and played with my hair, and she wouldn't leave my side.

KELLY: Yeah. So we had Jace and then Lexi came. We also had Alex.

CRYSTAL: She was three at the time. And then two weeks later, we get a 13-month-old baby who didn't sleep. We had a three-bedroom house with an office that was connected to our bedroom, so we changed that into a nursery/office. Now we're this ginormous family in one year. We have all these kids in our home and wow, it was crazy.

KELLY: Whoa. We are crazy.

Fast forward, some of our placements turned into adoptions. We did Weston's adoption and then Alex's adoption. That was actually on the news.

CRYSTAL: Oh, yeah because he was 18 at the time when he was adopted. He went back and forth about whether he wanted to be adopted or not.

KELLY: It was just kind of neat for him to know it was such a big deal that we adopted him.

CRYSTAL: And then we adopted Jace next. And then Lexi's adoption was finalized.

KELLY: Then we closed our home.

CRYSTAL: Yes, we're done. We're done.

> **Fostering is clearly a life mission for Crystal and Kelly, but that doesn't mean they're immune to the hardships that are possible.**

CRYSTAL: This is where I can say being a foster home is hard. We love what we do, but I know a lot of foster parents get angry and bitter when it comes to biological parents. You will send your child off to visits, and visits are hard. We are in support groups where people complain, "Well, my foster baby went on a visit, and the mom didn't feed him and didn't change him for three hours."

To me, I think, "Well, that's our job. Our job is to know that when I pick up the baby he will not be changed, and he will not have been fed." So I would have a bottle ready, and I would change the baby as soon as he got in the car. And hey, that was it.

It's not my job to put that parent down because they're having other struggles along with trying to learn how to be a parent.

> **There was one particular loss that was hard for Kelly to recover from. They nursed a baby back to health after Shaken Baby Syndrome, only to have him placed back with his birth family.**

CRYSTAL: We got the notification that our foster child, "B" was going back to his biological father. The biological father was not the one that did the abuse. It was someone else that did that. And the dad did work his services, and so he ended up getting custody back of the baby. The baby's grandmother was going to be the one that was going to actually step in and take care of him though, so he had gone on visits with the grandma, and the grandma just loved him, and the dad loved him, so he was going back to an amazing family. We knew our time with the baby was just to get him better, and to be the people that helped him along the way.

KELLY: But that's not how I felt at the time. That's not how I felt at all. Not saying anything bad about the family, but for me, I had this internal struggle because selfishly I wanted to keep him. But in my heart, I knew she loved her grandchild too. And this dad is really fighting for him. I learned to see it that way after, but it probably took me a while to kind of get over losing him. It was tough because we had already contacted attorneys because we thought it was going to adoption.

CRYSTAL: It's hard, but I think you do want kids back with their biological family, if it is a good home and a good fit. I'm absolutely for that.

MICHELE THE DOULA

> Before Michele and her wife walked down the adoption path, they considered becoming foster care parents. Michele realized fairly quickly though that she wasn't ready for the possible difficulties of fostering.

MICHELE: My wife, Ashling, always wanted to foster, so we went to the big "Family Building Expo" at the LGBTQ Center. We went to the adoption seminar and then the foster care one. And in the middle of the talk, I was basically weeping in the back, pretty much uncontrollably. Finally, this foster care lawyer lady came back to me and said, "I just want to give you a tip."

I said, "Great, yeah."

She said, "You are not a good fit for foster care."

I was like, "Yeah, I think I figured that out."

JAIMIE: Because you're so emotional?

MICHELE: Yeah. A lot of parents who have their children in foster care don't want to relinquish their rights. Maybe they're incarcerated or maybe they're fighting an addiction or something, whatever it is, they're saying "No, that's my kid. Just give me a minute."

Ashling still really wants to foster, and I said, "I need at least one baby that's mine, and then I can wrap my head around fostering."

CHAPTER 6

TRANS AND FERTILITY

"I was talking to my aunt about my daughter, and she asked me, 'So, are you going to use your sperm?' I said, 'Auntie...' And she said, 'Oh, wait, wait.' Yeah, yeah, she didn't get it." - Tiq Milan, Transman, Advocate, Public Speaker, Writer

We're six chapters into this book. How's it going so far? You love us, right? Don't feel at all pressured by the fact that we love you, like *a lot*.

At this point you should have become aware LGBTQ family planning is complicated. One thing we have learned is when you don't know something, it's important to do research. Another thing we've learned is it's important to resist the temptation to share your new-found knowledge on Twitter. Instead, be cool man, and when applicable, defer to real experts on the topic.

When it comes to the trans experience and fertility, we've talked to some pretty spectacular couples and advocates from the trans community. You'll be reading some of their stories below, but we thought the best way to open up this chapter is to have someone with more experience and knowledge give us the skinny.

So without further ado, here is Charlotte Clymer, writer,

LGBTQ advocate, and proud trans woman, to give a quick overview of the landscape for trans fertility today.

CHARLOTTE CLYMER

I'm often asked what I wish everyone knew about LGBTQ people (and transgender people, in particular), and my answer is quite simple: I wish the vast majority of heterosexual and cisgender people understood that LGBTQ people are just as boring and ordinary as everyone else. We have 9-5 jobs, kids, lawns that need to be cut, parking tickets, afterwork grocery store trips, terrible tastes in network reality television, and the utter, unyielding thrust of banality that comes with an engaged, responsible adulthood. Family planning for LGBTQ people is remarkably similar, nearing compete overlap, with that of our non-LGBTQ counterparts. Aside from specific process differences, we navigate the same emotional need of wanting a loving family in whatever form that takes shape.

As a proud transgender woman, for example, my own journey is not dissimilar from most cisgender women in how our personal lives and family outlooks are shaped by our reproductive health. The vast majority of cisgender women are compelled to account for the limited window of fertility that may shape their planning. The vast majority of trans women are compelled to negotiate the medical effects of transitioning on our own planning. When I sat down with my endocrinologist to begin hormone treatment, we discussed at length my own plans for the future and if that includes wanting children who share my biological makeup, and if so, I would need to consider storing sperm in a professional facility because sperm counts are dramatically decreased with estrogen intake. Suddenly, I went from an existence in which I didn't need to worry too much about my timing for children to having a hell of a lot of anxiety and planning pushed into my immediate reality.

All queer experiences matter, and the stories in this chapter illuminate both the considerable obstacles and the profound beauty of the LGBTQ community. If we are to be a society that respects the family as the core unit of who are as human beings, it is essential that we recognize all the ways in which families are wonderfully and validly made.

JAIMIE AND ROBIN

Thank you, Charlotte. Now let's hear from our guests.

MARK AND GREG

As a fertility doc, Mark is often asked to speak about LGBTQ family planning. It was there he learned that we all have to be more inclusive of trans folks when speaking about the process.

MARK: I speak every year at the LGBTQ Task Force. I speak for a big pharma company about family planning, and they provide a slide deck that I use. It's been set over the years, and it speaks in the binary.

So I was giving this presentation, and I got snapped. Basically, the audience started snapping at me because I was only talking about men and women and not people born with ovaries who are living as a man and not women who were born with testes but are living as women, or gender fluid.

It was an eye-opening moment. I always strive to be inclusive, but the slide deck I was talking with was not inclusive. But the good news was the company changed the deck.

I've always said there are no accidental pregnancies in the LGBTQ community, but actually, that's not true. If you're a trans person who has not been on hormonal suppression and your partner is a sperm source and you are living as a man, but you have a vagina, and you're having sex, you can get pregnant.

It's hard as a doctor to not talk about ovaries and testicles, but we're much more complicated than that.

TIQ

Tiq's journey to parenthood was a continuation of his personal transition. Early on, he was faced with trying to figure out if carrying on his genetics was important, as well as how to pick a sperm donor. Eventually, Tiq realized that the only things that mattered were the love he could provide his baby and the father he would become.

In this podcast excerpt, Tiq refers to "gender dysphoria". For those not familiar with that term it means the distress a person feels due to their birth-assigned sex and gender not matching their gender identity.

TIQ: We wanted kids, and it was really hard at first trying to figure out how to do that. But we figured it out, found a donor, boom, boom, bang.

It's a donor that we know. We said, "Hey, we're a queer couple, and this is what we want to do." He was cool. His mom is a lesbian. He was really responsive and respectful. He said, "Yeah, I'll shoot this in a cup for you."

JAIMIE: And you used your wife's egg?

TIQ: Yeah, I wasn't using anything from me. When I was with my girlfriend prior to my wife, she and I had talked about having a family too, but she wanted to carry my egg. And I don't get a period, I've been on T [testosterone] since 2007. I don't even know what that would look like. I had a lot of gender dysphoria around getting a period. I'm cool with the parts, you know, I got my top surgery, but that one thing, I couldn't do. And in order for her to carry my baby, I'd have to get off of T and let that come back. I couldn't do it. She was really putting a lot of pressure on me. My mother was really mad at her like how could she ask me to do something like that?

Then when my wife, Kim and I met, she understood that wasn't happening. She said, "I would never ask you to do that. I would never, ever, ever." So we found a donor who worked for us.

ROBIN: Is the donor in the kid's life in any way?

TIQ: Not at all. That was the whole thing. He already had a kid, and he had a relationship. He was just like, "Oh, you know, my mom's queer, I totally get this. Here you go."

We're working on baby number two now. The donor [for their soon-to-be second child] looks like my wife because we couldn't find anybody that looked like me. Trying to find anonymous donors is just so hard. There's just not a lot of black donors in Canada. In the entire country of Canada there are only something like 24 black donors. So we bought a bunch of sperm, and a couple of them were black guys, but a couple of them weren't.

JAIMIE: Wait, whoa.

ROBIN: You just bought random bunches of people? You didn't pick one donor and then buy 12 vials?

TIQ: No because the way we did it, we had to find sperm banks that would ship to Canada because we wanted to have our babies in Canada. And the one black guy that we found, we could only get like two vials from him. That was all that was left. There was another guy—my wife is Trinidadi—so this guy was like Trini and Asian, Chinese, something like that.

ROBIN: You're like, "Close enough."

TIQ: Yeah, close enough. We got sperm from three different donors. Three very different looking donors. And we have a choice. We have a number one choice, and then we're going to work our way down. We want to have them all on hand, just in case. We don't know how long it's gonna take.

And I'm the dad. It don't matter. It really doesn't matter. If I have a little Asian baby, guess what, that's my baby. That's my little Asian baby, and I love her. I mean, who cares. As a trans person, I know for me, I had to let go of this idea that my kids are ever gonna look like me or are going to share my DNA.

For me that wasn't difficult because those are the things I had to think about when I started my transition. I knew that I was about to come out as a trans person, and I may lose everybody in my life that I thought loved me and I have to be ready for that loss. I have to be ready for the long term implications of what I'm about to do to myself and to my body.

So yeah, there's a loss, that's just what it is. There's a lot that you gain, there's a lot that you lose, and there's a lot you have to negotiate. Those are the things that I really was intentional about. Knowing that I was going to lose some community. Knowing that I was gonna have to grieve the woman that I was and grieve the sisterhood and the community that I made and also understand that my kids are never going to share my DNA and probably won't look like me.

But that doesn't mean they can't be like me. One of the most important things that I've ever heard came from my dad was when I came out as a lesbian at 14. I only came out to him because his best friend at the time was a lesbian, and she said to me, "Your father knows you're a lesbian, and he is so hurt that you don't trust him enough to tell him."

So I sat him down, and I said, "Okay daddy, I'm gay."

And he said, "Baby, my job as your father is not to teach you who to be, I have no control over who you are. It's to teach you how to be in this world."

So for me, who my baby is don't have nothing to do with me. But how they are is something they're going to carry with them forever. How to love with their whole heart, how to lead with compassion, with empathy and to be kind, and to be strong. These are the things they're going to learn from me. How they look, that means nothing. That means absolutely nothing. I had to let that go a long time ago.

BETH AND JEN

Jen had a complicated path to parenthood because of gender identity and not being sure exactly where she landed on the gender spectrum.

JEN: I have a really complicated and confusing relationship with gender. I'm an army brat and also the child of an Irish immigrant. There was raging Catholicism, and raging, toxic masculinity in my family. My dad is amazing. He was not the toxic masculine figure, but, being on an army base, I grew up where this was criminalized. There was "Don't Ask, Don't Tell" and that kind of stuff.

I would watch music videos, or whatever, when I was little, and I would see the feminine woman with the man, and the feminine woman was very pretty to me, somebody I'd want to be with. And because I never saw a woman with that person, I thought, "Well I must be the guy."

I don't necessarily resonate with men in terms of gender, but I don't resonate with women either. In terms of body, and carrying children, it was never something that I thought about. And so I grew up, not only not knowing who I could be with as an adult, but also not knowing who I could have children with or if I could have children at all.

JULIA SCOTTI

Before stand-up comic Julia Scotti transitioned, she was lost personally. She spent lots of time getting married, having kids, and trying to find herself.

JULIA: I was at this point in my life where I needed to tell the world that I was transgender. I was still dealing with a little bit of shame. My generation, you didn't do this kind of thing. I didn't know what the hell was going on with me back then. I just kept getting married and making babies, and I was like, "I'm still not happy. Something's not right about what I'm feeling inside."

Back then, you were either gay, or straight.

ROBIN: There weren't as many buckets and options that we have today. Like gender-queer, queer and non-binary.

JULIA: I think gender's a bunch of bullshit anyway. Well, because I am substantially older, it was always, "Boys are boys, and girls are girls." And having gone through this, I realized that there was no absolute male and no absolute female. You're somewhere on this scale, it's like a gray scale. I talk about this in my act. I say, "You think I'm a freak because I had this surgery? Women get new boobs. They get new asses. They get new noses. Nobody says a damn thing, you know?"

Being trans and human is not an anomaly. There are a million different kinds of flowers. I just think of myself as a flower that just got discovered.

LARA AND JOANNE

> Lara wasn't sure she wanted kids until she met Joanne, mostly because of her shame and internalized transphobia. In contrast, Joanne always knew she wanted kids, but as a lesbian, she wasn't sure how she was going to make that happen.

LARA: We fell in love. We were inseparable. Before Joanne, I wasn't planning on having kids. I didn't want any kids to come from my transgender body, and it was mostly because of shame and internalized transphobia. I didn't feel like trans people should have children. I didn't feel worthy of being because I was trans because I was brought up that way. Society brought me up that way.

I didn't realize I was holding onto so much of that until Joanne. Joanne fell in love with my whole being and not just a fake me. And I learned that Joanne really wanted a baby, so I said, "Let's see if we can do this." I knew it would be hard, but I didn't realize how hard.

JOANNE: I always saw myself having a child. But I thought it'd be like Diane Keaton in *Baby Boom*, you know, a baby just shows up one day. I'd tell my mom, "I'm going to inherit a baby. Don't worry, it's going to just happen that way for me."

Then when I was dating women, I found myself so frustrated like, "If this comes up, what am I going to do?" And I thought, "Wouldn't it be cool if the person I fell in love with I could actually, you know, combine with?"

I was kind of obsessed with that. I used to read about how they were trying to get lab mice to smash eggs. And I thought, "Okay, rats are doing this, mice are doing this, I've got 50 to 100 years before they do it to a human. I don't know. I might be pretty dusty by then."

So when I met Lara, and she showed me a picture of herself before she transitioned, I was pretty blown away. I thought, "Well this is somebody in the middle of something pretty major."

Then we made out in the parking lot after.

LARA: We had the longest date I'd ever been on. We went to four different places.

JOANNE: After, I was driving home and I thought, "If this works out, we could have a kid."

> **Turns out they were in it for the long haul, and Lara and Joanne set their sights on having a baby. They decided that Lara would stop taking hormones so they could make a kid the old-fashioned way.**

LARA: I didn't realize how difficult it would be to go off hormones until I felt the deep trauma. When I transitioned, I was in a very bad place. I was suicidal. I was all the horrible mental health things you can think of, that was me. I felt like transitioning saved my life. And at the time, I thought, "Okay, I've found a solution to these problems, and it was transitioning."

When I stopped using estrogen, the testosterone became the dominant hormone, and all of the trauma and baggage all came back. I had to deal with all of that again, and I had to slowly watch my body change to the way it used to be before I transitioned.

JOANNE: I never want to speak for Lara, but what I did find during that time was people were scared to ask Lara questions for fear of offending her, which I get, I really do. So a lot of times people would ask me, "What's going on? What's that like?"

The best thing I could say to people was, "Imagine you do things every day to make yourself feel like you, right? You eat good food. You sleep well. And imagine you not only stop doing that, but you are doing stuff to make yourself feel awful."

When I said that to people, they went, "Oh. Okay."

And it was hard on me because sometimes I didn't know how to handle it. I felt like I was always watching out for Lara. Almost being a caregiver, which is a weird place to be when you're in a relationship with somebody. There were times when we didn't see friends because Lara didn't want to see anybody. And I had tremendous guilt.

After a while I was like, "What the heck am I doing to the person I love? Is this even worth it?"

Then Lara said, "I can't keep doing this."

LARA: I was off the hormones for a little over a year, but I had been trying for a year and a half where I would be off for a month or two, and I just couldn't stay off.

JOANNE: Lara was always mad at me, and that's not even me speaking out of school.

LARA: Yeah, I was pretty awful. Hormones affect your mind and body in ways you don't realize until you're experiencing it. There are studies out there that talk about how trans people's brains fire off in similar ways as their cisgender counterparts, based on their gender identity. So what I find, and not just for me, but other trans people's experiences that I've talked to, is that when you don't have the correct hormones it causes horrible mental health issues. And we just can't control it.

So I'm in this body and this mind, and I still love Joanne, but I'm begging her to break up with me.

JOANNE: I was like, "Yeah, I'm not going anywhere."

They decided to give up on trying to make a baby the old-fashioned way. It was just too hard. But they planned to bank some of Lara's sperm and allow Lara to get back on her hormones so she could feel like herself again. And that's when lightning struck.

JOANNE: There were two nights where the pregnancy could have happened.

JAIMIE: Oh, this wasn't in a fertility center?

JOANNE: Oh no, this was in the heat of the moment.

JAIMIE: You "baby danced".

JOANNE: I like that. We "baby danced" pretty hard one night. There was a nice calm night too. We weren't doing this on purpose anymore. We just thought things were over. We're still doing it to each other, like you do, but we thought, "We're just gonna bank sperm."

Around those same days, we were walking on Bleecker Street, and they were selling these tiny little dolls, and I was like, "You know what? I'm going to carry this in my wallet as a good luck charm." It was supposed to bring financial luck, but I thought "Hey, maybe the luck works for babies too."

A few days later we went to bank sperm, to actually bank it, but what we didn't realize I was already pregnant.

CHAPTER 7

MONEY AND YOUR LGBTQ FAMILY

"When we were 22, we thought, 'Oh, they can do that thing for lesbians where I'll carry yours and you carry mine.' You have this silly idea, and you don't realize it's going to cost $100 million dollars." - Laura Abby

Welcome to Chapter 7. In this chapter, we're talking money. The finances of making a baby can be daunting to an LGBTQ family. Here are some general, don't hold us to them, ballpark costs associated with adoption, surrogacy, and IVF/IUI.

For the folks without insurance going the science route:

- A typical IUI cycle costs $1,000 to $4,000 (depending on prescriptions) + sperm from a sperm bank which comes in at about $1,500 per cycle.

- IVF can cost close to $50,000 because many folks will need to cycle more than once.

For those without a uterus:

- Average cost of surrogacy using an egg donor is

currently between $150 to 200k

For the Adopters:

- Using an attorney (not with an agency) can range from $8,000 to $40,000

- Using an adoption agency, the average total cost is about $40k

- Adopting from another country, the cost range is approximately $20 to $40k

Did you just throw up in your mouth a bit? We did. When you see the numbers on paper, it's hard not to be outraged by the fact that most of the paths to parenthood for LGBTQ families are going to cost, and cost big.

One silver lining on this cloudy day is health insurance. Trends are moving in the direction toward insurance companies covering reproductive benefits for same-sex couples, but we're far from the mountaintop. We talked to a bunch of couples whose insurance companies did not offer reproductive benefits if the couple was not made up of a man and a woman.

Below are some stories from guests about the costs associated with making a family and their stories of victory or defeat in the insurance game.

But before we get to that, remember *you* can advocate for change with your employer when it comes to insurance coverages. If your company has an LGBTQ employee resource group, that's a great place to get involved. You can also be vocal and ask your company to make sure there is no infertility coverage discrimination in their insurance offerings.

ROBIN HERE

We were one of the lucky couples who had insurance. Long before same-sex marriage was legal in New York State, my former company offered insurance to domestic partners. I have to give a shout out to Viacom because not only did they offer benefits to my lady friend, but at the end of the year, they sent me a check refunding the amount of extra money I paid in taxes. What taxes am I talking about? Well, if you aren't married, the government looks at the benefits your domestic partner receives as added income, and you're taxed on that money.

Back to my point. My insurance offerings included the holy grail of fertility coverage—LGBTQ parents were covered the same as straight parents. For IVF we had coverage for one try plus a portion of the cost of the meds. We also had two plan choices, so if I exhausted my IVF try on the one plan, I could switch to the other during open enrollment, and we'd be covered for a second try.

We were fortunate in that we never had to walk down the IVF path (sorry Jaimie), but my coverage for IUI was also darn good. That was great news because when you do IUI, there are all kinds of tests that need to be done. First, they check the state of your eggs, your uterus and pretty much all your lady parts. Then when you're trying, there are tests on day 3, day 30, day 300. I can't remember the exact details, but I know I was regularly at that clinic. Luckily, my insurance covered most of the work as gynecological work, so I only paid a co-pay. Oh, and I also got a reduced rate on the IUI itself.

Altogether we paid about $1,200 a month in the purchasing and shipping of the sperm and about $200 a month to our reproductive endocrinologist for the check-ins and the IUIs. That put us all in at about $1,400 a month. Since it took me four tries to get pregnant with my first, we spent approximately $5,600 out of pocket.

We were one of the lucky couples. We didn't have to spend a boat load of money on IVF, and we had insurance that carried most of the burden of the IUIs. But before now, I never calculated exactly what it cost to make our kids. I'm a bit flabbergasted by the fact that my path to parenthood was easy, and we still forked over nearly $6,000 per kid.

At the time, I was so focused on having a baby that I didn't think about the people who don't have the money to create a family in the way they want to. But after talking to so many couples who borrowed money, liquidated pensions, or searched for "buy one get one half off" sperm sales, I realized my thinking had to change. Look, Mary and I will never be confused with a brave, crusader like Rosa Parks. Unlike that powerful woman, as gay people Mary and I have always been thankful they let us on the metaphorical bus at all. But now we realize it's time to fight. There's an inherent discrimination in the insurance system today, and we need to take this on because there should be an easier way. All LGBTQ people that want to have kids should be able to have them however they choose.

Period.

JAIMIE HERE TOO

I never kept a running tally, and I don't really know the exact amount we ended up spending to make our kids. I think I have a mental block against knowing the full extent of the damage we caused to our financial future. It seems everywhere we turned there was a new surprise expense to pay for. It became comedic after a while, only in the sense that if Anne and I didn't lighten the mood, the weight of all the debt we racked up would suffocate us before we even had our kids. We needed to be together to parent those expensive little buggers, so we had to laugh at the twists and turns along the way.

You've probably gathered by now that I'm not much of a planner. I'm a go-with-the-flow type gal. I head into most situations blindly and trust that things will work out, and usually they do. I'm also not very good at saving money. To be fair, I've never had the types of jobs that lend themselves to saving money. I've never had a 401K or stocks and bonds or whatever the rest of you all have in the 9 to 5 world. I sang and danced my way through early adulthood, jumping from job to job, paying my bills with tips between acting gigs, taking odd jobs to make ends meet. So when it came time to making our babies, there wasn't much extra in my bank account. Luckily for me, Anne had a steady career, a bit of savings *and* good health insurance. Our insurance covered unlimited IUIs and most of the meds associated with the procedures. All we had to do was buy the sperm, and Anne's savings more than covered that. We were golden. We figured it shouldn't take more than one or two tries to make each baby, and then we could use the leftover money to decorate the nursery. "Easy peasy, lemon squeezy," as my daughter says.

Turned out, getting Anne pregnant proved to be slightly more challenging than we had anticipated. During Anne's fifth round of IUI, our doctor suggested we switch to IVF. Apparently, in the science world, if something's not working, you switch the formula. So in the middle of Anne's cycle, while Anne was literally lying on the table with her feet in the stirrups, we agreed to take a different route with a more involved procedure. The co-pays for the new meds were heftier, and there were more meds to manage, but still, our savings more than covered them. Insurance had covered the IUIs, so we naively figured it would cover IVF as well.

Note to the wise, don't go into anything in the fertility world blindly, especially when it comes to insurance. Turns out IVF wasn't covered under our policy, IUI—sure, IVF—no way. The day before Anne's retrieval (that's where they put you to sleep to extract all your eggs to be harvested in a petri dish), we were brought into an office and shown a bill. I froze dead in my tracks when I saw the amount at the bottom of the page. And I thought Anne might spontaneously combust right there, swollen ovaries and all. How the hell did this happen? Why didn't someone explain this to us before the procedure?

It was all a big misunderstanding. *They* assumed we knew it wasn't covered, and *we* assumed insurance made sense. So silly of us. We had already gone through the required weeks of blood tests and ovary monitoring (that's totally not the technical term), and Anne's follicles were matured and ready to be extracted. All of the needed services had been rendered. There was no backing out now. A monstrous charge was staring back at us from the paper, and a chipper little financial lady was asking how we wanted to pay. We took deep breaths and handed over our credit card. Reality hit us hard in the ovaries that day my friends.

That first round of IVF cost us somewhere between $15,000 and $20,000. Luckily, we used our mileage credit card, so we racked up a hefty sum of miles when we finally paid it off with a loan taken out against Anne's retirement plan. There were some fun trips home to visit my folks paid for with those miles, let me tell you. We sure made lemonade out of those lemons. The true sweet part here is that Anne got pregnant on that IVF round, and our daughter was born after an uneventful, easy pregnancy. We got our baby and never thought about the money again. Until it was my turn.

You've already heard my extensive tale of infertility, so I'll just try to sum up the financial portion of the journey. In a nutshell, after about 10 IUIs, we did 2 IVF retrievals and 3 IVF transfers, all of which failed. This was all under the same insurance. We had to buy more sperm from our donor. When those vials didn't work, we spent extra money to buy him out of retirement and purchase *all* the extra vials he produced. At the end of my journey, I also did 6 months of weekly acupuncture, which thankfully my mom helped pay for because by that point we were tapped out. We took another loan out against Anne's retirement to pay off everything. Our second loan was for $30,000, and we're still paying it off. That's about as much thought as I want to put into this, but you guys can do the math. It was a lot.

But I have my babies now and that's all that matters. I would spend it all over again to have these little humans in my life.

The point of this cautionary tale? Don't assume anything when it comes to your fertility journey, especially when it comes to gays making babies. There are no givens, and there are no guarantees. Every insurance offers different coverage. Some are more inclusive of LGBTQ families than others, but none of them is perfect. We still have to be creative in making our very intentional families because we have to figure out how to navigate a world created for heterosexual folks. When embarking on an LGBTQ family making journey, expect the best and prepare for the worst, and maybe try to save some money along the way. But also remember, once your family is complete, however that pans out, you will not regret a single penny spent. Our families are proof of our resiliency and determination, and they're fucking beautiful. But don't take my word for it, read on.

THE TWO BARONS

> **Our favorite millennial couple without kids, The Two Barons, who we lovingly refer to as "Baron and Other Baron", are in the early stages of planning to have a child. Very early stages. Right now, they want to save money, so they have the freedom to create their family in whatever way they choose.**

OTHER BARON: Everyone in our generation has student loan debt. Everyone.

BARON: Yeah. And when you look at the cost of having a child as a gay person. It's super high. It's like a mortgage.

OTHER BARON: The thesis of this entire podcast is really that alternative families, or LGBTQ families, have to go about things intentionally. And because we're at this place in our lives where we're really laying the foundation for everything, we have to ask ourselves, "Are we going to have two kids? Or are we going to buy a home?" We have to think about those choices now because we are coming of age in a system that requires us to plan ahead like this.

BARON: I think we actually give more up. Most of my friends are like, "Homeownership? No ma'am." No payments. Like that's not happening.

ROBIN: I never even thought of the idea that you're saddled with student loans, and now making a baby on top of that is an equally expensive thing. Is that something that might stop you?

BARON: If I can have a child or two—I don't want more than two—and I can maintain my current lifestyle. And like, let's be real, I'm gonna need a nanny, and I'm gonna need a night nanny. Because guess what, I'm not getting up in the middle of the night. Well, I do have Other Baron for that.

OTHER BARON: How can millennials afford both having a child and avocado toast?

ROBIN: Are you guys ready to give something up? You may have to give some things up.

BARON: Oh, yeah. Absolutely.

OTHER BARON: Also let me say I feel like I was born to be a dad.

BARON: Yeah, we know.

OTHER BARON: I love kids. I absolutely want to have a child.

BARON: So my thing is, I do like kids, I think they're cute. I just wish I could send them away until they're like 15.

OTHER BARON: Six is a cute age.

JAIMIE: Maybe you guys should try babysitting first.

> **In the middle of our conversation, The Barons got a bit of sticker shock when they heard what it can cost on the surrogacy route.**

ROBIN: Unfortunately for gay men it's very expensive because you have to get the egg donor, and then you have to get the surrogate.

BARON: How much does that cost because I know it's expensive, but like how expensive are we talking?

JAIMIE: Some of the numbers we've heard are between $150,000 to $200,00.

OTHER BARON: Does insurance cover any of that?

ROBIN: Not really.

BARON: Wait, hold up, $200,000? I could have a Lamborghini for less than that.

OTHER BARON: That's why we have to start planning now.

ROBIN: We talked to some people, there's an organization called Time For Families, and that's run by these two guys Tony and Gary. They talked to us about scholarships and bundling deals, so there are things you can do.

BARON: God, I have to apply for a scholarship? Maybe we adopt. We just take the genetics out of this.

OTHER BARON: How hard is it to adopt? Like how do you adopt a kid?

BARON: I would like to look at the cost of both options because I think I would be really happy adopting a child, not from America, but like adopting a child and raising a child. I think I would really like that.

ROBIN: Well, I think it's a scale situation. Adoption is less money but more unknowns.

BARON: We're planning ahead, so we need to figure it out. Can you believe straight people can just bone?

GARY AND TONY

> After donating sperm to a lesbian couple, Tony and Gary assumed they could never afford to have kids of their own. But they were surprised to find out their neighbor

**left them quite a bit of cash in her will. Thank Buddha
for that because the amount they spent to have their
son through surrogacy is eye-popping, jaw-dropping and
heartburn-inducing.**

TONY: So I tracked everything that we spent, and our journey
was about $160,000.

GARY: This was nine years ago.

TONY: It's interesting because from an industry standpoint,
there are more options for men out there now. So it's leveled
the price out. There are still full-service agencies that will help
you, hold your hand through every step of the way. But there
are other agencies that will provide certain services, or you can
pick and choose which services you want. And it's amazing
because, while the organization [Time For Families] is geared
toward gay men and trans women—people who through social
infertility can't have children on their own—I've had straight
couples come to our event and say, "I have learned more in
two days than I did in four years of trying to understand what
surrogacy was."

KIM BERGMAN

**As one of the founders of Growing Generations, a full-
scale surrogacy agency, Kim knows all about why the
process costs so much. Basically, it has to do with all the
cooks in the kitchen, and some prep chefs too.**

KIM: I wish it wasn't so expensive, but there's a whole bunch of
parts that need to be paid for. The IVF, the lawyer, the insurance,
the surrogate's compensation. Surrogates are paid because they
are dealing with discomfort. They're dealing with risk. They're
dealing with their life being sort of dislocated or disrupted. So
that's why they're paid.

If you have embryos, if you're able to create your own embryos,
surrogacy can be somewhere around $120,000. If you need to

make embryos with your own eggs, that's about 15 to $20,000. And if you need to make embryos with an egg donor that's about $50,000.

ROBIN: On top of the $120,000?

KIM: For the egg donor portion, yeah.

ROBIN: So we're looking at like a solid $170,000. If you need help from every single person.

KIM: Yes, and it can be more, depending on what agency you're with, because if you don't get pregnant on the first try, you're going to have to pay for IVF again. Though in our agency, you only have one fee that carries you through the whole thing. The legal fee and the psych fee, the insurance, those are one-time fees. There are a lot of things that are set, so it doesn't become exponential. But if you need to do IVF, again, you're going to have to pay for the doctor, the medication, the surrogate's travel, her lost wages. It can add up.

ROBIN: How much does the surrogate make?

KIM: The surrogate's compensation is around from $25,000 to $50,000, depending on what agency it is with, where she lives, if she's done it before. Certain risk factors will have her compensation be higher. For example, if she's carrying twins or she's carrying for an HIV positive couple, even though there's no risk. It's psychological.

AIMEE AND MYRIAM

Some lucky couples have insurance that covers LGBTQ folks for IUI or IVF. Hooray! But often, whether you are straight or LGBTQ, there is a limit of one or two tries. That was the case for Aimee and Myriam, so they worked the system by doing the old "Insurance Carrier Switcheroo" during open enrollment.

MYRIAM: That's why I'm so grateful for the opportunity of having insurance. And it's sad for those who don't have it. But even using a doctor, both times, we were banking on the first try.

AIMEE: Because there was no money for more tries.

MYRIAM: You know, with the first one, we did it at home, but it didn't work, so then we went to the doctor, and by the grace of God, once we went to the doctor, it worked for us the first time, both times.

AIMEE: Then for our second kid, we waited until the next year, when we had the open enrollment, and switched insurance plans.

THE ABBYS

> Sam and Laura were incredibly frustrated their insurance carrier defined infertility as between a man and a woman, which made them ineligible, and excluded them from reproductive benefits.

JAIMIE: Were you guys paying out of pocket for this?

LAURA: Yes.

JAIMIE: Did you have insurance?

SAM: Yeah, we did.

JAIMIE: They just didn't cover it?

LAURA: No, and I spent so many hours on the phone with the insurance company, after reading their literature about how they define infertility. There was always the wording "male and female". And I'd say, "You're not hearing me. There's no man. We've been having sex for 12 months and have not gotten pregnant."

JAIMIE: It's a form of discrimination.

LAURA: Yeah, it is. But even with an infertility diagnosis, I wasn't expecting them to pay for all of it, but maybe some of the medication. Just a little something.

EMMA BROCKES

> Emma talks about the benefits of the public insurance system in England for general healthcare, but is open about how it's not great for fertility. Ultimately, she wanted control of the process and the ability to get access to care, so she was thrilled with the system in the US and our pay *a la cart* fertility process.

EMMA: I adore London, and I'm sure I'll end up back there at some point, but the NHS insurance—it's amazing if you are genuinely sick because obviously it's all free. The NHS will look after you from the cradle to the grave. That's what it's supposed to do, but in this one particular area, it's not set up to give you choice.

IVF is an incredibly expensive procedure, which means that the private sector hasn't developed to the extent that it has in the US. In terms of facilities, you've got a much narrower choice. And compared to the US fertility industry, the British one is massively regulated. There's a donor sperm shortage. A total shortage because they changed the law a few years ago, so that there's no such thing as anonymous donor sperm. All children have a right to trace now. That's a huge disincentive. So there's a waiting list at lots of clinics. Friends of mine who have done it in England, most of them have shipped sperm from the US.

ROBIN: Would they still pay for portions of it, but you just have to jump through a lot of hoops, or is it similar to the US?

EMMA: You can get it on NHS, but you won't. The waiting list is so long, so you would end up going to a private clinic [where you would pay for it yourself]. In your late 30s, you would qualify for a very few cycles. And at the private clinics I think, it is still either mandated or strongly recommended to offer counseling services to single women who want to have a baby.

JAIMIE: Is it the same for lesbian couples or gay couples?

EMMA: I don't think it is. I think it's the condition of being single and wanting a child that seemed to be deeply problematic.

ROBIN: So had you been married to a woman, it would have been an easier path?

EMMA: I think it would have been very easy because British laws are very liberal about that. It's interesting, it's the same deal with insurance companies. Insurance companies, obviously now have to, because of anti-discrimination laws, pay for gay couples to have fertility treatment, but they don't have to pay for single women. My insurance wouldn't cover it. So yeah, in the end, I just came running back into the arms of the American system, so happy that I could just put my credit card down and make it all happen in a couple of weeks.

MOLLY

> Molly is a financial planner by day who helps people plan for their financial future. She shared some of the best ways LGBTQ folks can save toward making their future babies.

MOLLY: My wife, Shannon, and I worked at the same company, at one point in time. And because we weren't married, we couldn't be on the same insurance plan. That meant we were paying single deductibles. It's amazing how many heterosexual friends, because this was back before marriage was legal, said things like, "Oh, I didn't think about that, you guys can't get married, so you have two different deductibles." It's those kind of things that people don't think about in their heterosexual world.

Shannon and I just went through that because I switched to a different company. I'm not allowed to be on her insurance anymore, so we're thinking, "Okay, which is better?" I put a spreadsheet together. She is charged a spousal surcharge on my insurance, but they gave her more in HSA, but my family deductible is smaller. We weighed all these options and had to make a tough decision. You've got to think about this stuff and be very cognizant of it.

ROBIN: When do you start planning? And how do you bifurcate planning for making kids and retirement? Especially when you're young and making 25 grand in an entry level job?

MOLLY: Well, it's hard when you're young. I was lucky that we had kids later. We were both 36 when we had the kids. First of all, I would suggest that you talk to three different people. First, a financial advisor or financial planner. Secondly, a CPA, in order to make sure that your taxes are doing okay. And the third one would be the attorney. An estate planning attorney. Somebody who can do wills, medical power of attorneys, items like that.

ROBIN: Do you need to be meeting with a lawyer that early on?

MOLLY: Yes, and here's why. Once things progress, it's good to have all these people in place, and be on your side, have a relationship with them.

ROBIN: Get a team.

MOLLY: Yeah, exactly. That's what we call it here too. You want to get your team together. People aren't going to be comfortable bringing me money to invest if they don't know me, right? So you have to develop relationships with these people ahead of time.

ROBIN: And you're happy to take meetings from the 24-year-old who comes in and says I only have $100?

MOLLY: Yes, there's not a lot of advisors who don't, but I take people like that because I was once a person like that too. And those people are eventually going to be my biggest clients, years down the road. I try and take people that don't have a lot of money to get them on a plan, even if they are not investing with me. If they're just investing in their 401k, I try to get them on the right plan and start with a budget. A lot of people don't know what they spend every month on food and gas and entertainment and going out. That's where I start. You've also got to develop that relationship with the attorney and the CPA, and it's going to cost you a little bit more.

ROBIN: What's the CPA doing for you?

MOLLY: Just your taxes and making sure that you're getting all the tax benefits.

ROBIN: Would you ever say to somebody, "Hey, I know you want to do surrogacy, but it's going to hurt your retirement, so maybe you should think about adoption because it's a cheaper route?"

MOLLY: I think it's more like tell me what you want to do, and we'll try our best to get there. It depends on the situation. You have people who walk in with nothing and they need $200,000. And I can't just pull money from the air, I'm not that good. But, it's all a matter of going back to budgeting. How much are you going to need? Figure out from a medical standpoint, how much is insurance going to pay for? How much are you going to need? That's what Shannon and I did, and of course, I made a spreadsheet. How much am I actually going to need at the end, and then let's budget for it and see if we can get there.

We also wanted to know what advice she had that was specific to LGBTQ folks.

MOLLY: Well, since marriage became legal, it's easier, I guess, but I would say a few things. Before you get married, you usually put as your beneficiary for your 401k and your IRA's somebody like a sibling or your parents or someone like that. After you get married, don't forget to change your beneficiaries to your partner. If you don't change your beneficiary, like say I had my brother listed, and I got married and Shannon didn't sign off on my brother as beneficiary, that would be null and void. Because usually, when you're married, 401Ks and IRAs go to the spouse automatically. And if people have life insurance, it's very important to update beneficiaries on that as well.

When we talked about our team, use your attorney to set up trusts. If something was to happen to Shannon and me, if we didn't have a trust set up, then it would go to the courts. And the people in our wills would have to go and say, "Hey, I need $10 for my son's shoes."

ROBIN: Wait, why? If you have a will and it says the money is going to your kids, why doesn't it?

MOLLY: The kids are underage, right? They become guardians, so they still have to go and ask for the money. If it's set up in a trust, the money goes into that trust, and the trustee can take the money when they need it.

ROBIN: So if this trust is set up, if they're over a certain age the trust goes to them. But if they're not above a certain age, then the guardian has access to the trust.

MOLLY: Right. And you can set it up a lot of different ways. I'm not an attorney, so you're going to want to verify all this with your attorney or your estate planning attorney, but trusts are a good thing especially when it comes to LGBT and that that type of situation.

PART TWO

YOUR LGBTQ FAMILY HAS A BABY: NOW WHAT?

CHAPTER 8

BEING OUT AS A FAMILY

"The transition to parenthood was really kind of dramatic.
It forced me to be much more out of the closet because I
wanted to be proud of my family." - Mark

Every LGBTQ person has a coming out story. Those early moments of talking about your sexuality can be loaded with angst and shame, but usually, the process of coming out gets easier as you go.

For many folks, there are moments where they may not feel the need to be out, and they decide to "pass" as straight. It might happen in an Uber ride where your extra friendly driver is either creepy or working overtime for five stars, and he asks you, the lesbian from Brooklyn, if you're on your way to meet your husband. You sigh, because all you want to do is shout out, "Mind your business!" As you open the app and give him one star.

He's now forced you to make a decision. Do you come out to this guy who you'll never see again? Do you owe it to every gay who has gone before you, not to mention those who will come after you, to educate this driver on why his question is ignorant? Or is it okay to say, "Yup. I'm on the way to meet my very attractive, stockbroker husband. He's from the Niagara Falls area. You probably don't know him. But we better stop talking because he gets very jealous. Did I mention he knows karate?"

However you choose to handle the situation is your right. Sometimes it's okay to not be Norma Rae standing on a table, screaming for unions. Sometimes it isn't anybody's business who you make out with.

But once you have kids, hiding your sexuality becomes a dicey choice that is loaded with consequences. Suddenly you need to make sure you are modeling pride for your child, but at the same time make sure you're not so gosh darn proud that your kid says, "Do you think maybe you could wear one less rainbow to the grocery store?"

The cold hard fact is that when you have a baby in an LGBTQ relationship, the number of times you'll be forced to be out as a family is multiplied exponentially from those early days with the Uber driver.

You'll have to deal with the public school system where forms say "Mother" and "Father", and they have events like "Daddy and Daughter Dances." You'll need to investigate daycares and summer camps to find out how they feel about same-sex families. At the dentist or the doctor, staff will inquire about family medical history and you'll need to talk openly about the donor. And you'll be asked, by absolute strangers, "Who's the real mom?" on more occasions than you'd ever imagine possible.

What we heard repeatedly from our guests is that these situations happen all the time, and often in front of the kids. So LGBTQ families have to be thoughtful and careful about how they handle being out as a family because the kids are *always* listening.

JAIMIE HERE

People never assume I'm gay upon first meeting me. I guess I've just got that straight girl look, whatever that is. I remember going to my first Ani DiFranco concert with my live-in girlfriend at the time (who totally looked gay) and spending way too much time figuring out my outfit for the night. I think I finally settled, after *many* wardrobe changes, on a pair of combat boots, rolled up jeans and a shirt with anchors on it. Don't ask what made me think anchors portrayed "lesbian" to the world. In my mind, anchors were the missing "I like girls" piece. I always had this fear of being seen as an imposter, like my long hair and flowy skirts made me too feminine to really be gay.

When I went to my first Dyke March, wearing my combat boots again of course, I carried a sign that said, "I won't give up until heterosexual is not the assumption." Such a badass, I know. But in my early lesbian years, I felt compelled to prove to the world that I was gay, and I used fashion and attitude to attempt that. None of it ever really worked though. Everyone always assumes I'm straight when first meeting me.

As I got older and more established in my lesbian ways, I learned to drop the fact that I was a lesbian into the conversation as quickly as possible when first meeting someone, to avoid any awkwardness later on. "Hi, I'm Jaimie. My wife couldn't be here tonight. Did I mention I have a wife?" Or something smooth like that. This way, the person wouldn't ask me questions about my husband, and we wouldn't have to have an awkward moment. I don't like to make people feel bad when they've been ignorant. I don't like to rock the boat. But I did this with people who mattered, people whom I knew would be staying in my life. Those who didn't matter however, like the bodega owner, or the cab driver, I let pass. Why waste my breath? I'll never see them again anyway.

Enter babies. Once those suckers came into my life, I realized that it is my job to model pride in our family to every person we meet because my kids are watching. I have to use the word "lesbian" with power and authority and not whisper it like it's a bad word. Have you ever noticed how many people whisper that word in conversation? It's really astounding. I never want my kids to feel ashamed that they have "lesbians" as mothers. I've got to let them know that my relationship and their family are both totally okay. And I have to believe it too. And I've worked really hard to believe it, even though mainstream society shows me, time and time again, that it's not the norm. There are people out there who actually think it's wrong, and I'm done condoning their ignorance. My kids deserve that.

So now, when the guy at Home Depot tells me how lucky I am to have grandma helping (yes, that happened, much to my wife's chagrin, I also look really young), I tell him, "She's not my mom, she's my wife, dude. Can you point me to the track lighting?" And then I have a laugh with my daughter and go about my gay day.

ROBIN HERE TOO

I was never one to be *out, Out, OUT!* when it came to my sexuality. I had a lot of internalized homophobia and it took me a minute to become comfortable with myself. My earliest coming out experiences with friends and family involved hour-long chats filled with tears and fears—both on my part while my friends patiently assured me that everything would be just fine because they loved me just the way I was. Thanks, friends.

Years later, when meeting a new person or starting a job, I became a pro at dropping in references about my wife or softball so that my lesbianism was quickly established, and we could all carry on with our days. There was no longer a process of coming out, it was just who I was, and I was very comfortable with that.

Then I got pregnant, and before the baby was even out of my uterus, I had to begin the coming out process all over again, but this time as an LGBTQ parent.

Being pregnant or having a baby meant we had to be out at the OBGYN waiting room while sitting amongst the heterosexual couples, out as we took a walk to the store with the baby, out in our apartment building, out at the playground as we met other parents. Whether or not we chose it, we were suddenly *out, Out, OUT!*

With that, came an onslaught of fears about how we would be treated as a nontraditional family.

I remember sitting with Mary in front of the administrator of the daycare where we wanted to score a coveted spot in the infant room. Our eyes darted about the place looking for health code violations, while simultaneously asking pointed questions like, "We're two moms. Is that going to be a problem for the staff or any of the teachers?" Since Mary and I weren't members of the KGB with vials of truth serum in our pockets, we had to trust this lady's answers. We had to believe that her staff would treat our children just like all the other kids when we weren't around.

As my kids have gotten older, I've spent time worrying about whether a classmate is *really* unavailable for a playdate or if the parents are big ol' homophobes. I've never gotten any indication of the latter, but that doesn't stop me from wondering about it.

The reality is that I'll never know what's in a parent's heart or mind when they cancel a playdate or aren't as chatty with me as they have been at past school events. But I can't waste my time focusing on that. Especially when that parent might just think I'm annoying. It happens.

Instead, I try to spend my time modeling pride in our family. And I hope that the result is that my kids will be so comfortable with our nontraditional family that they'll quickly drop in references to their two moms and how they play a lot of softball. And everyone will get it and move on with the conversation.

BRIAN ESSER

Brian, a dad of two boys through adoption, perfectly articulates the moment most LGBTQ families have experienced when a stranger mislabels their family.

BRIAN: One of the hard things you have to deal with is deciding when you're going to come out. I was with my three-year-old at the dentist, and the hygienist said something like, "Do Mom and Dad brush your teeth?" And I didn't say anything because I thought, "Oh, this probably doesn't mean anything to him."

Then the dentist came in, and the hygienist said something again, but the dentist corrected the hygienist, and my son's face lit up. He was so pleased that somebody really respected his family like that. I thought he didn't understand, and then I felt like the biggest dummy.

The thing is they're listening. They're always listening. And, there's a need to model pride in your family, so now I make an effort.

JUDY GOLD

Judy isn't just a stand-up comic, she's also a public figure who has used her platform to advocate and fight for visibility of LGBTQ families. And she was doing that long before there were a lot of our families out there. Here she is with her 22-year-old son Henry, talking about the fight.

JUDY: Back in 1996, when Henry was at daycare, we were the first lesbo parents that they'd ever had.

In general, back then we didn't have the rights that you guys have. You know, there were so many times, I don't even know if Henry remembers these, where we'd be at the airport and someone would say, "Who's the real mother?" I wrote an article a few years ago about when Ben got his tonsils out, and they kept saying, "Who's the real mom?" At the fucking hospital. So I changed the form.

And Henry would go to school, and the form would say 'Mother' and 'Father'. So I wrote to Christine Quinn [Speaker of the New York City Council]. I love her, and I said, "Listen, Henry's in kindergarten and it says 'Mother' and 'Father' on the form. It needs to say 'Guardian.'"

She was instrumental in changing that.

But believe me, I know, there are other people who have kids who dealt with this too. 9/11 was a big factor here in the city because there were so many kids who had lost one or two parents. But at every juncture, I said something. And I said that this is not a gay issue. This is a family issue.

I remember we would have to travel with our kids' birth certificates, identifying that we're both the parents. So Sharon and I got divorced, but before that, one time, Sharon was flying with our other son, Ben. And Ben was a little baby, and he was a lap child, but he was speaking at that age. And Henry and I dropped them off at the Provincetown airport. And they were getting on this tiny plane. And the flight attendant comes over and says, "Oh, is that your mommy?"

But I'm Mommy and Sharon's Mama, so Ben says, "No, my mommy just left."

They were like, "What?"

And Sharon was saying, "No. I'm the mama. I'm the mama!"

We had to go to lawyers to make sure everything would be okay if anything happened to each other because of situations like those two moms in Florida. They were two mothers and two kids, and one had a massive stroke at Disney World. They brought her to the hospital, and they wouldn't let the kids or the partner in to see the mom. They said, "No, this marriage is not valid." The fucking nurses said that. And this is not that long ago. That woman died alone in the ICU

ROBIN: Those kids never got to say goodbye to their mother.

JUDY: No.

How Judy modeled pride was not lost on her two kids.

And because of that, both Henry and Ben have always been out, open, and proud.

JUDY: There was a time, do you remember? You were playing baseball—he's a catcher. A guy from the other team said, "You're a faggot!" Or something like that, and Henry got up and said, "Don't use that word. I have two moms." And the coach from the other team came over and apologized.

HENRY: Then the coach came out to his team.

JUDY: Henry's really been an ambassador. He has been so profoundly outspoken about LGBTQ equality.

You know, there are so many times where I could say, "I'm not gonna explain this to this person, blah, blah, blah." And then, I realized, once these people know a gay person, when they like or love a gay person, the world will change.

And when these people go to a voting booth, and they have a visual, they'll think, "Do I want this person that I know not to have the same rights as me?"

So I found it really important, no matter who it is, to just be matter of fact about it. There's no emotion. And you can't be ashamed. That's why I knew I had to talk about this on stage. What kind of message would it be to say to my kids, "By the way, guys, we don't talk about this."

ROBIN: I can't even imagine you not doing that material. You seem just so open.

JUDY: Well I'm proud of them.

> **Judy also recalls the early days of parenting her sons and how much more difficult it was to be out and open. There was less support. There were fewer places where you could vacation and be accepted.**

JUDY: There was a documentary about the Rosie cruise [the first LGBTQ family cruise]. That cruise was one of the most amazing experiences. I mean, you have to realize this is was over 20 years ago. To get on the boat and see these families who were in the fucking closet, in the closet 51 weeks out of the year. And these kids. I remember at first the crew acted like, "Oh, what is this going to be like?" But by the end of the week they said, "These were the best behaved kids ever."

It was the most magical trip, and I think it was because these people all wanted these kids. They were all intentional families. And at that time, it was really multicultural and the love was—it was magic. It was fucking magic.

Of course, we got screamed at in the Bahamas [there were local protestors of the LGBTQ families coming to their island]. Do you remember?

HENRY: No, you didn't bring us off the boat. There was a lot of homophobia.

JUDY: That's right. I didn't want my kids to hear it.

STACEYANN CHIN

> As self-described activist, poet, and a single mom by choice, Staceyann had to educate her neighbors about her family. Lesson one: when Staceyann got pregnant, it did not mean she gave up her lesbian ways. Lesson two: gay women can have a baby without straight sex.

STACEYANN: There's a couple of things that happened when I got pregnant. Number one, I moved into Crown Heights when it wasn't sexy to live in Crown Heights. Most people there didn't have real life experience with a gay, but I'm walking around and I'm out on TV, I'm out on Broadway, just being gay. Like I'm a publicly practicing lesbian. And for maybe ten years, I worked on these people. I'm charming. I'm in the elevator and I make sure I smell good. I say good morning to the old ladies. I lift bags for them, and let them go first. I work hard at being a good neighbor so that people would know that a gay could be good. I'm standing up for all the dykes out here. So everyone gets to like me, and most of these folks are Caribbean, so they're very jocular. The old ladies are flirting with me. I'm like, "You really shouldn't be wearing that dress. It's way too short. You're gonna make me have inappropriate conversations with you." And they're dying and blushing. It's all very sweet.

Then, I show up pregnant, and they're just super confused because I'm a no gray area gay. Like, I am not slightly gay. I'm not partly gay. I'm super gay. And they're just looking, and they want to ask how did this happen? But it's the kind of thing they don't really want to ask. "Did you have a penis in you? Did you change your mind about the whole VJJ thing?" You can see it in their face. They don't think IVF. They think that you went somewhere and fucked a man.

So there were a bunch of ways that I had to come out as a lesbian when I was pregnant. Then I had the baby and then people who don't know me, but knew I was gay, they assumed I was straight now. Suddenly people got very excited, like, "You've finally done the thing you were made to do." As opposed to all of that carpet munching you've been doing all these years. "You've fulfilled your purpose."

So everybody in an LGBT family has to come out, all the time. Every day my daughter Zuri has to say, "That's not my father. It's my donor." And she has to say, "I don't have a dad" or "I only have my mom at home."

It's heartbreaking when she comes in and says, "I wish I had a dad." And I say, "Why do you wish you had a dad?" And she says, "Then I wouldn't have to tell everybody that I don't have a dad."

I don't believe not having a dad is the real issue. But being in a world where having the dad is normal is. In her class, there's the assumption that everybody's got a mom and dad, and a lot of the story books are about moms and dads. I mean even the fucking bear and raccoon movie has this heteronormative idea to them. The Daddy raccoon is always paying mad child support.

But, I got my daughter speaking out now. There's this commercial that says, "What little boy doesn't like trains and dinosaurs?" And I hear Zuri yelling at the TV, "What does she mean, which little boy? I'm a girl and I like trains and dinosaurs."

But the biggest thing she has to come out about is when we are together with her donor, Baba. When asked, she'll say he is where my sperm comes from, and my mom is where my egg comes from. People automatically put language of father in her mouth, and she always has to say, "He's not my father. He's my Baba." And some people even push back at her and say, "Well, he is your father." And she has to say that she comes from an LGBT family and she has to say, "My mom has a girl sweetheart."

So every day I give her the language, and I affirm. If I hear her having a particularly difficult time with one coming out process, like somebody is pushing back, I reach out to my community of hodgepodge gay, straight people and I say to them, "Over the next two weeks y'all are on duty to affirm." Whether she's having problems with having black girl hair in a white school or she's having the dad thing coming at her, people tell her, "You're so lucky to have your mom, and you have a Baba, and you have all these aunties who love you. Not everyone has a Baba. That's so special."

LIZ

A single mom, by choice, Liz struggles with whether or not she needs to tell friends and co-workers that she had her child using a sperm donor.

LIZ: It's not that it's a secret, but I choose not to tell people. I told my parents, of course, my brothers know, and just a few friends here and there. I think that it's not only my story to tell. It's also my son's. If I'm going to share, I want him to let me know that it's okay for me to share his story.

And I was so afraid that he was going to hear something that he was not ready to explain. That was my biggest fear that he was going to be somewhere, and two adults we're going to be talking, and then one kid was going to tell him, "Oh, I heard my mom saying this and that about you." And then he was going to feel ashamed or not know how to explain it because at the end of the day, he's just a child. So I said, "You know what? I'm going to keep this." And right now, the important people in my life know.

But whatever decision Liz made, there were moments in her life where people felt that it was totally appropriate to ask who her child's father was.

LIZ: You'd be surprised by the things that I get asked. A lot of people assume that my ex was the father of my child. I let anybody assume whatever they wanted to assume, and then after my son was born people started noticing that there was not a man around, they would ask, and I started saying, "No he's not part of our life. He's not in the picture."

Sometimes the story changed depending how many times that same person kept asking me the same question because it's like, "I already told you he's not in the picture. Why do you keep asking me how much child support am I getting? Or, does he come to visit?"

ROBIN: Are these neighbors?

LIZ: Neighbors. A few co-workers. So depending on what day you got me, I would say, "Oh, I get $1,000 a month of child support."

One day I just said, "You know, he died in a car accident." And then they stopped asking questions. But if I say, "No, he's just not part of our life." Then they say, "Oh, you mean he just left?

Oh, you mean he walked away?" It created more questions, so I killed him off.

I think the biggest thing that I went through was when I went to get my son's passport, you have to have the birth certificate, and there's no father's name on his birth certificate. The man behind the counter just did not understand why it didn't have a name on the birth certificate. And this was in an office where there was a lot of people and I was talking low because nobody needed to know why there was not a man's name on the birth certificate, so I said, "Because my son does not have a father."

"That can't be. That can't be. There has to be a man on the birth certificate."

"No there does not, sir. My son only has a mother. He does not have a father, and there's no need to have a man on the birth certificate."

I was there for 15 minutes trying to explain to this person that my birth certificate was correct because he told me I needed to go back and have my birth certificate issued correctly. I just got so frustrated that I said, "I just don't know who the man is. Can you process the passport please?" And all this time with a nine-month-old sitting there because I had to take him with me to get the passport.

He just looked at me like, "Okay, now we can process this."

EMMA BROCKES

> Emma found that being a single mom by choice opened her up to scrutiny from friends and colleagues. Sometimes it was for the sheer fact that she was having a baby on her own, but it was also because of how she chose a donor.

ROBIN: Did you ever feel like people were coming at you for making the choice of being a single mother?

EMMA: It was mainly men who felt somehow personally attacked by the sperm donor thing, which is really weird because I was seeing a woman anyway. It's not like I was being heterosexual.

One of them in particular, my friend, got really uptight about it and said it's like eugenics. "You don't give guys a chance to show you their charm."

I was like, "How is it you think I'm going to do that? I'm never going to meet this guy. This is insane."

Eventually, after I questioned him, it turned out that he believed he would not have been picked in this lineup of donors, and he was feeling less than because he didn't feel he was tall enough. But I will say this, none of my male friends would have been picked because none of them can catch a ball or throw. Some of them aren't tall enough. But then again, I would never be picked if I was an egg donor because half of my family are alcoholics. So that was that.

But I didn't mind that because it was like, "Okay, I understand what's going on there. It's got nothing to do with me. That's just you and your self-esteem."

The thing that I found trickier was when it got back to me that people who had been, to my face, relatively supportive. These weren't close friends, but it was colleagues who would take the position of high school friends. And it got back to me that someone at work had said that she thought what I was doing was problematic.

ROBIN: I want to punch her in the face for you.

JAIMIE: Go raise your own kids.

ROBIN: I bet she's a shitty mom.

EMMA: I had all those sentiments and more.

GARY AND TONY

These dads, who created their family using surrogacy, reflect on the fact that it can be difficult to travel as two men with a child.

GARY: When we would drive to Pittsburgh through coal country, where I grew up, it would make me very nervous. Once we stopped at Burger King, and there was an elderly couple sitting next to us.

TONY: This was when our son, Nicholas was a teeny baby.

GARY: I felt so naked, and I thought the woman was gonna say something to us.

TONY: We were both scared. We had come out as gay men a while ago, but when you have a child you have to come out again. And this was one of the first times that it really came up, and we were very nervous about it. And this woman came over and she said, "You know what? My daughter's gay. And I've always wanted her to have a family. So I'm so glad you guys are here." And it just melted our tension away. We realized, we're going to go through this world, and we're going to have a wonderful family that we're so proud of. And if you want to get to know us, come and talk to us, like this woman did.

We're right here.

RAE AND MARGIE

In the late 80s, these two ladies moved from NYC to Connecticut to raise their daughter, Emma. There weren't tons of other families like theirs in the suburbs, and that meant even more coming out as a family.

RAE: It felt very isolating. We were obviously a minority. But we wanted to make sure Emma was in a good place, so we interviewed every elementary school principal that was in the target area where we were looking to buy.

MARGIE: Some of them were pretty clueless, or they blushed when we talked about our family.

RAE: All of this was very stressful.

MARGIE: Over time, we found out there were other same-sex families raising a child in our area, as it turned out, even on our street. But they were not open. Our family was the only one that was open. They pretended that the parents were just friends. That was very common back then.

RAE: But I had the philosophy that if we kept this a secret, we would create a sick environment. That meant that no matter where we were, we had to be open about our relationship. And we had to be open about Emma. And that's how we lived our lives. We would both go to every parent-teacher conference. We both became brownie leaders.

MARGIE: My God, we were the most unconventional brownie leaders.

ROBIN: You weren't concerned about being a brownie leader and them coming after you for being lesbians?

RAE: Of course we were concerned.

MARGIE: But there was no room in the Brownies for our child, so we had to start a new troop. We built our own community. But I also think that people generally want to be welcoming and inclusive. We felt that people generally went out of their way to embrace our family. I certainly feel that way.

I think hiding is almost always a bad idea.

RAE: I feel like we were pioneers, and we set a tone. Years later, a number of young women who came out in West Hartford came to us and thanked us for being so open. Today, I still talk about my family in my work. I'm not closeted in any way. I can't be because I made this decision.

It wasn't just principals and Brownie troops that Rae and Margie had to deal with. The very event of giving birth to their daughter in the hospital required a call to a lawyer and another coming out.

RAE: In the hospital, the social worker thought that Margie was having the baby, and I was adopting, and Margie was giving the baby up for adoption. So Margie calls me and says, "They think I'm giving up Emma for adoption."

MARGIE: I'm sitting there with my stepmother and this social worker comes in asking me these weird questions. It quickly became clear that she thought I was giving up the baby. I said, "I'm not giving up the baby."

Then she's like, "Well then, who's that woman who keeps sneaking in at 530 a.m. through the garbage entrance?" Rae was on the phone with a lawyer right away, and ten minutes later, it was resolved.

RAE: You had to be hyper vigilant.

MARGIE: I'm sure it hasn't changed that much. It could be the cab driver or the candy store person, because people are always trying to figure out the relationship. They know that it's clearly not just friends, so they don't get it. That means that at any moment, you have to figure out how much of the story you want to tell.

MARK AND GREG

Being out as a family means that people feel like it's perfectly acceptable to ask personal questions and share unsolicited opinions. A stranger who had a lot of questions approached Dr. Mark, and he handled her politely, but with some serious boundaries.

MARK: I'll tell you a true story, I was rolling down the street in our little suburban Connecticut town with my two kids in the stroller. They're little at this point, and we have a double stroller, and it's great. I'm running by the beach, and I see someone who says, "Oh, you're giving your wife the day off."

I say, "No. We're a two-dad family."

She looks and she says, "Which one's yours?"

I say, "Well, they're both mine.

She kind of gives me that look, and she says, "Well, which one is really yours?"

Seriously, I don't even know this person. So I said to her, "Well, you can find out when they find out. They're gonna ask when they're about nine. So if you're still part of my life…"

MICHELE THE DOULA

> Michele and her wife have a daughter they adopted who is biracial. Michele is constantly dealing with questions about their family. And often, this can be a frustrating experience.

MICHELE: I want to say, "What is your real question? Do you actually want to know who had the baby? Like, do you actually want to know if she had a C-section or if she had a vaginal delivery? Is that what you actually want to know? Or do you want to know how she felt about her birth? Did you like your doctor? Did you feel empowered?"

It just takes a minute more to maybe try to be creative and think if that was your first impulse of a question, maybe 50 other people this week have already asked me that. So maybe just change it up.

JAIMIE: Well you have also a double whammy.

MICHELE: Yeah, we're two white moms and our baby is brown.

I just I think if it's gonna affect what you do with the child, then maybe it is okay to ask the question. But if you're just curious because we're kind of like a circus show, then by asking those questions, you're gonna make me feel like I'm a circus show.

JANA AND LINDA

Even in a school in a hip and progressive Brooklyn neighborhood, your kid might be confronted about their family differences. When that happened to Jana and Linda's kid, Linda jumped in and handled it with the school.

LINDA: Our kid's elementary school is super progressive, and so there was already that framework, but our daughter, Callie had a problem in kindergarten. A kid said to her, "Oh, you have two moms?" And then he just turned up his nose. And I saw her little shoulders fall, so I turned to him and I said, "Oh, how many moms do you have? Because I notice no moms are here."

I just snapped him down because I was like I don't care. I knew that wasn't nice, but he wasn't nice.

And I guess in fourth grade, she had a kid who was making fun of her. She came home, and she didn't want to tell us that something was wrong. But it was a kid making fun of her for having lesbian moms. Finally, we got it out of her what was wrong, and I emailed the teacher. By the time we got to school the next day, the teacher met Callie at the door. She said, "We love you. You're great. And we don't care. What he did was wrong."

He had to write an apology. The whole class had to talk about their families, and they watched "It's a Family" and then the whole class had to go around and talk about their family.

JAIMIE: So you were in the right progressive bubble.

LINDA: Yeah, we were in the right bubble.

JANA: Also, in her class, they had other kids who had two moms or two dads. So she had other kids who she could talk to about it, but she always would come home and talk about any issues that came up.

LINDA: My theory about this is always be honest. Don't make the kids lie about anything. Just be honest and see what happens. Expect acceptance. That's what they have always done. They don't know any other way to be, but to expect their family to be accepted.

CHAPTER 9

TALKING TO YOUR KIDS ABOUT THEIR FAMILY

"My theory, and the way I parented them about all this stuff is when they asked a question, I would answer it. And then I would say, 'Do you want to know more?'" - Judy Gold

Disclosure is a really important word for LGBTQ families, and a fancy new term we learned on a recent episode from an LGBTQ family building expert, who we lovingly refer to as, Lisa the Therapist.

Disclosure
Noun

> The act of talking to your child about how they were made and preparing them to handle their differences in a world that is predominantly heterosexual and cisgender.

When, where and how do you decide to talk to your kids about where they come from? For our families, this question is a doozy that requires some intensive thought.

To a certain extent the decision to talk to our kids has

already been made for us because we can't pass as "traditional" families. At some point, whether it be in elementary school or daycare, kids recognize that LGBTQ families are different from other families, and they start asking questions.

There's a lot of research out there suggesting that the earlier you talk to your kids about their story, the better it is for them. But it's important to make your conversations age-appropriate and let the kid lead. Don't answer more than is asked. Start small and add to the conversation over time.

The good news is there are more and more families like us out there, and that means there is more support. There are books to read to your kids, educational resources available online, support groups, therapists that specialize in family building, and LGBTQ family classes and programming at community centers.

What we heard from family after family is that while the conversation can be uncomfortable for some parents, the kids seem to take it in stride and adjust to their family structure.

This doesn't mean there won't be bumps in the road. But as intentional as we have to be in making our families, chances are good that behavior will carry over into the way we parent. Below are just a few examples of the families we talked to who are striving to help their kids become comfortable and proud of who they are and how they got here.

ROBIN HERE

Mary and I always said we'd be open with our kids about our family story. It's not like we were brave warriors, it was more like we knew we didn't have a choice. Even if our kids weren't smart, at some point they'd figure out that one of us ladies was not a dad.

In the early days of parenting, we thought all we needed to do to address the situation was use language like, "Some families have a dad and a mom, others have just a dad and some families, like ours, have two moms." And then we'd head to Universal

Harry Potter and all would be right in the world.

That was our approach, and we felt like we were winning. Until our daughter, who was about three at the time, started yelling at strange men on the street, "That's my daddy!" as she skipped toward them.

This was alarming because the first guy she went up to was most certainly homeless, but it was also surprising because of the timing. I knew we would have to deal with the fact that we were a two-mom family, but I thought it would be when our kids were in middle school, and they were ashamed of us. Yes, they might be ashamed because they have two moms, but it could also be because we wear ugly outfits like Old Navy jeans and free t-shirts from my day job.

Anyway, when the moment arrived a decade early, Mary and I both knew we needed to up our game on the disclosure conversation, and stat. So I found what has to be the most specific family origin book ever written, called "My Family." It's sold by the Donor Conception Network, and they have options for almost any situation one could imagine—two dads with a borrowed uterus, a mom married to a dad whose sperm is broken, or even a gay dad and a pack of lesbians on a commune. Okay, maybe not that specific.

I picked out the book for two women who bought sperm on the Internet as easy as buying a bathing suit from J. Crew. I popped that bad boy into my cart and checked express shipping.

We decided to not make a big deal of it, and we put the book into rotation between "Good Night Moon" and our other family favorite, "I Like it When." We didn't debate the points of the story or even chat about it with our daughter, but we read it and re-read it each night before moving on to the rest of our bedtime routine. We were prepared if she asked any questions. This felt like just the right amount for information for her age.

Over time, our daughter, Maxine stopped mentioning her daddy. And two years later, I arrived at her elementary school to pick her up. When I walked into the classroom, I saw Maxine happily playing Magna-Tiles with another girl. Her little friend saw me and speed-walked over, placed her hands on her hips, and said, "Does Maxine really have two moms?"

Her tone wasn't mean, but it was incredulous, as if two moms was mathematically impossible.

I looked the little girl in the eye and said, "Of course she does."

The little girl made a "huh, that's weird" face, shrugged her shoulders and walked back to the play area.

Maxine smiled, ear-to-ear, like she was the proudest girl in the whole world because she was different, special even. Then she said, "I told you I had two moms." And then gave the girl a hug and skipped over to me so we could head home.

We don't think it will always be like this, but we hope that maybe, just maybe, it will.

JAIMIE HERE TOO

My kids are both young, so we haven't had many conversations about their donor yet. We have a book that describes how two moms make babies. It's ripe with words like sperm and ovaries, and it's packed with illustrations to boot. We bring it out regularly to read together at bedtime, but our oldest is more interested in reading about kitty cats and unicorns than sperm banks and doctors, and I don't blame her.

Experts we interviewed on the podcast have said that kids ask questions when they're ready to hear the answers, and we trust experts, so we're following our children's lead on this one. We do make a point of affirming to them how lucky they are to have two moms, and I think we have every children's book on our shelves ever written about kids who have two moms, and we do our best to read to them whenever they'll let us. But like I said, we mostly read about kitty cats. Kitty cats in space suits, kitty cats who practice magic, kitty cats who fly, kitty cats who dance, and so on and so forth, you get the picture.

There was that one fun time when Rose insisted that our

not-so-friendly cab driver was her dad. He was not amused, but she proclaimed it loud and proud anyway, over and over again, just to make sure he heard her. I think he might have been less unhinged by Rose's continual declarations than of our continual reply, "He's not your dad, sweetie. You have two moms." He did his best to ignore the whole scene until Rose changed her tune from, "He's my dad" to "He's a pig." That was a fun moment, and I said, "That's a compliment, sir. She really loves pigs." He was not amused, and we couldn't get out of the cab fast enough.

Based on that experience I am nervously awaiting the donor conversations that I'm sure are soon to come. Luckily, I get to hear all of our guest's stories on this topic, which are preparing me for the inevitable. I now know that these conversations come in all sorts of shapes and sizes, and much like the rest of parenting, I'll never really be prepared no matter how much I plan.

LISA THE THERAPIST

Lisa is a therapist and a founder of The Center for Family Building. She breaks down, in an easily accessible way, what disclosure is and the best way to go about it in your family.

JAIMIE: When you say disclosure, what do you mean?

LISA: How you talk about your donor. How you talk about being adopted. How you talk about the feeling of being uncomfortable about this thing or that. Do you want to talk to people about it? Do you want to talk about having two moms? Do you want to talk about your donor? Do you *not* want to talk about it?

If a kid says to another kid on the playground, "Gosh, you don't look like your mom," how is that child going to respond? The answer may depend upon how they feel about the question or who is asking. And that answer might be different if they have a donor or come from a foster care system. But the kid has to be able to put that all together, to respond in a way that's comfortable for them.

I teach a Tip Top Program at adoption camps, and at the NYC LGBTQ Center. It's a program that helps parents and children learn about disclosure issues. We have a very full curriculum, and we break kids up by age group, and we split them from the parents. For the kids, it starts with some icebreaker activities, for instance, we'll give them a rope and we'll say, "Jump over the rope if you like chocolate ice cream."

"Jump over the rope if you like to ride a bike."

"Jump over the rope if you have two moms or two dads."

Everybody jumps over the rope. And they look at each other like, "Oh my god, this is the only time I've been around everybody like me."

Now we start in a place where they can let their shoulders down a little bit. And we start to educate them about their origins. We do a lot of art projects that help to elicit information about how they feel about their origins, how they feel about their donor, how they feel about their parents. Then we start to move into the feeling realm, when we start to educate them about if I'm nervous, my heart's beating, or my palms are sweating, so they can put the feelings together. Lastly, we teach them how to put all these things together with disclosure issues. We show them their different choices, and they can choose to walk away from somebody who asks them a rude question. Or they can decide if they want to teach them something. Or if they want to share their personal story.

After we do this, the parents and the kids come together, and we have the children show the parents what they've learned. So the parents now learn all these things about their kids and how the kids are really feeling. And, you know, some kids are soapbox kids, "I want to tell the world everything." Some kids are more private. And so it's an opportunity for the parents to talk to their children around these issues.

The last workshop we did, we had one child who said, "It's really hard for me to have two moms." And his moms didn't know he felt this way. But it was so good because he was able to talk to them. Now this is something they can explore together because they're on the same page. You want the parents to be the allies for their children so their children can talk to them. You want them to be able to feel the door is open for them to talk to their parents.

> **Lisa also suggested other communication tools when working through disclosure issues, because the more ways we can "drop seeds" of information to our children the better.**

LISA: There's a theory that started in the adoption community that's now very prevalent in the donor community. It's called the "Drop the Seed" theory. Essentially it means that it's good to keep dropping seeds. And I have a life book that I created because there really weren't any books that addressed everybody. The life book goes through different stages of your experience to have a child. I think children, even teenagers, like to learn things in context. You can put information about your donor in there. There's lots of information about the roots of the family, whether that be the donor and the parents or the birth parents and the parents, and then the whole family tree. It's a way for children to see, in pictorial form, how they came into the world. They can look at it as they feel comfortable.

JAIMIE: I love this. I never thought about how heteronormative baby books are.

ROBIN: It seems like it's more of a "where you come from" book, which wouldn't really be addressed in regular baby books because in traditional families, you came from your parents.

LISA: Right. This is your story. It's how you came into the world. And your kids can look at it or not look at it. There may be times in their life where it's really important to them and times when it's not. I've seen twins where one says, "Oh, my gosh, I have to find out who my donor is." And the other one says, "I couldn't care less." A lot of it's going to be temperament, too. As you drop those seeds with your kids, you'll see how they develop and see how they feel about it.

I put my kids through the Tip Top Program as well. And one of my kids was really, really into it. She talked and talked and talked. The other one would not say a word. She'd say, "Oh, my god, I can't believe we have to do this camp. It's so annoying." But one day I came into her room and she had pulled her life book off her bookshelf, and she was looking at it. You just don't know.

You just keep dropping the seeds.

STACEYANN CHIN

There was no special moment when Staceyann told her daughter, Zuri, about how she was made. It's just always been a part of their conversation.

STACEYANN: My daughter has always known, and she'll tell you, "My sperm came from Baba, and my egg came from my mom. Then the doctor put them together and like, whisked them around. Then they put the egg back in my mom, in her uterus. I was in there for like nine months and the doctor could have cut me out or I could come out through the vagina. But I wouldn't come out through the vagina, maybe because it was like ickey. And so he had to cut the thing, and he pulled me out. When I came out, I didn't cry and he was like, 'Why isn't she crying?' It was because I didn't have anything to cry about."

LIZ

A single mom by choice, Liz knew the moment would come when her son would ask where his dad was. She

shared his conception story with him from the beginning. He knew that his mom used a sperm donor and that he had siblings from that same donor, but he never truly understood what that meant. But Liz had her speech ready for the day he asked for more details.

LIZ: I've been practicing for nine years. I did role playing. I had books that said exactly what to say when he said this, and how to answer that. And when the moment came, it did not go anything like I practiced. I think I screwed it up big time because oh my god, I was so nervous.

He came in the room and said, "Mom, how come I don't have a dad?" I started hyperventilating, and I wanted the ground to open up and just swallow me. I started stuttering, but I knew I had to stay strong and come up with something because at that moment, nothing I read was in my brain. I couldn't remember anything that I had practiced or any of the information from the books I read.

I thought, "Okay, now what?"

So I left it very simple. We already had discussions that families are different because he was obsessed with having a dad. He would come up with stories when he was little. "I went to the park today with my dad." And I thought, "What is he talking about?" And then he would play with a toy and he would tell someone, "Oh, my dad gave me that for Christmas." I thought, "Okay." But I never corrected him. At that moment, if he felt that a father gave him that toy then that father gave him that toy. I figured sooner or later he's gonna know.

So we'd already had the conversation that his family is Mom, Abuela, and Abuelo and Tio and Tia. And he would explain it like that because we were at dinner once and a little girl asked him, "Where's your dad?" And he goes, "Oh, I don't have a dad. I have a mom and a grandma and a grandpa, an auntie and an uncle." And I thought at least he's getting what I'm saying.

That day, I was not expecting that question. He came to me and said, "Mom, how come I don't have a dad?" And he immediately started crying. Then I started crying because when you see your son cry, you cry. I hugged him and I told him, "Okay, you know Mommy wanted a baby and Mommy wasn't married. So Mommy went to the doctor and the doctor helped Mommy get pregnant. There's this kind person that donated the parts mommy needed, so mommy could have a baby."

And then he kept asking me if he was going to meet this person one day. And I said, "Yes when you're old enough, 18, we can try and locate him and see if you can communicate." He made me promise him that was a possibility. At that moment, I promised the world. I mean whatever you want. That's when he acknowledged the siblings [of the same donor] because that's when he asked me did my brothers and sisters do the same thing? I said, "Yes. Their mommies did the same thing. And that's how come you guys are related because that same person donated what those mommies needed."

Then he kind of understood why they were siblings. That's when everything clicked. Then he asked me was this a secret? I think he asked that because he was just hearing about it and nobody in my family talks about it. I said it was not a secret, and if he wanted to discuss this with anybody he could. He could discuss it with me or with his siblings, if their mommies allow it, or we can discuss it with your doctor. I've been putting away money for his therapy, because you know somewhere along the line, I'm gonna screw up.

I said, "Who would you like to discuss it with?"

He said, "Right now, only with you."

So I said, "Okay then, every time you have a question, I want you to come and ask me your questions and I'll tell you as much as I can."

For three days in a row, that kid asked me questions. The same questions. "Are you sure I'm going to meet him one day?"

I said, "Yes, when you're 18, we can try to locate him and see if you can meet."

Then he asked me if he could meet the donor with the other kids so he wouldn't have to do it by himself. I said, "I'm sure that once you and your other siblings are old enough, you guys can discuss that and maybe do it together. But that's something you need to wait until you're older and you need to discuss it and everybody has to be on the same page. Everybody needs to feel comfortable."

TIQ

Tiq decided that his coming out days were behind him. When raising his child, his daughter's origin story will always include the fact that gender is a spectrum.

TIQ: Our kid is always going to know that gender is a variety. That it's not a binary experience. Two of my daughter's godmothers are butch women and another one of her godparents is a trans woman. Our doula is a gender non-conforming person. And I'm her dad, and I'm trans. She's going to be brought up around people of different genders, so I don't think there's ever going to be a moment where I have to come out to my daughter. It'll just be, "Oh yeah, my daddy's a trans guy. And my babysitter is gender non-conforming, and this is who they are." This will be part of her language. She's going to be brought up with that truth, that gender is a spectrum.

I don't ever want to come out to her. My coming out days are done. I'm almost 40 years old. I'm done coming out. I'm here. So that's it. That's how we're going to deal with that.

She's always going to know that she can be anywhere on that spectrum that she wants. Right now we gender her as "she" because she is only one years old, so she can't make those types of decisions. But when she gets to the point where she wants to make decisions about her gender and how she wants to show up in the world, then I say do whatever the fuck you want to do.

My kids are around a bunch of queers all the time. We really want her to understand that even though you do learn lessons outside of the home, the greatest lessons that you learn are the ones that you learn in between these four walls, and you'll carry that with you everywhere that you go.

I think what makes us LGBT folks, queer and lesbian, gay-identified people, really good parents is that we're raising our children with the openness that we may not necessarily have been raised with because heterosexuality doesn't allow for that openness around gender or gender expression or sexuality. We come into parenthood as intentional parents. I wasn't planned. I'm sure a lot of us weren't. That doesn't happen in our community.

I think that makes us better prepared. I have patience for my baby, and I'm ready for the change in life that happens when you have a kid. I've had to dial things back a little bit and certain things up a little bit, but I knew that's what I was getting into because I wanted her. We worked really hard to have her. We paid money. You know what I'm saying?

CAMILLA

As a social worker and an adoptive mom, Camilla believes it's important to talk about where your child comes from to normalize it, and to talk about pride in your own family story.

CAMILLA: You have a job as a parent of an adopted child to normalize it 100%. I think that is done by talking about it right from the beginning. And how you talk about it is really important. You want to be clear that it isn't anything to be ashamed of. That all families are made in lots of different ways. It's also important to value that difference, right? Saying, "This was an important part of who you are." It's important to communicate to the kid that's okay and that their story is of value, and you're proud of it.

I do think it's easier, on some level, for LGBTQ families because we've had the experience dealing with stereotypes and everything else, and that is helpful for kids.

ROBIN: You get comfortable by having the conversation. That's how it happened for me. The more I talked about it, the more comfortable I got.

CAMILLA: Yes. Exactly. Exactly.

BRIAN ESSER

Always the lawyer, Brian believes in being straightforward with his kids when talking about their family story.

BRIAN: Some people really give their kids like a script that the kids almost regurgitate back. And I'm not judging people who do that, I mean, do it your way, but we've tried to give our kids age-appropriate information and let them think about how they feel about it, and let them internalize their own story.

GARY AND TONY

Because Gary and Tony used an egg donor and a surrogate, there are multiple layers to their story and lots of people involved. But they've tackled all of that with an openness about their family as well as an open relationship with their egg donor and their surrogate.

GARY: Some of the donors we met said, "I don't even want to know what comes of my egg, let alone meet you."

TONY: We were lucky because Holly, our egg donor, was completely open. And Shannon, our gestational carrier, was also open to having an ongoing relationship with us. We call on Christmas, and one of the things we started doing was taking pictures of Nicholas like every month, and we send Holly and Shannon postcards so they have a whole catalog of pictures of Nicholas growing up.

JAIMIE: Nicholas knows them both?

TONY: Nicholas knows everything. Holly's his egg mama, and he calls Shannon his belly Mama.

GARY: We go home to see our moms a lot, and one time Nicholas said, "I want to have a mom."

I said, "You do have a mom. You have Holly and Shannon."

He said, "Can I talk to them?"

This was about three years ago. And I said, "Sure."

I called Shannon and I said, "Nicholas just said this, and this is how I responded. Do you mind that?"

She said, "No, not at all."

It went that quick, and they talked on the phone for like five seconds. Then he threw it down and went and did something else. Later, I heard him tell a classmate who said something about him not having a mother, "Oh, I have two."

TONY: There's lots of studies now about alternative families through surrogacy and also about children's welfare and health and their emotional capability of understanding this information. And the studies are showing that the earlier you share the origin story with your child, the better they will adapt to it. So from the beginning, we've been very open and honest about it.

One of my favorite stories. I went to pick him up after school, and his friend Sebastian was in the class. I walked in, and he saw me and said, "Hey Nicholas, how come you have two dads?"

And without missing a beat Nicholas said, "Because I'm lucky."

It just melted my heart. It was the greatest answer in the world.

TOM

Since Tom is a sperm donor, his kids don't live with him. That has allowed him the choice of when and how to tell his parents, brothers and sisters that he had kids.

TOM: When I told my parents, it was interesting. The reaction was not terribly emotional. I guess you could say with my parents being in their mid-to-late 70s and Italian American Roman Catholics, their reactions were not unexpected. I showed them a picture of the kids, and now they know that the door is always open for them to meet the kids. But, by choice, they've never met them.

My siblings have met the kids though. I hosted a brunch about three years ago. And they were very excited to meet them. The biggest water works moment for me in the whole process was when my twin brother said let's take a picture with the boys. So I'm sitting on the couch, and I thought, "Holy fuck! I'm sitting here with my twin brother and my twin sons." And I had this huge smile on my face.

Every single time I see that picture I know exactly what I was thinking at that moment.

EMMA T.

Emma, daughter to Rae and Margie, felt a lot of pride in her family because of how open her moms were about their family story.

EMMA: My parents were so open about everything. Anything I asked was answered. That was the policy. So I knew where babies came from a lot earlier than other people. I asked things earlier, but I also got truthful answers. Like I was spoken to as an adult, even as a child.

JAIMIE: They didn't tell you that you came from a stork?

EMMA: No, not only did they not lie about that stuff, but they answered honestly almost beyond expectation. They really were honest, and I think I grew up therefore with a lot of pride, and not with shame about our family.

SENATOR ZACH WAHLS

You might remember Zach Wahls as the young man who went viral giving a speech to the Iowa House of Representatives to support his two-mom-family. Now he's a State Senator and shared how open his moms were about their family when he was growing up.

ZACH: My moms were very straightforward with me about the donor. There are no secrets. They shared a recording that the cryobank did on a CD. I think that's pretty normal. He had filled out a questionnaire. I could read that. We have a donor number, and my mom made up a name for him. It was Wolfgang because that was the name that she had threatened to name me when she was talking about her pregnancy with my grandparents.

My mom Terry, God bless her, from before I could understand, told me stories about how I came to be. She talked about artificial insemination right out of the gate. I literally don't remember a time when I didn't know. There was never a moment where she sat me down and we talked about it. I just always knew.

MARK AND GREG

Mark and Greg are each the biological father of one of their children. People are often curious which person fathered which child. Early on, they had to decide how they would handle these types of questions.

MARK: Even amongst our closest friends and family, we have not said who's genetically whose. We feel like it's important for our kids to be the ones to find out first. And they haven't asked yet.

GREG: That said, as they get older you can kind of tell.

MARK: They'll ask eventually. There's a lot of data on donor conceived children for gay men and lesbian women. It basically says right around three, four or five, kids want to know who's tummy they were in. And right around eight, nine, or ten, they want to know whose sperm or egg did you use.

JULIA SCOTTI

Julia had a choice of living her truth as a transgender woman and telling her kids about who she was, or living a lie and feeling suicidal. As hard as it was to be open with her children, she doesn't regret her choice.

JULIA: I've never regretted it. But, losing my children, for as long as I lost them, was the worst part of it though. You know, I really just tried to stay in their lives. I didn't move to the west coast because I wanted to be close to them. I wanted to be their mom. And I didn't realize that at the time, but in looking back, their mother and I were always butting heads about who was mom, without actually saying it.

Right before I transitioned, I was still living as dad. And because you have to live a year in your new gender, and it was coming up soon, I had to tell them. It was hard. I think it was harder for my daughter than it was for my son. She was a little bit older than her brother. My daughter was just twelve and my son was nine. And I was asked to stay away. Not by them, but I felt like if I inserted myself in their lives because I'm selfish, and I wanted them so badly, then I would not be doing what's best for them. It was a "Sophie's Choice" kind of thing.

But also I was told that they didn't want me in their lives. I knew they were angry with me, but I've always felt like, together, we could have worked it all out.

That wasn't the case. There was so much Sturm and Drang at that point. I just said, "Look, I'm just going to go away." And that's the way it was for 14 years. I was always hoping that they were going to grow up someday and come back. I tried every now and then, I would send them an instant message, "Hey, how you doing?" And nothing.

Then one day, God bless my son, about three or four years ago, I sent him a birthday present or something like that, and he answered me. We started to talk again. Next thing I knew, we were having breakfast at a diner, and little by little, we talked it out. And his sister came a little bit later.

Now my son has aspirations to be a comedian. He's a great writer. He's a musician. I mean, he's a cool guy. And my daughter is living in San Francisco.

ROBIN: Did you have feelings about the fact that their other mom was instrumental in that lost time?

JULIA: I went through a lot of years where I hated her for doing that. But one of the things I've learned, coming out as trans and developing is that you can't hold onto the hate. I would hate everybody, you know? You can't have expectations about the way people should respond because when you do, you're putting your expectations on how they should behave, and that's wrong. They have their own expectations about how they should behave.

I just I had to learn to stop having expectations, and that's not easy.

CHAPTER 10

ALL TYPES OF FAMILIES

"When people ask, 'Who's the dad?' I think, 'Get over yourself. I don't know. Open your mind. There's no dad.' It's like you're looking at an orange piece of paper and you're thinking, 'Where's the red?' You're not seeing what you're seeing. You're seeing the thing that you've been primed to see." - Emma T.

As a community, we have to think nontraditionally about our family set-up. Our favorite millennial guest from Season Three, Baron (see Chapter 2), put it best, we can't just "bone" like the straights do. We have to think "outside the box" to make a baby.

We believe all the choices suggest some unconventional thinking is needed when it comes to family structure and parenting roles. We're also hypothesizing that some of our choices around creative family structure are because we've been excluded from traditions like marriage or health care benefits. Without the constraints of heteronormative rules and regulations, we *get the privilege* of thinking nontraditionally. And because of that type of thinking, we've stretched the definition of what it means to be a family.

In our interviews, we heard from folks who created

community outside their immediate family, such as enlisting friends as honorary "aunts" and "uncles" or having multiple sets of godparents in order to have a larger support system. LGBTQ parents have gotten creative naming ourselves. We've talked to some Moms, a Mom Tobi and even a Heepa. And there were some Dads, Pappas and one Baba. And we chatted with folks who have relationships with surrogates, donor siblings, egg donors and even biological parents.

We can't always be labeled or put into a traditional box, but each family makes up a little part of our rainbow, and that's a beautiful thing, goddammit.

Oh, and our families are thriving too. So take that, folks who want to keep us down!

ROBIN HERE

I don't come from a traditional family. My parents split up when I was 12, and I lived with my mom who was definitely not like other moms. She wore short shorts, halter tops and more makeup than is worn on the set of a high def movie today. Growing up, we were never close with our extended family. In Mary's family, there's way less drinking and way more of the Lord.

Once I started adulting, I knew I was on my own, and I needed to create a family network. So I pretty much stole my friends' families. If we were friends, and you came from a good home, I was at your house holding sparklers at the fourth of July pool party, bringing gifts for the Secret Santa exchange, and volunteering to create the calendar for the yearly beach vacation that I invited myself to. And when I jokingly called your mom "Mom," I was not kidding. I weaseled my way into families so stealthily that you thought I was always there. That might have been because I made sure I was in every picture too. That's an important part of stealing someone's family, establishing proof of belonging.

Oddly enough though, my "make-a-family" philosophy

did not extend to the LGBTQ world when we first had kids. I wanted our immediate family to be Mary, me and our kids, and no one else. My reasons centered on wanting the traditional family I never had, but they were also deeply connected to the way we have to make our families. I resented that we had to rely on a stranger and his sperm. Just because we needed a thing from him, didn't mean he was a part of our family.

But after we had our first kid, we wanted to have our second using the same donor. Turned out he was out of stock and retired from donating. After a few moments of panicking, someone gave us the advice that we could sign up on the sibling donor registry board of our sperm bank and see if anyone had leftover sperm from our donor. I signed up for that reason only. I wasn't interested in making friends or a family.

Then we started corresponding with these folks. A woman named Liz responded immediately. She had a son by the same donor, and she declared us family. That moment felt exactly like when a co-worker comes at you for a hug and you put out your hand to shake. However, I stayed in contact with her even though she didn't have any extra sperm.

Then a woman from the West Coast reached out. She had one vial of sperm left, but she wasn't ready to part with it. We emailed back and forth while she decided, and surprisingly enough, she turned out to be quite nice too.

Then I spoke with a woman in Bogota, Columbia who had one more vial, and she offered it to us, without cost. After a bunch of calls trying to figure out international sperm shipping, she suggested I get on a plane to Bogota and get my IUI done by her doctor. It was a crazy suggestion, and of course, I did it. In Bogota, I met her family, and they treated me like family. I met her son, who is my daughter's sibling. These wonderful people, and a little boy who had similar eyes to my daughter, chipped away at my closed off heart. How could I not open the door to all these wonderful people trying to help us?

I ended up setting up a private Facebook group for the

families who used the same donor. We started meeting other families as they came to town. And with each picture posted or conversation or visit my feelings shifted. I don't know if I got more confident in our immediate family unit or if I felt like it doesn't have to be Mary and I against the world. Whatever the reason, I now have a real connection with these folks. We're all on our own separate paths, with our own families, but the universe has brought us together, and we are a family of sorts.

So in our immediate family we call the kids from the same donor "siblings". We distinguish between the word "sibling" and "brother" or "sister" because that's what works for us. We hope that a connection to the donor siblings will help our kids feel a sense of their full identity and where they come from. We also hope it will help them not feel like they have a missing piece. And if they have issues, they now have a group of people they can talk to who will understand *exactly* what they are going through.

JAIMIE HERE TOO

I just teared up watching a video of my friends' daughter giving the commencement speech for her 5th grade graduation. I sent a text to her moms saying, "We've raised such a smart, articulate young lady." I'm half joking of course—clearly I didn't help with any of her linguistic eloquence, but I do feel a strong sense of pride in the young lady she is becoming. I've been in her life since she was born. She calls me Aunt Jaimie, and I consider her my niece. She and my daughter fight and make up like only cousins can, and her moms are our best friends. We even share a group text titled "BFFs" because we're that annoyingly close. They may not be blood, but they are family. In fact, there's a whole group of us lesbian moms who've stayed close throughout the making of our babies and the rearing of them. Our children refer to all the moms as "Aunt So-and-So", and the kids are growing up as close as cousins can. We do have one straight dad in the mix, but the kids keep it real and call him

"Aunt Pat". He likes it and we're all glad to be able to keep the theme going. We rent houses together for holidays and regularly meet for barbecues. In many ways we're closer than even my extended family back home.

I'm not telling you this to make you jealous that you don't have an "Aunt Pat" of your own (although you should be, he's awesome), but to illustrate how creative us LGBTQ folks get to be when designing our families. In my case, we wanted our kids to see themselves reflected in the families around them, and so we created a world that would do that for them. My daughter may only have one other two-mom family in her school, but she knows handfuls of them in her personal life, and they are her Family. When the Family and Aunt Pat are around, our kids get to live in a space where their particular family make-up is not the exception but the norm which is not the case in the rest of the world. This is the beauty of our families. Since there are no set molds for our families, we can create the community we need in whatever way we want, the sky's the limit. I'm really proud of the community Anne and I have created to surround our family. They're fucking beautiful and I wouldn't have it any other way.

BRIAN ESSER

Brian's kids were both adopted from different families. He feels it's important to let each child define how they think about their birth families, so they keep an open relationship with the birth parents, and those relationships are evolving over time.

BRIAN: My kids have different birth families, and they know their birth families. It's open. A shout out to my husband. He's the one who really manages this relationship. He sends letters and pictures on a really consistent basis. Like a lot. To the point where the agency said, "Maybe you just want to send these directly instead of sending through us?"

We see them for visits once or twice a year as well. I sort of feel for my son's birth mothers the way I feel about my first cousins. They're people who I see a couple times a year, have a certain fondness for, but they're not people that I'm hanging out with every weekend or anything like that.

ROBIN: Do they call the birth mother's "mom" or by their first names?

BRIAN: First names. My older son is from Pennsylvania, so he refers to them as his Pennsylvania family. Then my younger son was born in Connecticut, and he refers to them as his Connecticut family.

It's just a nice way to describe it without putting a lot of language around it.

TOM

> As a sperm donor to a lesbian couple, one might think Tom's job ended after the donations, but the kids think of him as more than a donor.

TOM: I think I've been really blessed with how everything has played out. They've kept me engaged, they've kept me involved. Even if they go away for a weekend, they send me a picture and say, "We went to Sesame Place."

And I don't feel like, "Hey, they didn't ask me." I think, "Oh good, they went away."

I call the moms my pseudo wives. And it's funny, at one of the kid's birthdays, one mom was snapping at the other one. And the other mom said, "Don't yell at me in front of our husband!" It's a joke, but I'm the male figure they see most often.

The whole thing is great. It's like a great balance for me.

> When the kids were first born, Tom was living in another state, but since returning, he remains very much in their lives. He sees them on a non-scheduled, but consistent

basis. And the kids call him Tom, but they also refer to him as their father.

TOM: I moved to Chicago two months after my daughter was born, which was a predetermined move for me. I came home every six months and visited my immediate family as well as [the family he donated to], and it was good because it gave the moms an opportunity to establish their life without me there.

Now that I'm back, I see them about every six weeks. It kind of averages out that way when you figure holidays and birthdays. Something's always happening.

Recently, my daughter drew a picture at school, and she said, "This is my family. My moms, my dad, my brothers and me." And so it's in their consciousness. For me, it's not part of my every day because I don't wake up with them, but when I'm with them I feel like, "Oh, yeah."

They don't call me dad. They call me Tom, but they know I'm their dad. I get cards at Father's Day and everything. I'm glad I didn't have a cocktail before this interview because I would be crying right now. That part of this journey has been mind-blowingly amazing.

When I first got back from Chicago, like in that first year, my daughter had a birthday party, and I went to their house, and they all had these temporary tattoos on their arms. And I said, "Well, where's mine? I want one."

The moms gave me one, and they said, "Look, now we're all a family."

JANA AND LINDA

Jana and Linda created a blended family over time. Since Linda had the children with her ex-wife, Jana had to find her place as a parent with Linda and the kids. The result wasn't a stepmom title. Instead, the kids call her Heepa.

JANA: I just liked how Linda was handling our new relationship. Everything was really about the kids, and I grew up in a home where it wasn't about the kids other than the kids being used as pawns, so to speak. Linda wasn't about that. Fast forward a couple of months, we would just hang out. We'd go to dinner, we'd go to movies, and we were getting to know each other in a different way, and it was pretty awesome.

ROBIN: What's interesting is it's like the anti-lesbian story. You didn't go on two dates and move in. It was a slow courting of the whole family.

JANA: Yeah. I didn't spend a night at Linda's house for maybe five months into the relationship. She was like, "Go home!"

LINDA: Because I didn't want the kids to fall in love. If it didn't work out, it would just break their hearts.

JANA: I just have to say that Linda thought I would be the rebound girl. I'm just tossing that in there right now.

It was really interesting because we developed this relationship and I really fell in love with the kids. Of course I fell in love with Linda, but when she would start to work my nerves, I would say, "Oh my god. I just can't be in this relationship. She's driving me crazy." Then I would say, "But I love the kids. I have to make it work with her because I love the kids." I respected the relationship that the kids had with Linda's ex, Vicki. I wasn't trying to come in and move anybody out. I had something different to bring to the family. I was about having a good time. I would take the kids to the park. We've been together 17 years, so for the first 10 years of our relationship the kids called me Heehee because I would say, "Let's go to the park. Hee Hee!" and I would make that noise. So all the kids called me Hee Hee, and actually one day I was in line going to the movies, and I heard a grown-up say, "Hee Hee." So everybody called me that.

ROBIN: They still call you that?

JANA: Well, it kind of morphed. Now the kids call me Heepa. It's kind of cool.

LINDA: Our family is very crazy with nicknames.

JANA: Yeah, Heepa or Heehaw because I'm from Texas. Or Yeehaw.

JAIMIE: And that's their own special name for you because you are their mom.

JANA: Yeah, Yeah.

LIZ

> Sometimes defining the family goes beyond the parents and the donor. Robin, this book's co-author, and Liz are a new type of family. They each have a child from the same sperm donor, making their kids siblings.

ROBIN: Liz was my entry point into meeting the other families who used the same donor. We actually got in contact with Liz because we needed more sperm when I was ready to have a second child and our donor was out of sperm and out of the program.

And so I registered on the sibling registry board and when I got onto the site, Liz was the first person that popped up. My goal wasn't to make new friends or redefine our family. My goal was to see if anyone had extra sperm.

Liz said, "I don't have any more sperm, but we're family."

I thought, "I'm so scared."

LIZ: I knew it was going to be tricky and different and maybe difficult. But I said, "You know what? I'm going to put myself out there, introduce myself and build some type of relationship, and then let my son Julian take over and decide what type of relationship he wants with his siblings."

But at least I wanted him to get to know them and know that they were out there. My biggest fear was I didn't want him to feel that he was alone in this process. I wanted him to know that there were others just like him going through the same thing he was feeling, because I can't relate to what he's going to be feeling not having the standard family that everyone else has.

> **Liz and Robin are in a secret Facebook group that includes most of the families who used the same donor. There are somewhere in the neighborhood of 12 to 15 families in the group. Some folks vacation together, others participate in the Facebook group, occasionally posting a picture or a comment.**

LIZ: The way I think of it is, at the end of the day, you have total control over how much you let these people into your life. Just because you put yourself out there and say, "Hi, I have a child from the same donor as you," doesn't mean there has to be more. You can just leave it at that.

ROBIN: That's true. We have varying levels of connection in our group. I've never done any of the vacations, but anytime anyone's in town, I always say, "Let's get together."

LIZ: Right. Right. When I went to New York, and I reached out to Robin, and I asked her, "Do you want the kids to know that there's any relationship between them?"

She said, "I don't feel comfortable."

And we said, "Absolutely. Then we won't mention it."

I told my son, "We're going to meet a friend that lives in New York. They have two kids, and you're going to be able to play with the kids."

We left it at that. You don't want to invade anyone's privacy or the way they want to raise their child or impose yourself on them. You just want to know that they're out there. And then once you know that they're out there, then you have total control of deciding how much you want these people in your life. You have to decide what you feel comfortable with. And I don't think you should feel pressure, but it's really nice to know.

ROBIN: We've changed over time. The day after your visit, we ended up telling my daughter, Maxine who Julian [Liz's son] was. Then we started talking about what it means to be a sibling because for us it was more complicated for my kids because they were so young, and they had to understand that they are brother and sister, but they come from different donors, so it felt confusing to explain. I didn't want to share it until I knew I could explain "brother and sister" and "siblings".

LIZ: I will admit from my side, I was just going to register my son in this sibling registry board. I was going to learn that there were other families out there and that was going to be the end of that. It never occurred to me that I would be going on vacations with these people. But I thought, it's a few days, it's for my son and then I go home, back to my life and back to our day-to-day. And my son had a wonderful memory to look back on because I have all the pictures. I've created little books for him with names of who they're from and where they live with each mom. And he has that.

Plus I made a promise to my father. One of my father's biggest concerns was, "What if Julian goes away to college and meets a sister and they started dating?" He was so concerned, so I said, "Don't worry. I'm going to pick an open donor and then I'm going to register him, and if he does have any siblings, maybe we can communicate and he will know that they are out there and then I'll let him choose what type of relationship he wants with them."

MAKEDA AND SADIE

As kids of LGBTQ families in the 80s, it's interesting to hear that friends and co-authors, Makeda and Sadie, both embrace siblings from their donors. They also

both believe in the notion that family is not created but chosen.

SADIE: I have talked to people who feel vastly different than I do, but for me, it was kind of cool to know them [the two kids she knows who share the same donor]. I see them around and it's like, they've always kind of been family, right? So it's very much like, "Oh, hey, how are you doing? I love you. You're awesome."

I think I was raised to believe that family is chosen. Family does not have to be blood.

MAKEDA: I'm nodding my head along with Sadie around chosen family because that's the way I grew up as well. I was definitely raised by my two moms, Corrinne and Annette, but I also feel like I have this extended family full of lesbian feminists who are of my moms' generation, and they have actually shaped me, and continue to shape me, and who I call my "OWLs"— Older Wiser Lesbians. They're really the community that raised me. They are my chosen family.

LISA AND JENNIFER

These two ladies welcome their relationships with the donor siblings and their families. It's always been a part of their family story.

ROBIN: You guys are in touch with other families who had kids by your donor. Do you call them siblings?

LISA: I call them siblings. They are our son's siblings. The way that happened was the sperm bank has a donor sibling registry, and when our son was born, we registered him. And someone who had already given birth with the same donor had put a message on that board, because the board only pertains to that one donor, and they had started a closed, secret Facebook page. It was basically, "Anyone who wants to join, come on over." And that's what we did.

JENNIFER: It started when they were babies.

LISA: Yeah. And we slowly got to know each other a little bit on Facebook. We're spread out all over the country. And over time, we started to meet up with some people. There's a family in Philadelphia. There was one other family in New York.

JENNIFER: I think we have a few social hub type people among the parents. And they generated this idea of, "Oh, let's all go on vacation together." And so we went to Club Med in Florida when the oldest kids were four.

LISA: Yeah, they were all born the same year.

JAIMIE: How many are there?

LISA: We think there's about 18 or 20.

JAIMIE: And they're all in the group?

LISA: No, they're not there. Most are. We think there are one or two that are not. I've actually managed to identify them.

JENNIFER: Because Lisa has a second career in her as a private investigator.

LISA: I'm a sleuth.

ROBIN: What's the makeup of the families? Gays?

JENNIFER: It's like six lesbian couples, and the rest are single moms. But two of the single moms are lesbians, and the rest are straight.

JENNIFER: It also turned out it was a whole bunch of families who are kind of in the same phase of their lives, right? Families who all have kids the same age, and who all got pregnant the same way.

LISA: We all picked the same donor, so there's some similarities amongst us. We're all attracted to the same donor.

JENNIFER: And they all liked each other right away. So we all went on vacation, and it was so fun, and we had such a good time.

JAIMIE: I would have been so nervous for this.

JENNIFER: We were nervous.

LISA: But then we did it again two years later.

JENNIFER: Now, I don't know what happened, but we started planning the next one for another two years hence. And some-how it became, "Let's just do it this summer." So now we're going to go on vacation with them two years in a row.

LISA: Yeah, I mean, I love it. I think it's a very rich part of this experience.

JENNIFER: It's been really rich. People think it's strange from the outside.

LISA: But it doesn't feel that way.

JENNIFER: It does not feel strange. The more people and the more connections that you have in this world where we're all so alienated from each other, why wouldn't you want that? And yes, I get that the relationship is not one where we have a template that everyone's familiar with, but I think the next generation will have an easier time of it.

My cousin Emma's moms are lesbians, and she's part of the first generation of donor conceived children. She has no idea who she is on that half of her genetics, and she doesn't have a way of finding out. She was in her 20s when we were planning all of this. And we were able to talk to her about that, and that's part of why we chose a known donor. Part of why we think that the relationships with the other siblings is really important. And we feel really lucky we were able to learn from the previous generation.

LISA: It's also something our son knows about. He's met 80% of his siblings.

JENNIFER: So he won't accidentally marry any of them.

ROBIN: We all worry about that. Let's face it.

LISA: I was so concerned. I was so worried how are we going to explain this? And when are we going to explain it? I think that first year we went on vacation when he was four, we just put it out there. You know, these people are your brothers and sisters.

ROBIN: You say brothers and sisters?

LISA: We do.

JENNIFER: Lisa does. I don't.

LISA: But it was all very seamless, and children don't ask anything more than they're ready to know. So he just accepted it. I think at this point, he knows that it's different. He doesn't live with them. And he sees other families where brothers and sisters live together. He hasn't really started asking a lot of questions yet, but he knows that his situation is somewhat unique. But it's out there now.

It's really special, and it's a great story.

EMMA BROCKES

> When Emma and her partner were dating, they each decided to have their own kids. They live in the same apartment building, but on different floors, so they each are single parents who help with the other's kids. Emma may not have complete clarity on the wording of their family, but she is very clear that it works for them.

ROBIN: How does your family work?

EMMA: I have no idea, honestly. So the reason we live upstairs, downstairs is just the real estate market. It just happened. It's the Universe. I was living in Brooklyn. She was in Manhattan. And we didn't know what we were doing. Half of me thought I should move to be near my best friend who was further into Brooklyn because I thought he was my most reliable emotional crutch. Then all the cues in life tell you that that's inappropriate, and that even if you tenuously connected to someone romantically, then that is the person you're supposed to bond with to have a kid, but it wasn't appropriate in our case. The one thing we knew was that we were not suited as co-parents. It's weird, but we just knew.

ROBIN: Do you have different parenting styles?

EMMA: I mean, not in a way that causes conflict when we hang out. But I think if there was actual 100% shared responsibility, there would be a power struggle. The fact that neither of us represents a threat to the other one's authority means that there's a balance.

ROBIN: Because you're in the same building, I imagine a TV sitcom with people going up and down stairs.

EMMA: Well, we sold the sitcom funnily enough. Yeah, the pilot script just landed. But, we use the fire escape, not the outside, but the interior. We also really annoy people by going one stop on the elevator all the time.

ROBIN: Do you say girlfriend?

EMMA: No. No. No. This language is so tricky. It doesn't work for some reason. That term does not work for us. I suppose first of all, it feels age inappropriate. Like my dad doesn't have a girlfriend either. He has a partner, which L [Emma's partner], whenever I use that word, she's always like, "You make him sound like he's gay." Which I think is nonsense. Unmarried people have partners. Anyway, partner is the nearest one.

ROBIN: I'm assuming you're not dating other people?

EMMA: Exactly. Right.

JAIMIE: So in your early stages of dating, she said, "Oh, hi, I know I just met you, but I'm gonna have a baby."

ROBIN: And she was very clear, "It's my baby"?

EMMA: Yeah, totally clear. And I found that insane because I was like, "What is that?" That didn't make any sense to me. Actually, I would have been more alarmed if she'd said "Let's have a baby together." Then I would have just walked. But as it was, I was like, "Wow, interesting. Okay, I'll stick around." Because it's not my problem.

JAIMIE: Did you guys have a conversation about what your role was going to be?

EMMA: We're not awesome at having conversations about things. It was sort of apparent because I supported her throughout the entire process. I was involved, but I understood absolutely that this was not going to be my baby. That was crucial. Again, and I feel like I'm on such thin ice with this language, but it was not my baby. And that's not because it wasn't genetically mine. It was just that structurally it was not my baby because I had no rights and responsibilities. I wanted my own baby.

ROBIN: Will it progress? Would you move in? Or is this how it is?

EMMA: Well, I think at some point, we both went through phases of assuming we were just incredibly slow burn. That we needed all these legal protections because we're both highly controlling, I guess in some way we must be. But that probably or possibly, it would morph into something more conventional.

Actually, that's not been the case. What turned out to be the case is that this is exactly the level that we need to be interacting and it works really well. There's massive moral support. There's an extra adult who the kids see every day. And what is really interesting is that they're incredibly close, but of their own discernment. I think they understand that it's a difference. It's a category difference. It's not a second parent.

ROBIN: I assume the separate apartments helps with that.

EMMA: Right. It's a big show. Exactly.

ROBIN: I'm assuming that you spend some nights in your apartment, some nights in her apartment?

EMMA: We kind of don't just because the kids just can't manage it. It doesn't work. Like it just ends up everyone being awake at two in the morning. It's like cousins. I have to find a better way to talk about it because it sounds so dysfunctional.

JAIMIE: It sounds like you are very sure in it, and it works for you.

EMMA: It's very unconventional. It's only possible because it's two women because obviously if I had been dating a guy, I couldn't have gone off and had a sperm donor baby. That would have been too much. So to me, it's sort of emblematic of the fact that women together can just create models that don't exist in the male dominated world.

ROBIN: Has anyone ever asked the kids to describe their family?

EMMA: My girls aren't quite old enough. Although I'm trying to integrate it all from day one like you're supposed to, but they're showing zero interest. Every time I go down the slipstream of where they came from, they just zone out. I think the way that is, we're probably going to present it, just for family history at school is "single parent". Given that I can't put into words, I can't really expect a five-year-old to do it.

As they get older, though, it will require some extra bit of narrative. I think we just explain it like a different way of being a family. In the day-to-day, there's no ambiguity, it's like, "These are the pillars of the kids' lives." They're here and they're completely solid. And they're completely reliable. It's not complicated. It's just when you hold it up against the model of what is should be, that it starts to look kind of a deranged. Especially heterosexual couples who I talk to.

Many of my female friends are like, "Oh, my God, if I could get away with living in a different house, that would be awesome."

RAE AND MARGIE

Rae and Margie set about creating a wide network of adults to help raise and guide their daughter, Emma.

RAE: We have a "Team Emma". We had a naming ceremony. It happened in the first 30 days. In some places, you would name godparents, we had guardians and a number of the men and women who were in our lives really assumed spiritually, a guardianship. Not all of them have come through and been there, but -

MARGIE: A lot of them have.

RAE: And they even set aside money for her education. They connect with her on every holiday and are friends with her now that she's an adult.

STACEYANN CHIN

When you're a single mom or an LGBTQ family, you create your community and family. Staceyann learned that the folks who supported her during her pregnancy were not necessarily the folks who would be hanging out with her at the playground.

STACEYANN: For my pregnancy, I was on bedrest and broke. And all these black lesbians, black straight women, black gay men, black straight people, and one or two white people, they really showed up with groceries and getting me to the hospital.

I was bleeding all the time, so sometimes there would be like a gush of blood, which meant I would have to go straight to the hospital and someone had to sleep at my house. And I had to eat at six in the morning on the dot. If I didn't eat at six, I'd be sick the rest of the day. So somebody had to rise at five in the morning and make me breakfast. That required a whole bunch of love.

I'm not suffering right now, and I'm fucking irascible, so you can imagine what I was like as a suffering pregnant woman stuck in a bed. The pregnancy was difficult. I had shit to do, like my rent was due all the time. Just shit had to be paid for, and people just showed up with groceries and food. Fans sent me shit.

My whole family has been absent from my life and so at the baby shower and those kinds of events, it was just good friends who showed up. Walter Mosley, he's a writer, he's Zuri's godfather, he bought the crib, and one month I was going to be evicted, and he wrote a check. Different people showed up in that way.

But then it's interesting that the people who were around to help me through the pregnancy, they weren't really around after. Like maybe they weren't kid people, so a different community has emerged at different times. It changes because the needs change, the timing changes. I've learned about community because in my head I was gonna be in community with all these fly lesbians who were going to be in my house, and I thought it's gonna be so cute because they're going to be holding the baby, and we're gonna have all these sexy parties, while we're breastfeeding.

Then all the sexy lesbians who were around, and who lent themselves to me during pregnancy, they were like, "I'm not coming over to your house to sit with a crying child. No."

I would be like, "Hey, can you watch the baby? I have a job this evening and the sitter canceled."

"Oh, man. I just made plans to have drinks with a friend."

Then there's a silence where I'm hoping they'll be like, "Okay, I'll cancel my plans."

But, no. They be like, "I'm going to motherfucking drinks. And that's what I'm doing."

And these people inviting me out like, "I haven't seen you in so long. We're having drinks at nine o'clock in the city."

I'm not going to go pay $12 for a fucking drink, take a cab downtown, and then pay somebody $20 an hour to watch my kid. I'm like, "No. No. No. The rent."

Different priorities. So now, I have people who have kids. One of my closest friends is an old dyke who is retired, and all her kids are grown, so she can pick up Zuri from school some days. She can hang out with me during the day. I'm friends with a math teacher. People at her school are in my community because I'm in the school all the motherfucking time. I'm friends with wealthy white women. And I have to go home and pray because it's a problematic friendship because I like them so much, but I'm supposed to be hating you because it's like sleeping with the enemy.

That's kind of life with anything, whether someone came out of your chocha or not, you look up and you're like "I never would have guessed that you and I would be friends."

CHAPTER 11

NON-BIO, ADOPTIVE, AND STEP PARENTS

"And now we're raising a child, and everybody asks,
'Who's the real mother? Who's the biological mother?'
And everywhere we went people asked this
question." - Rae

When creating an LGBTQ family, there's almost no way around it, someone else, other than the couple or a single parent, will lend DNA to the project. Except those very lucky trans couples who are able to make a baby together, most families need a little help. That means only one parent will have DNA associated with the child. And in some cases, like adoption or fostering, neither parent will have a genetic connection.

Welcome to the world of bio and non-bio parents. For some couples this is all, "No big deal, man." The non-bio parent might experience some small feelings of loss of not giving birth, or the end of their family genetics, but when their baby pops out, they know they are the parent, and they never look back. For others, there's a fundamental feeling of otherness and feelings of being left out.

In either case, LGBTQ families have to deal with seemingly innocent questions like, "Who's the *real* dad?" One of our biggest fears is that some idiot will to refuse to recognize the non-bio parent. And when travelling to another country that may or may not recognize our families, all of us wonder if we're supposed to fill out one customs form or walk up together to that menacing looking customs officer.

Outside of the dilemma between bio and non-bio, there's yet another way our families are different from the straights, in that many cisgender heterosexual families follow societal guidelines as to what is a parent's role. Those roles have been ingrained in all of us from a young age. Sure Mr. Mom exists, we know this because we saw that classic 80s movie with Michael Keaton, but that scenario is definitely the outlier, rather than the norm.

In our LGBTQ families, we don't have defined roles. Most families choose who does a task based on who does it better. We think this is leaps and bounds better than a system where the woman does diapers because the woman has always done diapers since the beginning of time. In our homes, if one parent is better at math, they do the bills. If the other is sporty and outdoorsy, they become "Coach Mom." And the parent with a more flexible work schedule can be the one that attends the millions of school functions where attendance is *critical*. For example, in Jaimie's house, she *knows* that Anne is much better at folding laundry than she is, so it's only natural that Anne be the one to handle that task. It all works.

We get a clean slate and get to define, relationship by relationship, who makes what decision. And though the bio/non-bio issue is ever present, we're fighting as individuals, as couples, as a community to make sure ignorant questions aren't asked, and to make sure we are all seen as parents. Not bio or non-bio, just parents.

JAIMIE HERE

You all know by now I have a high opinion of my mom.

I would catch a grenade for that woman. If she had a twin, I would still choose her. She is the sunshine of my life. Song lyrics aside, she means the world to me, and I believe there's a reason for that.

She was and always will be a first-class nurturer. When my brother and I needed comfort, we ran to her. If we got sick, she took care of us. When we needed a break, she blasted music for impromptu dance parties. She was loving and patient and self-less and fun. She was everything. Dad was the adventure guy, and the fix it guy, and he was always there, but we chose my mom for most things.

Once I became a parent and started struggling, whenever I tried to get my dad's advice he would say, "I learned early on to just let your mom handle that. She was so good at it, and she wanted to do it so bad." But I wish he hadn't. I got so used to my mom handling everything as a child that when my dad wanted to read to me at bedtime or comfort me after a nightmare, I would pitch a fit until my mom gave in and did it instead. I learned to only want her, and I wish that wasn't the case. I wish my dad and I had bonded more during my childhood. I wish I hadn't pushed him away.

Now that I'm a parent, I want to fix the missteps of my childhood. Mama, you did an amazing job. You lift me up. How sweet it is to be loved by you. But I'm also a gay parent, and Anne and I both have the added gift of each being both the bio-mom and non-bio mom. This adds in a layer that most fami-lies don't have to navigate. For me personally, I feel a constant current of trepidation that Rose will inevitably choose Anne over me, because they share a bloodline.

On top of that, Anne and I both grew up favoring one parent over the other, and we are each determined to not become the second fiddle parent. We want, no, we *need* everything to be equal. Maybe that's not a bad thing because it challenges us to create a whole new picture for what our particular family looks like. We are both fully committed to 50/50 parenting.

We split everything. We are co-parenting the shit out of these little chickens.

Splitting everything has its challenges. We have to make sure we are on the same page about everything. I can't change a routine without consulting Anne first. And if she wants to change something, I need to be willing and open to try things her way, no matter how strongly my alpha mommy instincts kick in. We split bedtime down the middle. I do one night with one kid, Anne does the next. If a child asks for the other parent at bedtime, it sounds cruel, but we tell them, "No, you get me tonight." Luckily, after a few nights of screaming, both children fell in line with this one and it worked out. Our children don't have screaming fits like I did when my mom would leave me with my dad for the day (so sorry, dad). And we trust each other implicitly with parenting decisions. It hasn't always been easy. I still get worried when Rose wants Anne more than me that genetics will win out and she'll ultimately choose her bio-mom over me. And when Orion is screaming for me, but it's not my night, it kills me not to run to him. But we are committed to this, so we suffer through the tough things too.

So there you have it. I'm a bio mom/non-bio mom living and co-parenting with a bio mom/non-bio mom, and that is guiding our parenting decisions. This mommy and mama are doing it their own way, and so far we're doing all right. Talk to me in ten years and we'll see where I stand then, but so far our new mold is holding. It's morphed a bit from a pure 50/50 strategy to more of a tag-team, pass-off to whoever is closer in proximity to either child at a given moment since we added the second kid. But no parent in our house has the market cornered on any given task, and we like it that way. Except folding laundry, Anne's way better at that. You should see those creases.

ROBIN HERE TOO

I was the one who carried both of our kids. Despite choosing a donor with Mary's hair color and skin tone (eye color too, but we both have blue eyes), both kids ended up looking just like me. Actually, my son is the spitting image of the tomboy I was way back when, and my daughter looks like me, but prettier.

So I can see myself in my kids. That is both a good thing and a bad thing. I see physical resemblances, which I guess feels comforting? But I also see all my worst traits bubbling under the surface too. And I spend an inordinate amount of time worrying that they'll love booze just a little bit too much, like most of my relatives.

I think that makes me like every other straight, bio parent on the planet.

I've never had to deal with the issue of being the non-bio parent, but Mary has. And since this is all about Mary, let's get that answer straight from Mary.

MARY HERE

I didn't mourn not having any genes in the kids. Truthfully, I was thrilled that we didn't use my DNA because if our kids were born without arms or were clinically depressed, I would have been plagued with guilt for eternity that it was all my fault.

Also, I never really worried about *other* people wondering if I was the "real mom." That wasn't something I was afraid of. Instead, I spent most of my time worrying that Robin and the kids wouldn't think of me as the "real mom." I was afraid that as the non-bio parent, I would be relegated to following Robin around, holding the diaper bag. It wasn't until the kids were born that I felt like I was their mom.

ROBIN AGAIN

For me, what's interesting is as our kids get older, I see so much of Mary in them. Maxine, like Mary, has no idea where she's going, even with Google maps. I once saw her walk by our bedroom, with her pants down, heading in the wrong direction for the bathroom. When I said, "'Um, where are you going, and why are your pants down?" She laughed, hit her forehead with the palm of her hand and said, "That's funny." And then turned around and shuffled toward the bathroom. That's so Mary, except Mary generally leaves her pants on until she gets to the bathroom.

Maxine leads with kindness and is content to stay inside, just like Mary who calls herself "indoorsy". Henry is a gamer who would use every moment of his free time to develop Minecraft games, just like Mary who plays "Grand Theft Auto" each night after the kids and I have gone to bed.

I remember one day recently, Maxine asked me if I hadn't married Mary, would she still be the same kid? That question is so layered that I momentarily stopped. What she was really asking was if I had chosen the same sperm, but been a single mom by choice or had a different partner, would she turn out the same? She was also working out the fact that she doesn't physically come from Mary, but realized that so much of who she is, is a direct result of Mary.

That was some deep shit.

After I thought the question through, I answered her by saying, "Nope. I don't think you would be the same kid." And that's true for me because bio or not, whether Mary believes it or not, she is a driving force in our family.

In our family, we ended up with a dynamic where Mary is the more nurturing, apple pie-baking parent who is more likely to buy them a doughnut and say, "Don't tell your mom." And I'm the more authoritarian, parent who is feared, but who also plays sports with them. I also set up the doctors' appointments and show up to curriculum shares at school where I'm often overheard telling other parents, "Oh, you sent the birthday party invite to Mary? Don't do that. Her inbox is like a black hole."

We're not a jumble of DNA, but we are a jumble of roles. We each take on what we do well, and for now, it all seems to work. I suppose you should check back in with me when my kids are in high school, and possibly absolute turds, to see if I'm still glowing about how we've laid things out. But for now,

I'm feeling fairly to moderately confident.

RAE AND MARGIE

Rae and Margie used an anonymous sperm donor with Margie's egg. As the non-bio parent, Rae has always had complicated feelings about not being the bio mom, and that started before their baby was even born.

RAE: About Emma's birth—and this is a great story—we wanted to do it right, so we took the Bradley method of childbirth. Those classes went on forever.

ROBIN: What is the Bradley method?

MARGIE: I don't know. I just remember having to draw pictures of my uterus

RAE: They were very concerned that I should understand the father's role. And so I felt very awkward, but we would go for two hours and I would say, "Breathe. Breathe." I'm not a good counter, so I was failing at the Bradley method.

Then one day they said, "Okay, we're going to separate the mothers and the fathers." I just stood there, and they said, "Rae, you're going with the fathers." And so I was so effective in the father's group because I talked about being isolated and excluded.

ROBIN: Because you're were the only father who was talking about her feelings.

RAE: Right? Do you know they asked me to become a permanent member of the fathers' group?

MARGIE: It takes a woman to be a good man.

Once Emma was born, Rae's feelings of isolation and being left out continued. She was constantly asked who the real mom was. And this was before second parent adoption, so that led to her also feeling insecure about

not having full legal parental rights.

JAIMIE: Rae, a couple times it's come up that you were a little uncomfortable with being the non-bio parent. What was that like for you?

RAE: I was hoping you'd pass over that. I thought we'd run out of time, and we wouldn't get to it. Well, first of all, I had been in a lot of therapy, and I thought I was doing really well. I had a good relationship. We had a lot of fun walking around and doing things in New York. And now we're raising a child and everybody asks, "Who's the real mother? Who's the biological mother?" Everywhere we went, people asked this question.

I was also worried about not having a legal relationship. I always worried if Margie got a cold, something would happen. You know her family is perfectly nice, but they didn't sign a legal document recognizing that I was the co-parent.

ROBIN: Did you ask them to?

RAE: No, but we should have. I think I would have felt better

And I think Emma had a hard time having two mothers, but I think even in a traditional relationship my child would have had a hard time. I'm very creative. I'm all over the place. If we go shopping, I buy multiple choices. So I think it was hard for her and I think it was hard for me.

However, I realized that Emma was here to teach me lessons, and that I had to look at this relationship from a spiritual point of view and what lessons I had to learn.

JAIMIE: And you say that you think Emma had a hard time having two moms?

MARGIE: I don't agree with that. There was a power struggle. I mean, I think there are certainly many families where one child doesn't get along as easily with the father or maybe later the mother, depending.

But I think Rae has a very strong personality. She's extremely loving and very creative, but she has a very strong personality. And I think that there was a personality struggle. Emma has a strong personality too. And let's face it, I'm so fabulous everyone wanted my attention. Who wouldn't fight over me?

It was, at times, very difficult, but I think it was difficult as it might have been in any other family configuration.

ROBIN: Sounds like personality based, not lesbian based.

MARGIE: That's what I think. But when you're already feeling insecure in this kind of nontraditional situation, and you don't have the legal or biological ties, you know Rae took that very personally, and it was very difficult.

EMMA T.

> **Emma, daughter to Rae and Margie, talks about being aware of Rae's insecurities when she was younger. It resulted in her calling both her moms by their given names versus "mom" or "mommy."**

EMMA: I call my moms by their names. I've done that since I was like eight. I don't know how this is with other people, but if there's a mother who's your biological mother and there's a non-biological mother, and there are insecurities from the non-biological mom. I mean there were insecurities from just being a human, and from being a lesbian. My mom Rae is not bi. She was a lesbian in the 50s. She didn't want to go with a guy to prom. She knew she was gay. And Rae just could never blend, and I think that created insecurity. Plus, life is hard, and shit happens.

And there were not the legal things in place to protect our family that are available today. So my moms did a whole bunch of legal papers, and their lawyer did every single paper that you would need for an adoption to try to protect them. But there were times like when we were in Puerto Rico, Rae and I went ahead of Margie because she had to work or something, and Rae was terrified that something would happen, and no one would think she was the mom. One day I ran away in the grocery store and the cops found me and brought me back and said, "Is this your mom?" and pointed to Rae and she was terrified that I would say no because I was like three and mad at her because we didn't always get along.

It all just became a lot. And it felt like if I just call them by their names, we don't have to go into this stuff of who's the more superior mom.

JAIMIE: Before that, what did you call them?

EMMA: I think it was Margie was Mommy and Rae might have been Rae and that was probably not cool. This is so hazy and foggy and gets re-written over time in my brain, but something was wrong with whatever and she always wanted to be Mommy Rae and I'm like, I'm not calling you two names. I never went for that.

But eight is when something started to shift—and that was pretty early because I had little kid friends like, "Why are you calling them by their names? It's so weird. Are you professional associates or what?"

I get uncomfortable talking about this because it's uncomfortable. But this is important because this is the real shit.

LISA THE THERAPIST

> Lisa is an expert therapist on all things LGBTQ parenting. Lisa sums up the chatter about non-bio parents vs. bio parents with a very simple, yet deep statement—parents often gravitate to the kids they get along with better. Genetics have little to do with it.

JAIMIE: Do you talk to a lot of couples about bio parent versus non-bio parent anxieties or issues that come up in families?

LISA: Yeah, it can be a big issue. People typically will ask, "Who's the real mom?" And that can feel so horrible and upsetting and insulting too.

JAIMIE: Oh yeah. The first time we got asked, I got so angry. I don't even remember Anne's answer. But I remember thinking, "If she says she's the mom, I'm going to kill her."

LISA: Yeah. It's terrible.

JAIMIE: But it's well-meaning people that I love who say it. They just don't think it through. And I feel like having a conversation with a therapist about this issue is a good idea.

LISA: Patients typically ask me right away, "If I'm not the bio mom, am I going to be less connected?" And I always tell them it's usually about temperament. I see so many families who have a bio kid, and their partner has the other child or they have a bio-kid and an adopted child. And they often gravitate to the child who they like better, you know, who they get along with better.

People just automatically assume that just because you're not biologically related there's some difference.

ACTOR DAVID BEACH

David's house is a two-dad house, but he has often found himself in the position of either being called "mom" or having to call himself "mom" in order to make folks understand their family dynamic.

DAVID: I remember going to the playground and kids would climb to the top of the monkey bars and be scared to get back down, and they'd cry, "Mom!"

I think that Sadie [his daughter] thought the word "mom" meant

"I need a little help up here." So she would climb up too high, and she'd yell out, "Mom!"

I would walk over and say, "Yup. That's me. I'm just getting my kid. Sometimes she calls me Mom."

Then you know how people say, "Oh, you can't get out of jury duty. But, sometimes it's just better to go down there with the kids to try to get off." So I took Sadie with me, and I had her in the Bjorn, and I walked down there because I'm cheap, and I finally got there, and I said, "I can't do jury duty because I have childcare issues, blah, blah, blah."

And the judge says, "Well, where's her mom?"

I said, "I'm her mom."

He said, "What?"

"I'm her mom. You can just write that down. I'm her mom."

I was so tired, and mad at the fact that he really said, "You have to go to jury duty, and you should just give that kid to her mom." I was like, "Don't do that."

I did get off jury duty though.

But just because David was a good sport about the "mom" thing doesn't mean he wanted his husband to send him a gift on Mother's Day.

DAVID: One time Russell was traveling for work, and it was Mother's Day, and someone rang our buzzer and said, "There's flowers down here for you."

Russell had sent me a bouquet for Mother's Day. And I was not into it. I'm not the mom. Don't try to be heteronormative on me when you're off in a hotel room having scotch by yourself. I still want Father's Day as part mine.

Something about that was so painful at the time because I was just so tired. If your spouse is away, and you're taking care of a kid all by yourself, you're tired. Also, couldn't he have just given me a gift certificate for a massage? I don't need flowers.

But then he wrote the sweetest note about the fact that we can take all the holidays that we want and make them whatever we want. And in the end it all was great. But it was that kind of thing, "Oh, no, not flowers on Mother's Day."

BETH AND JEN

> **Jen adopted her daughter, Mia, with her ex-wife. Now she's remarried to Beth, which means that in their immediate family, neither Beth nor Jen share DNA with Mia. Jen doesn't have worries or concerns over not being the bio mom though.**

JEN: I think because of the way I viewed gender for myself, I have always been really great with not being included DNA-wise. I've read articles, especially when we learned we were going to adopt, that say that babies are 80% nurture, 20% nature, and if you get a baby at birth, their muscles actually grow into looking like you because they imitate your face. And so when you stand above a baby and make facial expressions, they imitate that, and their muscles grow that way.

I don't know, I've just never worried about it.

> **Beth is the stepmom to Mia. She has been in her life since she was very young, and their relationship is seamless now, but early on, Beth struggled to find her place in the family.**

BETH: It wasn't always easy.

JEN: Yeah, we had to figure out a really good middle ground.

BETH: I struggled a lot in the beginning with what's appropriate for my level of involvement. Even like, "Should I come to Trick or Treat?" Or, "Do I get to come to the dance?"

JEN: Mia's almost seven, and Beth has been in her life since she was three, so Mia doesn't remember life without her. She calls Beth, "Bethie" and sometimes "Mama B." We don't push it either way.

BETH: She can call me whatever she wants. I feel lucky for the age that I got to come in because I came from a blended family. My parents split when I was around kindergarten, first grade. My mom got remarried when I was 11, and I made it really hard on that dude because I had my mom to myself for a few years before that. And so I feel super lucky that Mia feels like this is the way her life has always been, and she's not like, "Who are you? You're not my mom."

> **Beth and Jen plan on adding to their family by having a baby together. This has brought up more fears for Beth, though.**

BETH: The difficulties for me always come down to insecurities. When Jen and I start to go through the process to have a baby, in my head, I'm afraid I'll be thinking, "You've done this before. There's all these experiences that you've had before with somebody else."

Even as a parent with Mia, I think, "Well, you have two moms. What do you need me for? What's my place?"

Mia's other mother is a great mom. I respect her as a person. It's almost easier when you don't like them. It makes it easier when there's some kind of spite, but I respect her as a parent. I respect how she has treated me since the beginning.

JEN: There's a unique set-up when it's all women involved. Beth didn't have Mia, neither did any of us.

BETH: Yeah, nobody else did either.

> **One of the secrets to the success of bringing their family together was letting Mia lead the way.**

BETH: Mia won my heart over so quickly. I felt like, "I just want to be in your life however I can. I want to hang out with you. I want to spend time with you." And we moved very slowly with her. We let Mia make a lot of decisions when it came to how quickly I immersed myself in their lives.

JEN: I said that I wanted the first sleepover to be Mia's invitation. It had been almost a year when she said, "Mommy has room in her bed, if you want to sleep over."

BETH: It was dark. I was crying and I said, "Okay." We felt like, not like Mia's in charge or anything, but she got to decide how she let me in. I was kind of dating them both together. It was also separate relationships that I was building with each of them. Ours was moving at one pace, and then I wanted to form my own relationship with Mia at the speed that she felt comfortable with too, which I think has been really great because now she and I have our own special dynamic. It's not just the three of us or nothing. Jen and I have a thing, and Mia and I have a thing, and then we all have a thing.

JEN: There are days that I work late that Beth goes and gets her from school. Mia never says, "Where's Mommy?" She knows exactly what's going on. We have the village. We're really lucky.

JANA AND LINDA

> When you have five parents raising two kids in two different households, defined roles and being on the same page is very important. Jana and Linda parented in partnership with Linda's ex as well as the bio dad, who was also in the kids' lives. Fortunately for Jana and Linda, everyone agreed that Linda would be the ringleader.

ROBIN: You've alluded to the fact that the dynamic with your family worked really well. Your ex had them part of the time, you had them predominantly. Once Jana was added into the picture. Did you hit any bumps in the road with custody or disagreements in parenting?

LINDA: Minor disagreements in parenting, but I think everyone kind of thought I was the one who decided on the bigger parenting rules, and then pretty much everyone fell in line. Not everybody always agreed, but as a group, we agreed that we shouldn't be having all kinds of squabbles. And I'm really coldly practical, and so my thing was, "Let's put the kids first. What's best for them? Kids need rules, so let's give them rules." Certainly, we have varying degrees of strictness and varying degrees of permissiveness.

ROBIN: I'm looking over at you Heepa [Jana].

LINDA: Heepa's a little strict.

JANA: Southern mama over here. Throw some manners up in the mix.

LINDA: And Vicky's a little more loose. But we were pretty much on the same page. We didn't have giant stuff. I think there was some tension sometimes when Papa [the donor] would come from Peru. If he hadn't seen the kids for a while he'd be behind, and you know kids don't want to be treated like they're younger. So we'd have to bring him up to speed, and there'd be a little bit of tension around that.

JANA: It's like, "Papa, she's five. She doesn't need a bottle anymore. No seriously, she's walking. You don't need to carry her. She's wearing heels right now."

LINDA: There was stuff like that, but I think that it wasn't a huge giant thing.

JANA: It wasn't, you know, for us it was about consistency. So whatever happened at our house happened at Vicki's house, and we got to understand how kids can be a little manipulative because they figured we don't talk, but we did.

PATRICIA AND KELLEN

Patricia and Kellen make a great two-mom duo, but it wasn't always that way. Patricia had to deal with her feelings of being the "second mom".

PATRICIA: We're a good tag team. Because we learned early on, if things are getting too hot, tag it out. I need a break.

ROBIN: That's why we're lucky we have two moms

PATRICIA: I'm sure there are guys that would do that, but it's very different, I think. I have a wife, and a wife is different than a husband.

But I was kind of like, "I am determined not to be the second or the side parent over here. Actually, that's what led me to the big decision to stop teaching at Equinox. We had a nanny who was doing pick up, drop off, the feedings, the bedtime, and I said, "No. I need that job. I need those kind of really basic roles. That's the part I'm doing." So I made a total lifestyle change, and I said, "I'm taking over this piece."

We went to couples therapy because we didn't know how to relate. I'll tell you, generally I'm the sideline driver, and I like it. Kellen's super strong, and she likes her way. And I like her way, so I go her way. We're a perfect match.

Well, then kids come into play, and I'm not a sideliner anymore. I have big, strong opinions, and so that broke the dynamic that had been happening. I didn't like how she was doing certain things, and she didn't like how I was doing certain things. We had major explosions.

I said, "We gotta get into therapy. We need some outside help because I think I'm right, and I think you're wrong. And you think you're right." We're both very fiery.

One thing the therapist told me that was super helpful was, "You don't want to neuter the other parent. You've got to let the other parent be a parent. If she doesn't do bedtime the way you do bedtime, well the kids will get to see both ways. It's a good thing and it's okay to have two different opinions."

That made a big difference for me because although I still push for my way, we're working you know? We actually have a good conversation because we always start by saying, "Listen, we know we agree on one thing, we want to be better parents, and we don't have to be right." I always say, "I don't have to be right about this, but I want to bring this conversation up, and this is what I want to talk about."

We always affirm, which I think is so very important. You gotta get out of the hot-headedness. That takes practice too, and it takes a real desire not to escalate something and not want to just be right.

CHAPTER 12

INTERSECTIONALITY: RACE, RELIGION AND GENDER FLUIDITY

One of the lovely things about our families is that we're as diverse as the rainbow flags that fly at our favorite bars. Our homes are filled with parents and kids from all races, religions and stations along the gender spectrum. And that's just how we like it.

With all this diversity come considerations and responsibilities, because as a parent, you may be raising a child that's not of the same race or from the same country of origin as you. You or your child might be exploring gender and/or sexuality. Or you might be on the hunt for a religion, a God, Buddha, Mother Nature, a tree, or a rock that accepts both you and your family. You do you!

These can be complex situations. It's important for our families to build diverse communities, to be aware of how our differences can impact our kids, and to bring in support when needed.

What we heard on these topics is there are a lot of families crushing it on this front. Our guests are getting ahead of the situation, being deliberate in their decision making and putting the kids first. But we didn't expect any less because who better to tackle these huge questions than LGBTQ folks who have faced discrimination throughout their lives?

JAIMIE HERE

When it comes to religion, my relationship with God is somewhat less than ordinary. I was raised to understand religion, but to never subscribe to a particular one. My religious rearing came more in the form of a "Don't drink the Kool Aid" approach than a "Let's save our souls" message. At my house we studied religion from a bird's eye view. We had shelves full of religious books, from The Bhagavad Gita, to The Book of Mormon, to the Koran, to many different versions of the Bible, which we perused frequently. We often spent dinnertime discussing and dissecting the ideas behind whatever specific religion my dad honed in on for the evening. He taught us to be wary of all religions, and to know enough about as many of them as possible, so that if religion came a-knockin', we could intelligently debate the discrepancies inherent in every doctrine and definitively decline the upcoming prayer circle invitation.

And one time, religion actually did come a-knockin'. Two sweet, Mormon boys knocked on our door at dinnertime. Instead of politely sending them on their way like most folks, my dad asked them to come back after dinner for a family discussion. I was mortified as only a tween can be. He wanted his kids to hear a true theological debate so we could take it out into the world and shout it to the mountain tops, or whatever. I just wanted to go to my room and finish level 9 of Super Mario Brothers. They did come back, ready to spout some serious Joseph Smith doctrine. My dad jumped right in and asked the boys what they thought of his theory that "proselytizing inevitably ostracizes the proselytizer, forcing him or her to run back to the warm embrace of their faithful community, therefore solidifying his conviction in his church and community," while I rolled my eyes and the boys stared at him confusedly. They were so sweet and young, I cringed under my teased bangs at their innocence. Thankfully my father ended up taking pity on them when he realized they were not as prepared as he was for such a debate. They just wanted to spread the word of their Lord. They went on their merry but befuddled way, and I was able to crush that level 9 castle after all. Yeah baby.

So I was taught to see religions from an outsider's point of view, and to see the good and the bad inherent in all of them. We visited houses of worship as intellectuals, not worshippers. I held fast to the religious skepticism my dad ingrained in me on these visits, but surprisingly I found myself moved from time to time. I've been to a gospel church and lost myself in the music. I've been enraptured by the scents of frankincense and myrrh in a Catholic pew. I've also found enlightenment in the teachings of the Buddha and Jesus and Ganesh and Mohammed and Alan Watts and the Dalai Lama and Oprah Winfrey. I was given the freedom to forge my own path into my spirituality and that has worked for me.

Anne and I have agreed to raise our kids without the umbrella of religion reigning over them. I am not morally corrupt despite not having a church to guide me as a child, so I'm not afraid that my children will be. Anne may have a strong moral compass because of her Catholic rearing, but she didn't feel warm fuzziness from the church when she came out as a lesbian. So we're raising our kids with an open mind to all religions, but we're not subscribing to any particular one. We're teaching them right from wrong, and we're teaching them to respect everyone's beliefs, regardless of what deity they choose to worship. We're also teaching them to be educated when it comes to joining any particular group, be it religious or secular. We realize that this is controversial and downright blasphemous in many circles because we've been told this by a handful of folks. But we don't expect others to do it our way. You do you, boo.

Our way is working just fine for us, and that's what matters.

ROBIN HERE TOO

Religion is a topic I have been thinking a lot about lately. Mostly I'm wondering if I'm dropping the ball when it comes to exposing my kids to some form of religion.

In my house growing up, there was no religion at all. There was no talk about God, unless my mom was pissed at me and yelling, "Jesus Christ, Punky!" We didn't go to church, but my mom did have a bright yellow t-shirt with sparkly, iron-on letters that read, "The Meek Shall Inherit the Shit!" I had no idea what that meant and wore it to my neighbor's house once, only to be sent home to change.

At some point, I noticed that other families went to church, and I wondered what all the hubbub was about. I asked my mom if we could go to church. The next Sunday, she sent me to church with the neighbors.

Mary, on the other hand, was raised in a house where she was required to go to church three or four times a week. She believes that the relationship that mattered most to her mother, without question, was with God. That didn't sit well with Mary. She also hated that her mother's God said, "Worship me, love me or you will burn in hell for eternity." Where is the love in that? The fact that this God didn't love the gays was just one more reason for Mary to hate organized religion.

So now Mary visibly shudders if I mention wanting to teach our kids about spirituality. Though, if I'm really pushing her on the pluses of the church, she acknowledges that she got morals and ethics that weren't a high priority in my house growing up. If the salt and pepper shakers were cute on the restaurant table, my dad would say, "Rosie. Give me your purse." Then he would wrap them in a napkin and jam them in.

For now, we've agreed to disagree on what the kids need in terms of religion because Mary's too triggered to hear anything about it in a positive light. But she says that whatever I want to do with them is fine, as long as she doesn't have to go. Ultimately, she just wants the kids to feel that they have a choice in what to believe or not.

Fair enough.

I like the idea of our kids having some connection to a God or the Universe or a practice where they can be still and listen to their instincts. Whatever that looks like. I do agree with Mary though that they should be able to choose what feels right for themselves.

My plan is what I call a "World Religion Tour". We're going to visit all different kinds of religions, like a Unitarian Church, a progressive temple, maybe something to do with Buddhism or a meditation class. It can be any religion or church as long as they accept us LGBTQs.

It still stinks that we have to ask, "Are we welcome here?" And we have to research places that will accept LGBTQ folks, but I'm feeling like the greater good will outweigh that negativity.

RELIGION AND LGBTQS

"When I realized what my attraction was, I realized it was not a surprise to God. And He realized that it was a surprise to me." - Aimee

AIMEE AND MYRIAM

Aimee and Myriam were on a religious journey before they even thought of having kids. Both needed to find a house where they could worship that felt right. But luckily, neither of them felt that God didn't love them because they were gay.

AIMEE: You don't even think about kissing, or at least I didn't. I wanted so badly to be as close to God as I could possibly be, so I turned everything off. I had no thought of any kind of attraction until high school or college.

I went to an all-girls junior high school and an all-girls college, and it never bothered me that there were no guys there because I really wasn't interested in guys. I realized, "Oh, my gosh, I'm not interested in guys!"

At that point, there were some other various kinds of crazy things going on in my life. And so I stepped away from the church, but not from God.

Eventually, when I realized that I have same-sex attraction, I still had a relationship with God. I never felt a sense that God all of a sudden said, "Wait, you're gay?" And took his love away from me or took that relationship away from me. The relationship was steady, constant my whole life. When I realized what my attraction was, I realized it was not a surprise to God, and he realized that it *was* a surprise to me.

So if anything, when I met Myriam, I was in the midst of all this craziness. And I was trying to find what my relationship with God is going to look like with the church and trying to figure out could I be in His presence? Could we have this depth of relationship that we had before? Myriam was trying to find faith as well, so when we met each other, it was total Kismet. When God wants to do something, he can do it anyway he wants to.

> **They found a church that felt right for both of them. It was a different kind of church than Myriam was used to, but it felt like home, and that church was welcoming of their family.**

MYRIAM: Yeah, that connection happened, and I thought, "Whoa, this is different."

But ever since then, I just follow, and I'm glad that I follow because that was where I found my freedom. That was where I found my freedom to be gay and Christian. It's hard for people to fathom that you can be gay and Christian or whatever the case may be. But once you find that personally, it doesn't matter what anybody says.

AIMEE: The thing is that there's so much biblical, theological debate. You might have heard about the Clabber scriptures and Leviticus and all the various scriptures that are used to falsely justify that God doesn't like gay people. The saddest part is that the Bible was used to justify slavery. It was used to justify the oppression of women. It was used to justify all. If you're a person who's in power, you can interpret things and use them the way you want to. If you happen to be a person who wants to oppress others, you will find a scripture that can apply to what you want.

It's sad, because if we focused more on the fact that God is love, and we experienced the depth of that relationship, and build our faith from that up, then you'd see the way those conflicts are. And it's just like, wait a second, the God I know, who loves me and woke me up this morning, gave me breath in my body, is not the same God who's going to make me burn in hell because I fell in love with Myriam.

You can go back and forth to those scriptures all day long, and you'll never convince someone that doesn't want to be convinced. If you start with that relationship first, you can't unconvince somebody who's already in love.

Myriam and Aimee also needed their very religious families to accept their family, which included their kids.

AIMEE: In my family, they're okay with me being gay, but it took time.

ROBIN: What about your family, Myriam?

MYRIAM: I'm very grateful. My mom is very loving to me and Aimee and the kids, but I think it's more. It was other people's impressions she was worried about.

AIMEE: But it doesn't bother me so much. Her mom is of a certain generation, and she loves us, and I don't feel like I'm betraying all of lesbianism to let her be where she is and stay in that space. I think it bothers Myriam more than it bothers me.

MYRIAM: It does bother me because I want her to accept that Aimee is my wife, which she does recognize. These days, I think she recognizes it's not going to change, 23 years later. I think the fact that I can talk to her about Aimee or I can talk to her about our kids. You take the little victories and add them up.

AIMEE: When you're together for 23 years—we've been together longer than half the couples in our families—and they're asking us for relationship advice, it's a little hard for them to be like, "You know, we don't believe in being gay!"

JAIMIE: How did your mom take the fact that you carried Myriam's egg?

ROBIN: Does she understand that?

MYRIAM: Oh, yeah. I think every time when she asked the question it was more like, "So they can do that?"

But in the midst of that she's still trying to understand. Her questions are like, "Oh, so was it the same sperm?"

She just keeps asking, and I recognize that's just her trying to get it. But-

AIMEE: Her mother was sort of quiet through the whole thing. She was like "Oh you're pregnant. Oh, okay." I forget exactly what her comment was, but it was something along the lines of she wanted to see the child. It was kind of like she wanted to make sure that it didn't have three heads and five arms.

But once she did, she was kind of like, "Oh, okay. I guess something worked."

GENDER FLUIDITY AND SEXUALITY EXPLORATION

"Because you were taught when you were little 'that's too feminine' or 'that's too masculine' or 'that's too this' or 'that's to that'. So we have these triggers that we aren't even aware of, but as a parent who has a very fluid child, you have to check your triggers. You have to constantly think, 'Do I have a problem with this? Why do I have a problem with this?'" - Dani

ROMAINE

Radio host Romaine Patterson's daughter came out as bisexual. That left Romaine with all kinds of concerns for what comes next.

ROMAINE: My daughter, at 11, has come out as bisexual. I never wanted a gay kid, and not because I think there's anything wrong with being gay. I'm the youngest of eight children, four of us are gay. I mean, the chances of her being gay were probably pretty high. I think without question it's a genetic thing.

But I didn't want a gay kid for a few reasons. One, I came out in high school in Wyoming, and that was hard. In college, one of my best friends was killed for being gay. You know the story, Matthew Sheppard from Wyoming. He was a good friend of mine.

The other reason I didn't want my kid to be gay, and this again, I'm a very selfish person you're going to notice that in this interview, but I did not want my child to get away with what I did. My parents, even though they had many gay children, they like to live in a land of denial. And I fucked my way through high school. I had a great girlfriend at the time, so it was really only one person, but we fucked all the time. I would say she slept over at my house at least two or three nights a week. So my daughter is a mini me, and I just think if you're a teenager and you want to have sex, you gotta get real creative. It can't be that easy. It was too easy.

Anyway, my daughter had a boyfriend for the longest time. It was like a cute little friend/boyfriend. Then she broke up with him to become a "single pringle", as she put it. Then a week later she was "takin' bacon" because she found herself a girlfriend. And I'm terrified because I know what comes next. She's gonna have a sleepover with her girlfriend, shit's going to go down. My wife said, "Romaine, you're being dramatic. This is never going to happen."

Fast forward to two weeks ago. My daughter and her friends hatched a plan to have a sleepover at one of their friends' houses. They're like, "Okay, now we're going to find an unsuspecting parent, we're gonna make them host the sleepover." And they did. They got one of the single dads.

On the way there, I said, "Hey, who's gonna be at this thing?" She starts listing off all these names, and then Emily's name is just kind of slightly slid in. And I said, "Emily, as in your girlfriend?"

She said, "Yeah, but it's no big deal, Mom."

I shoot this look over at my wife. "Told you so."

I knew this was going to happen. I knew. I knew.

So my wife says, "They're too young. Stop being dramatic."

The next morning, I pick her up and I said, "So where did everybody sleep last night?"

And she said, "Oh, well, some people slept on the bed. Some people slept on the floor."

I said, "Where did your girlfriend sleep?"

"Oh, she slept in the bed with me."

I said, "Yeah, that's it. No more sleepovers. I'm done."

Because this is my worst nightmare coming to life. I'm sure nothing happened because they're 11, but I'm done.

JAIMIE: But isn't it great that your daughter is emulating you and your wife's relationship in some way? Doesn't it feel good that she's fluid and has no problem liking a girl?

ROMAINE: No. It's a problem. I mean, granted, I'm relieved that she's not gonna get knocked up in high school like all my sisters did. I mean, listen, there are some real bonuses to her being lesbian versus being straight.

EMMA T.

> Emma is the daughter of two moms, but she never struggled with gender. She knew exactly who she was and what felt right, even at a young age.

EMMA: My earliest memories of anything that could be related to gender was when I was three, and my parents bought me jeans, and I didn't want to wear them. I was like, "That's for boys."

My gender expression was very loud, and it was, "I want pink, Little Mermaid, and the ballet." I remember being repulsed by jeans. But I remember I felt so girly, and I had two moms so that was easy to do.

> As Emma got older and started dating, the world of men opened up, and they were like unicorns to her. She knew of them, but not really about them. They were shiny, new and sparkly.

EMMA: What happened with men is that they were exotic, and that was a lot of my passion for men and a lot of what my truly promiscuous phase was really a lot about. What I saw versus my other girlfriends, was how exotic I found men. And they didn't. They were into men, but they weren't like, "Wow, it's so crazy that he thinks this way!"

They were more like, "Well, I have a dad and some brothers, and that's a thing that men do."

I just thought men were so enchanting. That phase has come to a close, but it lasted a long time.

> **Emma believes that gender roles come more from self and society than the home, but she also knows it's not quite that simple.**

EMMA: Well I'm going to disabuse you of one notion, which is that what you do in your house is what the kid gets. People forget that society is everywhere. Whatever you do in your house, it matters. It matters a lot with attachment and nurturing. And being a good mom matters, but gender roles are not coming from your house. They're coming from TV and school and walking down the street.

I did not get gender roles from my house because there were none to get. What I want to tell you though is that you don't escape any of the bad gender stuff just because your house is awesome. You still pick up the toxic. You still know that you're in defiance of something, like when I make sure that my boyfriend is sharing the housework with me, I'm in defiance of something. And now that I live with my boyfriend, I'm very aware that I'm not modeling what I saw, but doing my own thing, and it's because he's not a woman.

DANI AND MIKE

> **Dani and Mike are a straight couple whose son Leo is gender non-conforming. They've been supportive of Leo's love of dresses from the very beginning.**

DANI: He's just a very unique creature. He's a unique soul. He's never really been interested in anything that's traditionally been associated with male play, male colors, or male television shows. He's always gravitated towards sparkles and purple and pink and princesses, since he could reach for something.

ROBIN: At first, did you think, "Oh, this is just a boy who likes sparkly things?"

DANI: I think the moment where I thought, "Oh, this is something we have to process differently" was when there was a holiday break from preschool. I think he was three, and he got a "Sofia the First" princess dress for Christmas, and he wouldn't take it off. Like wouldn't take it off.

MIKE: It wasn't his first dress. But it was the one and he would not take it off.

DANI: Like hysterically crying when we took it off. All day, every day. And the preschool had a no costumes rule, and I thought, "Crap, this is a costume" but for him it was not a costume. For him this was his dress. He needed to wear this dress.

So we called up his preschool teacher, and we were anticipating that they were going to say he couldn't wear it, but we got so lucky. The preschool administrator is this profound human, who is rather gender non-conforming herself. She has purple hair and a giant chest tattoo and is in her sixties.

MIKE: And her hair is usually not more than about a centimeter long.

DANI: She's got a punk rock heart. And she said, "Oh, no, no, no. Everything's fine. He can wear whatever he wants. Let him do him."

ROBIN: For me, I had my own bunged up feelings with this kind of stuff because we are two moms, and I was afraid people would judge me.

MIKE: Like you have an agenda, and you're trying to make your kid gay.

ROBIN: Yeah, and one day my son wanted to wear his sister's pink coat, and in hindsight I feel so stupid for thinking this, but

I remember saying, "Let's switch coats back." I was really facilitating him not wearing that coat. Now I think, "Why couldn't I just let it be?"

DANI: Because you're also a victim of your own repressed homophobia.

ROBIN: You're right.

DANI: Because you were taught when you were little that's too feminine or that's too masculine or that's too this or that's to that. We have these triggers that we aren't even aware of, but as a parent who has a very fluid child, you have to check your triggers. You have to constantly think, "Do I have a problem with this? Why do I have a problem with this?"

ROBIN: Did you know how to do that on your own or did you have help?

DANI: Yes and no. Once he got the dress, I knew I had to get him something besides the dress because it was falling apart, and it was dirty. That's when I went online, and I bought him a rainbow of tutus. And he would wear them over his clothes.

JAIMIE: The day they came, was it the happiest day of his life?

DANI: Oh, yeah. He didn't take them off for two years. He would wear them till they disintegrated.

I work in the entertainment industry. And I interface with a ton of actors, and all these grown men say to me, "I wish I had a princess party."

"I wish I didn't have to put the leotard on in the closet while my sister listened at the door to make sure my mother didn't come upstairs and catch me in the leotard."

"I wish my dad hadn't burned my Barbies when I was at school."

"I wish my mother didn't tell me that all the *My Little Ponies* were too expensive."

A lot of what we pulled from was all the people in our lives who would have been very gender non-conforming had they been allowed to be. I asked questions like, "What would you like to have happened?"

> **Dani and Mike created a loving home where Leo could explore his gender without question, but when he went into his neighborhood elementary school, his experience was quite different.**

DANI: We sent him to the public school that he was zoned for.

MIKE: He was so excited to go. Over the summer he kept saying, "Is it time yet?" He'd planned out what he was going to wear the first day. It was very reminiscent of what Dani wore to her first day of kindergarten.

DANI: But with an extra tutu.

MIKE: And he went to school, but he was immediately miserable.

DANI: Crying, hysterical, holding onto my leg, didn't want to be dropped off. And when I would pick him up, he'd say, "Where have you been?" And I'd say, "What do you mean? It's only been two hours."

So he's miserable, and I can't get the teacher to call me back.

MIKE: Yeah, we were trying to reach out to figure out what was wrong.

DANI: Three weeks in, still no response. So a friend said we should reach out to the parent teacher coordinator. And I thought that was a good idea, so I emailed, and she said, "Yeah, I remember you. I remember meeting Leo. You should meet with the principal."

I said, "Okay, if that's what you think is best."

So we set up a meeting with the principal, and that's when it all kind of went to hell. She said things like, "We've done the two moms thing and the two dads thing, but never the gender non-conforming thing."

MIKE: "This is new territory for us."

DANI: Then, "Do you have research? If you do, you should bullet point things and highlight them because teachers don't like to read."

MIKE: She also said, "You know, it's just so confusing for some of the other kids. I think it would be simpler if he was trans."

DANI: And, "I don't understand why this is such a problem because we put him in *that* classroom because she was the teacher that was least likely to have a problem with this issue."

I remember what I was wearing, I remember the time of day. It's like trauma burned into my brain. Our faces were like—

MIKE: Eyes like saucers.

> **Unfortunately, the situation with their school did not get better. After Dani and Mike complained about the staff, the school retaliated, and the family is currently in litigation with the DOE. For now, Leo is being homeschooled.**

DANI: I think we were so burnt by the DOE, that no matter how wonderful the replacement school they offered was, we were not going to keep him there.

We also didn't want to put him back into that binary way of sorting kids because that is part of what's teaching him that he's wrong, that his existence is wrong. Boys are over here, and girls are over there.

So he goes to a program where they learn by doing. They go on field trips, and they run a diner. I do drama Fridays.

MIKE: But you can do only up to three days a week because it's for homeschool families. It's not a school.

DANI: He has a tutor two days a week where they do reading, writing, and math. And he takes guitar. He takes dance, and he swims, and he has a sewing class. Then he also does movies. His first movie, he was the title character. It's called. "A Kid Like Jake", and it's about a gender non-conforming four-year-old in Brooklyn.

JAIMIE: So despite the whole turmoil that happened in this lawsuit. He's okay?

DANI: Yeah, he's okay.

> **Dani and Mike's son is a tween now, but they feel strongly that they would allow their son to take hormones as he approaches puberty, if that's what he wants to do.**

DANI: The way I explain all this to people who don't understand it is to say, "Well if your kid has asthma, you can medicate them so they don't have asthma anymore, or you can worry about your neighbor who doesn't think you should be medicating them because they don't think asthma is really a thing. You can watch your kid suffer and not give them medication, and that will please your neighbor who you don't really know, or you can medicate them and help them. Oh, and at the same time you have somebody across the country who says asthma is the worst thing ever, and they're going to get lobbyists to make sure that everyone knows that asthma is terrible."

MIKE: Also, "The asthmatics are going to hell."

DANI: To that, I say, "No. I'm gonna fight you because I live with somebody who has asthma. And they're suffering on a regular basis, and it's a very simple, easy fix. Let them wear a tutu or give them the asthma medication."

Our son's never had any body dysmorphia. He loves his body.

He's got nothing but self-confidence. And I think that he's just been given the space to figure things out, and if he was really showing signs of being tormented by his body, then we would be having a different discussion, with a therapist, with a medical professional because it would be a medical necessity, right?

RACE AND LGBTQ FAMILIES

"When talking about difference, talking about race, it needs to be in age-appropriate ways. You're going to talk to a 3-year-old differently from the way you're going to talk to a ten-year-old or a 16-year-old. You have to be prepared. That's your work as a parent." - Camilla

TIFFANY AND CARISSA

Millennial couple Tiffany and Carissa were in the process of trying to get pregnant at the time of our interview. As a mixed-race couple, they found that they had to think carefully as to what race their donor would be.

TIFFANY: We're very visibly of different races. Carissa is very, very white and I am very, very black. We look like a conversation that folks in the US have been having since Africans were first brought here and enslaved a long time ago.

ROBIN: And there's a whole other layer because you're two women.

TIFFANY: For sure. So we have very different backgrounds but a very similar experience when it comes to being queer folk. I'm pretty high femme most of the time and Carissa is pretty straightforward butch, and so it adds a whole 'nother layer. I watch how people treat both of us sometimes, and it can get dicey.

ROBIN: It's almost like maybe you don't even know what the real issue is.

TIFFANY: Yeah, and who has time to parse this shit out?

CARISSA: That delves into our looking at race when it comes to our family and our children because we have looked at donors. We have a list at the cryobank, and it includes donors who are white and donors who are black. So there have been a couple of conversations surrounding the list.

TIFFANY: I went to predominantly white institutions my entire life, and I am so used to being treated weirdly because I am dark-skinned, and I have very, very nappy hair. I like my nappy hair. And I like my big nose with my African features. I like them, but I did get a lot of shade from it.

ROBIN: How do you choose a donor that emulates the two of you, but also helps you hold on to your heritage?

CARISSA: It's been a hard conversation because I don't have any feelings about the baby looking like me. I mean, the thing is that there's no way to know what the baby will end up looking like regardless of the color of the donor.

TIFFANY: No, no, no. It's all over the place. But then also, initially, when we started down this path, legislatively speaking, Michigan is really hostile to queer people, in particular queer people who want to become parents. And my worst fear is that folks who want to be mean will use those loopholes and gaps in our coverage as an opportunity to do something mean. So my rationale was maybe we do need to look for a medium brown donor, somewhere in between both of us. That looks like either of us could have carried. I get nerve racked that somebody will try to be mean, especially with Carissa being so visibly queer all of the time.

ROBIN: How are you going to make this decision?

TIFFANY: We're really looking at just general markers.

CARISSA: Interests, honestly.

ROBIN: So you're just opening the pool up? And you're saying it could be either and you'll choose the person, not the color?

CARISSA: Tiffany has told me that I should make the decision from the top five.

TIFFANY: Honestly, I hit a point where I was just like, "I don't care anymore." I want a baby.

MICHELE THE DOULA

Michele and her wife adopted a baby who is biracial. Their goal is to make sure they immerse their daughter in the African American community, and she has access to support.

MICHELE: Our daughter is mixed-race and that comes with a lot of responsibility on our part. To make sure that she knows what that means, to be black and beautiful and brave. That's one of the things we say all the time.

One of the choices that we made was to move to Philly. It's really easy as a white person to just have all your friends be white. So we chose to move into a neighborhood that is going to make that a little harder for us, and make sure that she has a black pediatrician, and friends, and their friends, and their parents, and black schools. I want her to see all the different ways that she can be. I want her to grow up being fluent in African American culture.

There's a way of coping with cultural violence that I have not known how to do. And I cannot teach her how to deal with the myriad of microaggressions that she's going to have. And I don't know how to talk to her about how to flow with nuance around an entire culture that is not in support of her being as big and beautiful as she can be. So that education has to come from somebody else, from her community. And it's my job to foster, to reach out and find that community.

My goal, and I've often made this joke, and I'm sure I'm going to piss somebody off, but there's a stereotype of white moms with mixed race, or black children, that their hair is really not together. So my goal is that on her first day of going to Howard, when she meets her roommate in the dorm, she's going to unpack a little picture of her little mommies, and her roommate's gonna go, "Huh, you have two white moms?"

She's gonna say, "Yeah."

Then the roommate's going to say, "I would have never known. Your hair is awesome."

That is my goal, and her birth mother says, "That is a very layered goal."

CAMILLA

> As a social worker and therapist, Camilla was well versed in how to speak to her daughter about their differences in race. But, she also tried to make sure to have people in place in their life that her daughter could look to in order to see herself and her cultural origins.

CAMILLA: When talking about difference, talking about race, it needs to be in age-appropriate ways. You're going to talk to a 3-year-old differently from the way you're going to talk to a ten-year-old or a 16-year-old. You have to be prepared. That's your work as a parent. Okay, you have an adorable, biracial, African American or Mexican child, and you're white parents. That child is going to be out in the world at some point by themselves, and you have to be able to help them. You have to be able to give them tools.

JAIMIE: When a four-year-old says, "Why is your mommy white?"

CAMILLA: Yep. I can tell you a funny story. My daughter was on the playground and a kid said, "Is that your mom? She doesn't look like you."

And my daughter said, "Well, she's not Chinese."

Which I thought was so obvious and so much from her perspective. That was probably when she was five or six. But I think that came out of a lot of conversations about her story.

JAIMIE: How does she identify?

CAMILLA: I don't want to speak for her, but I will just give my perspective on it. I think, as with many trans-racially adopted kids who live in fairly white communities, there is a divide that there is part of them that feels comfortable or somewhat comfortable in a white environment, and also feels very much identified as whatever identity feel strongest to them. My daughter very much celebrates her Chinese identity. But also knows that she's not in a Chinese family. Most of her friends now are non-white. That really began to happen in high school.

JAIMIE: Do you remember any of the other things that you did to meld the two cultures together? How much time did you focus on that?

CAMILLA: I would say it wasn't the major focus of our lives, but for some people it's more so. I think it depends on the family. We celebrate Chinese New Year. We spend time with Chinese friends, but we're not steeped in the culture in any deep way. I do think when people are adopting transracially, it's really important to have people in your life who are similar in race and culture to the child you're adopting. I think whether that's friends, teachers, practitioners, your neighborhood, the kinds of things you do, or role models.

CHAPTER 13

THE LEGALESE OF LGBTQ FAMILIES

"And that, unfortunately, is playing out across the country, in laws... To deny someone their wedding flowers or their wedding cake for any of these religious exemption laws is opening up a door that I think even the most rabid conservatives would find fearful." - Tony

It's Chapter 13, and it's high time we said something we've been dying to say since the introduction—our families are freaking fabulous. We're not kidding. We love the crap out of us. But, if we're being honest, we recognize there are folks out there that don't wish us good will. Can you imagine?

We can't keep going with this book without spending some time talking about the law and the legal rights of LGBTQ families. Really, this chapter should be called *Cover Your Ass*, because that's what we're talking about here, covering our asses against people that don't think we have the right to marry or raise wonderful little kids.

The ability to get married and have it recognized by the federal government was a huge step forward for our families, and it was a political win that many of us never thought we'd see in our lifetime. That change allowed us certain protections, like the ability to collect Social Security should something happen to our spouses, and the right to have both our names on the birth certificate of our children.

But one thing that's still heavily, and sometimes heatedly, debated is the need for second parent adoption. What's second parent adoption, you ask?

Second Parent Adoption
Noun

> A legal procedure that lets a same-sex or transgender parent adopt a child their partner is the biological or adopted parent of, without terminating the first parent's parental rights.

Some folks are thrilled that second parent adoption is a path to secure parental rights. It allows them to breathe a sigh of relief that their families can't be challenged. Others resent that it's something we have to undertake. It can be costly and requires the help of a lawyer, so that's another thing to consider.

Outside of parental rights, it's critical our families have wills in place that include the declaration of guardianships just in case something happens to one or both parents.

Of the families we talked to, many had legal agreements in place, but not all. Some were delayed in getting their i's dotted and t's crossed. Others had things locked up tight before the baby was even in the womb. And some moved forward on a handshake and a prayer, and it's 25 years later, and it all worked like a charm.

Now, we're not lawyers, and we're not even lucky enough to play one on TV, so we're definitely not handing out legal advice in this chapter. If you're looking for that, Google the crap out of the best LGBTQ practices in your region or head straight over to Lambda Legal. But we can say this, the lawyers we spoke to all agreed that when in doubt, it's better to have legal paperwork in place because it's a topsy-turvy world out there, and you never know what's going to happen next.

JAIMIE HERE

Okay you guys. Do I even have to write this story? You should know me well enough by now to know that I was not one of those queer folks who had legal measures in place before my children were born. Remember? I'm the fly-by-the-seat-of-my-pants co-host with a slew of documents sitting in the *If These Ovaries Could Talk* shared Google Drive that I have yet to open. Robin reminds me frequently, "Please take a look at those files and let me know your thoughts." Robin's so organized and persistent. We make a great team, but back to my family. To be honest, Anne and I chose not to complete second parent adoption in part because of my supreme procrastination skills, but also because we didn't think it was necessary.

Right after our first child was born, a court case in New York deemed Second Parent Adoption unnecessary. When a lesbian couple showed up in Judge Lopez Torres courtroom in 2014, they were told that the new same-sex marriage law vetoed the need for adoption. The judge also said it was her strong belief that all married couples, gay or straight, should be treated equally. Her argument made sense to Anne and me. Now that us gays could get married, we shouldn't have to adopt our children, dammit. Straight couples don't adopt the babies they make together. Why should we? Both of our names were on the birth certificate, so we thought we were golden. No need to fill out endless paperwork or come up with our past 30 years of residences. We were married, and our family was legit in the eyes of the law.

Turns out that judge was a tad bit idyllic in her ruling. I've since learned through interviews with lawyers, social workers and family therapists on the podcast, that we are not as safe as we'd like to be at this moment in time in our country or else-where. Unfortunately, we live in a country with a hodgepodge of laws both supporting and not supporting same-sex couples, and it all depends on where you live as to whether your parental rights are safe. Everyone we spoke to strongly advises the extra insurance of second parent adoption to fully protect our families. That silly judge made her decision based on how the world should be, not how it is. While I loved the sentiment, it looked like Anne and I were going to have to bite the bullet and fill out some forms.

Have I mentioned how much I hate filling out forms? It's almost as much as I hate remembering every address where I've ever lived. Needless to say, this second parent adoption thing has taken a bit of time. But we are in the process! We have a lawyer, and our paperwork is in. We're halfway through this bad boy. It only took us about a year to get here, so give me another year or so and we'll be done. Our children who are our children will really be our children. I'm very much looking forward to that day.

You'll also be happy to know that Anne and I did actually establish a will right after our daughter was born. We were on it. We have yet to update it for our son, however. We'll be doing that soon. It's on the list. In the shared Google Drive. I'll be looking at that shortly. Seriously. Robin, stop looking at me that way. I'm on it.

ROBIN HERE TOO

If you've listened to even one episode of our podcast, you know where I stand on the question of "To get legal paperwork?" or "To *not* get legal paperwork?" for your LGBTQ family. My position is squarely in the camp of "Get that business handled, people!" Yes, I am looking at you, Jaimie.

No judgement to the folks who go forward on a wing and a prayer, but I'm way too nervous, uptight, controlling and always picturing the other shoe dropping to play fast and loose with the law. It also might be that I want my family legally bound to me forever because at some point they're going to get annoyed with me and try to leave. I intend to make that difficult. Please don't leave me, Mary.

I'm also all about Google Documents, folders and binders, and organization and plans. So before we were even pregnant, I researched what we would need in order to keep ourselves protected. Then I added the legal insurance onto my benefits plan at work and found an in-network attorney who did both wills and adoptions.

The will part was easy enough. We already had a will that said, "Burn me up and spread the ashes somewhere pretty." And also, "Pull the plug if shit gets dark." So knowing we were going to have kids, we did an addendum to the original will that designated our wishes for guardianship should, God forbid, Mary and I both croak. Let's not have that happen, Universe. At least not for a long time.

Then we set forth on second parent adoption. In this arena, I did some serious LGBTQ drafting off one of our lesbian couple friends who had gone to the expensive LGBTQ lawyer that was popular at the time. Always a gal looking for a discount, instead of paying that same lawyer oodles of cash, our good friends gave us a copy of that paperwork (seriously, thank you ladies), and then I had my in-network lawyer recreate the same documents.

I had all of my paperwork completed before the kid was born, so I just needed a couple of birth details and the birth certificate, and then we could get before a judge and make it legal.

I admit to equal parts love and hatred for the second parent adoption process. I am thrilled that we have the legal recourse to have Mary's parental rights recognized through adoption, so our family can't be challenged. That's not something I thought would have been possible back in the 90s. But as I filled out the paperwork, and attempted to remember all the addresses I lived at for the last 25 years (no easy task for a lady who moved 19 times in New York City alone), prepared for the home study, made an appointment for Mary to be fingerprinted, I felt enraged that we had to go through this process. After all, it's not as if I had these kids alone or in a previous marriage. We had these children together. We picked out the sperm together. She held my hand as the doctor did the IUIs. And she held both my leg and my hand as I gave birth. Why should she have to establish legal guardianship when we created our children together?

But for now, the paperwork is done, and we are protected. That, to me, is the most important part.

One note before I leave you. I'm not recommending that anyone follow my bargain hunting lawyer tactics. But if you're a former poor kid like me who can't stop himself or herself from trying to save money, keep in mind that going that route meant we had to be really buttoned up on the research. Second parent adoption wasn't something our lawyer was familiar with, and the same was true on the guardianship paperwork. Our person wasn't giving us advice, she was just replicating paperwork from another lawyer and filing or notarizing. I think there's something to be said for going to someone who specializes in LGBTQ family planning who will have the up-to-the-minute legal advice about our community.

BRIAN ESSER

Brian is an LGBTQ family lawyer, so he has some strong feelings about the importance of putting protections in place for our families. Starting with second parent adoption.

BRIAN: Let's start with this. It is still the recommendation of all of the major advocacy organizations and family law scholars and Family Law practitioners that the non-biological parent get some sort of court order. Whether it's a second parent adoption or judgment of parentage, in states where you can get one of those, stating that you're legally recognized parent, so that you have an order that's entitled to full faith and credit under the US Constitution.

ROBIN: Being on the birth certificate doesn't cut it?

BRIAN: In pretty much all states, a birth certificate is proof of identity and proof of citizenship.

JAIMIE: That's it?

BRIAN: Yep. It's not proof of parentage, so relying on the birth certificate alone is not enough. You need some sort of court order saying definitively that you're a parent. In pretty much all states there's a presumption of parentage based on your marriage. And I try to be gender expansive when I describe this and sometimes it makes it less clear, but the spouse of the person who gives birth to a child is presumed to be that child's other legal parent.

ROBIN: Even if it's a same-sex marriage?

BRIAN: Even if it's a same-sex marriage.

ROBIN: Then doesn't that cover it?

BRIAN: That's just a presumption. It's a rebuttable presumption of parentage, so that means that somebody could come in and question the non-biological parent's parentage at some point.

Now, in New York, we have a really strong presumption. It's really difficult to rebut. It will most likely hold up as long as you're in New York. But I have a friend who practices in Missouri, and she says in Missouri, genetics is king. You go into court there, and any suggestion that this person is not the biological parent, and they may look at you like, "Hmm. Two ladies. Oh, no, we know what's going on here." And then there goes your parental rights.

Then you've also got states like, not to pick on Alabama, but there are states like Alabama where the courts and the state government generally are very hostile to LGBTQ families. There was actually a case that went all the way up to the US Supreme Court where a family had done a second parent adoption in Georgia and then moved to Alabama at some point in time.

And the Alabama court said, "We don't have to recognize your Georgia second parent adoption." They said that it wasn't clear under Georgia law at the time as to whether it was possible to do a second parent adoption.

The other thing is social security benefits. If you have that second parent adoption, if the non-bio parent were to pass away, your application for survivor benefits is approved almost immediately. I've heard of delays of up to a year if there's not that second parent adoption, and you're relying on the marriage because it goes up to the council's office, and they have to analyze whether this presumption of parentage existed under state law.

My feeling, and the general consensus is, their heart is in the right place with these judges who are saying that it's unnecessary to get second parent adoption, but it's really unrealistic. When you consider, I think it was in Mississippi, where there was a judge who held that an unknown sperm donor was a child's other legal parent, instead of this woman's wife. Then she basically had no standing to seek custody and visitation.

ROBIN: What if you're in a state where you don't have second parent adoption?

BRIAN: In all states now, for a married couple, you have second parent adoption. But if you're an unmarried couple, there are still a couple of states that won't allow you to get that second parent adoption.

Other than that, I tell my clients that we can correct a lot of mistakes with second parent adoption. From time to time, I'll meet some folks who rather than going the donor route and paying for donor sperm or having a known donor, somebody just does their thing with a guy one night who may or may not know that she's trying to get pregnant. That happens, and that's the kind of stuff you can work around. There's usually a workaround.

> **Brian also believes that it's important to put agreements in place when using a known sperm donor, even if it may not be 100 percent legally recognized yet.**

BRIAN: I do recommend having a sperm donor agreement for two reasons. One is the courts in New York are definitely moving toward recognizing sperm donor agreements. They haven't quite gotten there yet.

ROBIN: Meaning they didn't recognize these agreements before?

BRIAN: Yeah, basically. A donor could be sued for child support or a donor could sue to have visitation or custody.

ROBIN: So you're doing it to make yourself feel better, and if something happens, hopefully you get a liberal judge who's with you?

BRIAN: Yeah, but the other real benefit is that it makes you stop and think about what your arrangement is. I can't tell you how many times I have clients come in and say, "We've talked about everything. This is going to be really easy. We just need you to write up the agreement."

And I say, "Okay, great. So have you talked about this?"

And they say, "Hmm, that's a good question. I'll get back to you on that."

"Have you talked about this?"

"Ah, no, actually we don't know what he wants to be called."

"What about confidentiality? Who are you going to tell, or is this a secret?"

Things like that.

And from time to time, I've had people who start having these conversations, and maybe the donor's girlfriend starts to get wobbly, and they don't move forward. On some level you've dodged a bullet. If you're not all on the same page about what the relationship is going to look like, you shouldn't move forward with it.

> **Brian is not just a lawyer, but also a gay dad who adopted and therefore had to undergo home studies as part of the adoption process. He knows that the process helps LGBTQ families secure parental rights. But he still experienced all the nerves that came along with letting a stranger into your home to assess your parental fitness.**

BRIAN: First you sign up with the agency. You send them a little application, and they do a little interview with you. Then they bring you in and you go to a class, and then you do a home study, so the social worker comes to your house.

And it was nerve-racking. We stressed about it. If you've never gone through a home study before, it's really super stressful. We made sure that our appointment was the day after our house cleaning guy came. We had scones that we baked. We had the whole thing. We're bakers.

ROBIN: I would have bought the scones.

BRIAN: But you want the scones and you also want the house to smell nice. It's a two-fer.

CAMILLA

> **Camilla is a gay mom and a social worker who conducts home visits that are required for second parent adoption. The good news, she's not there to judge you. She's there to write the report and help you secure your parental rights.**

CAMILLA: A second parent adoption is the vehicle that we have in order to secure families. The problem is, you're already very successful at being families and it feels like a bit of an intrusion [to have to complete the process and the home study].

ROBIN: It's hard to look at it like a good thing that you get to do versus something we have to do. You're forcing me to do something that we wouldn't have to do-

CAMILLA: If we were straight. Mm hmm.

So with second parent adoption, the social worker has to come to your house and has to interview you and your partner/ spouse, both together and separately. And if your kids are old enough, they will have a brief conversation with your kid.

JAIMIE: I'm so excited for you, or whoever it is, to talk to my daughter. I think it would go something like, "So Rose, you have two moms?"

"I have two poops."

Something to that effect.

CAMILLA: Yeah. So there is paperwork. Basically, the home study has a certain format. I ask people about their decision to adopt, which usually in second parent adoption is to secure the legal relationship of the non-biological parent. How they came to create a family, and what that process was like for them. We look at your own family background. There's an autobiographical piece, particularly of the adoptive parent, but also I include bio-information about the biological parent. That's about what was important growing up. Who was your family, your siblings? What's your relationship like with them? If your parents are still alive, what's their role in your life now? Also, I ask about your child, what they're doing now, school or whatever. What your parenting style is. What's important to you in raising a child? Financial information, employment information. In some courts there are requirements for reference letters, but not in all courts. And, your community, your home. People are really afraid that their home isn't clean enough.

JAIMIE: Yeah, that's my question. What would you do if you came in and my house was a complete mess, which it can be with two kids. Would there be negative notes?

CAMILLA: No.

ROBIN: You're hitting on something that I've been thinking about. If a straight couple were maybe not stellar parents, no one judges them and comes to write a report on their parenting. And because second parent adoption is something we have to do to secure our parental rights, is there an ethical dilemma for you as a gay woman, if you come in and someone appears to be only so-so parents?

CAMILLA: It's very rare that somebody who's gotten this far is not approved to be an adoptive parent. Certainly, it happens. But there have to be pretty severe reasons for that, usually related to child endangerment.

I think what is really important when parents are doing an adoption home study is that they are honest with the social worker because you wouldn't want something to come up later. Like, say, on a fingerprint check. If you didn't tell the social worker, or whoever you're working with that looks much worse.

JAIMIE: I'm thinking, "Of course, I'd be honest." But I can see how it might be scary to share things from your past that are all over and done with because you'd think, "What if they tell me I can't be a parent?"

ROBIN: Well, I got arrested in college.

JAIMIE: There you go.

ROBIN: For a fake ID because we were all drunk, it was college, that's what we did. But I did some program called "Diversion" and it was supposed to be sealed and then expunged. So before our second parent adoption I made sure it was not on my record, but now I'm thinking I should have told somebody about that.

CAMILLA: That happens a lot, minor infractions, and somebody will say, "Well, yeah I got picked up for putting up a poster."

So I'm going to write that in, even though it's very minor, but what I also say is since that time, there has never been an incident of arrest or conviction. Sometimes, it's even more serious. Yet, if there's evidence of change, that's what's really important. If somebody has an arrest record, and yet they are clearly a really good parent, that's greater evidence to me than what they did when they were 22.

ROBIN: Do you have any tips for nontraditional families in terms of the home study and second parent adoption?

CAMILLA: Be honest and relax. I'm sorry that we have to do this, but it is a good insurance. It's insurance if you travel, if you move to another state, even if you don't think that's ever going to happen, you don't know what's gonna happen in ten years. Also, just the issue of inheritance, people can do funny things.

RAE AND MARGIE

Even back in the 80s, lesbians had to do what amounted to a home study. Rae and Margie were not just pioneers in LGBTQ parenting, but also in LGBTQ drafting. Their friends all prepared them for how to answer the questions in order to pass the evaluation.

MARGIE: Remember they had a social worker that had to interview us?

RAE: We had to have psych evals.

MARGIE: We were coached by our friends, you know.

RAE: Every lesbian in New York loved the ballet, concerts and had a wide range of straight, male friends.

JAIMIE: You had to say this?

MARGIE: I don't know, but we were coached.

RAE: They were looking for those answers.

MARGIE: I mean we were really the "Better Homes and Gardens" approved lesbians.

RAE: We rehearsed.

ROBIN: They didn't want to hear you talking about a commune with all women.

MARGIE: And excluding men. No that wouldn't have been good. I mean it wasn't us anyway, but it wouldn't have been good. So we passed with flying colors because we rehearsed.

ROBIN: They were like, "God these lesbians all love that ballet!"

JAIMIE: Don't they know we rehearse? I mean aren't they on to it?

MARGIE: I'm sure the social worker was also a lesbian. I mean who knows, but…

GARY AND TONY

> Tony is an LGBTQ family lawyer, and even with documents in place, he and Gary still worry because of the current climate around LGBTQ rights. His advice, in legal terms we all understand, is to cover your behinds.

ROBIN: In the news recently, there was a story about the Oklahoma governor who signed a law saying that if you run an adoption agency, and it's against your adoption agency's beliefs, you don't have to place children with LGBTQ folks.

TONY: That's essentially what it is. And that, unfortunately, is playing out across the country in laws more than just adoption laws. Adoption laws really cut to the core because they're going for your family or for your possibility of family.

Being able to say, "No, I just don't feel right with that." To deny someone their wedding flowers or their wedding cake for any of these religious exemption laws, is opening up a door, that I think even the most rabid conservatives would find fearful. If it goes to it's logical, inevitable end, it could be anything. I just don't feel comfortable with that. It could be the excuse that excludes a black child or a Jewish child or an overweight person, anyone.

It's really sad, and it's one of the reasons also why I think gay families are families by design. They are families that are intended and intentional.

GARY: There are no drunken surrogacies.

JAIMIE: God, if only.

TONY: Can you imagine?

ROBIN: I got loaded and ordered eggs off the internet.

GARY: Honey, whose eggs are these?

ROBIN: You'd have to be loaded for about a year and a half, which at that point, don't have children.

TONY: It's crazy, but we have to protect our families. I mean, not only are we carefully planning how to have them, but once we have them, we have to make sure that for gay men you have at least a pre or post-birth order, which happens in the state where your surrogate gives birth, and it terminates the rights of the surrogate mother, sometimes the rights of the egg donor, and sometimes the rights of the surrogate mother's husband. We had to have a pre-birth order.

GARY: We traveled frequently to visit our parents and had to drive through several states that didn't recognize our marriage.

So when we packed up the car, Tony always got the Ziploc bag filled with the papers in case we were in one of these states.

TONY: You're lucky that you live in New York right now because the law is protecting our families and it's recognizing our families in a way that states like Oklahoma are not, and I think that's the fear that we have. That's the reason why we chose to do a second parent adoption after the pre-birth order.

ROBIN: With a surrogacy, the sperm donor's the recognized parent, and then the other one has to do the second parent adoption?

TONY: Yes.

GARY: But when we reissued Nicholas' birth certificate, they did not have gender specific or gender-neutral birth certificates, so on his birth certificate, I'm his mother.

> Gary and Tony have a child of their own through surrogacy, but they also donated sperm. And what's interesting is when they donated sperm, counter to the advice he gives out, they did not have legal paperwork in place.

ROBIN: You're a lawyer. Was there back-and-forth about the legal when you donated sperm? Did you say upfront, "We want to be in the kid's life?"

GARY: Not really. We said, if you want any contact or no contact, we're totally open. Whatever happens.

TONY: We knew from the start it was their family. We were very, very clear that we were surrendering the parental rights to whoever was the non-biological mom, and our plan was to do that through second parent adoption. Whatever relationship we have with the children afterward was up to them, and that has evolved over time.

They said that they wanted us to play a part, but we didn't try to define it. We kind of trusted in the Universe, which from a lawyer's perspective is probably not the best thing to do. I know, I draft those contracts, so I understand that. But I think they knew because I practice this kind of law, that the conversation and our relationship and our word was bond. So we went through the second parent adoption process, and they have their family now.

JUDY GOLD

> Judy and her wife split up before they finalized the second parent adoption on their second child. There are so many things that could have gone wrong in this situation, and it serves as a reminder of the importance that families like ours get legal protections in place as soon as possible.

JUDY: My ex-wife had our first kid. I adopted him immediately. I had done all the paperwork before he was born. When he was born, all we needed was the court date. But when Ben was born, I had him, and Sharon never did the second parent adoption. Then we ended up breaking up when Ben was about two and a half and Henry was seven and a half. And she still hadn't adopted him.

ROBIN: Was that problematic for the breakup?

JUDY: It was because we weren't together. There was no genetic link to Sharon. There was no legal marriage. We were domestic partners, but we were not at the same address.

I was upset about the breakup, and a lot of people were saying, "No, don't let her adopt him." And I was like, "Shut the fuck up. We had these kids together." I didn't want Henry going back and forth, and Ben just staying with me, that's ridiculous. We're a family. This is who we are.

That's the thing about how important it is that we have these rights because she's not genetically linked, but she's his mother, you know?

So we got a lawyer, and it was a precedent setting case in the state of New York. And we went to the judge's chambers. And I'll never forget, she said to the boys, "Do you know what's going on in here?" And I don't know if she asked them to explain it, or they said yes, but after, she said, "I'm going to grant this."

And Henry leaned over to Ben and hugged him and said, "Now we're full brothers."

It's so funny because you say they're not genetically linked. You know, people are always like, and this is really annoying, "Well he's yours and he's Sharons." No! That's so fucking ridiculous.

TIQ

Tiq and his wife used a known donor, and instead of going to a lawyer, they LGBTQ drafted off a friend who had created a family in a similar way.

TIQ: A friend of mine, a trans guy, who's a lawyer at the ACLU, had a known donor as well. So he just gave me the contract that he used, and he said, "Just switch it up." So I did that. Got it notarized and boom.

NEE NEE

Nee Nee created a nontraditional family with her best friend and his husband. Their understanding was they would raise the child together, but in separate houses. It seemed like a good idea at the time, but Nee Nee's story is now a cautionary tale. It shows how things can go south in self-designed families. Especially when a legal plan is not completed.

NEE NEE: My family started constructing itself about eight years ago. It was with two really good friends, two men who were married. We vacationed together, and we spent a lot of time together. We decided to venture beyond friendship and create a child together. We had agreed that the child would spend the first year with me, and we would do sleep overs and weekends together and family trips. We were trying to create a new type of family. Fast forward to now. We just wrapped up a litigious situation, and the deconstruction of our family has been taking place since not too long after the child was born. It was very messy.

Initially, our plan was to see how it plays out, but we did have a bit of a framework. We sat down with the attorney and said, "Once the child is in school, this is what it's going to look like. And once the child is of a certain age, this is what it's going to look like. This is our idea."

ROBIN: Did you have things decided like you can't move out of state or how close you need to be to each other?

NEE NEE: We weren't allowed to move 35 miles away from one another.

ROBIN: Were the legal conversations easy?

NEE NEE: Oh, yeah. In the beginning, for sure. The attorney said she could draft something, but it wouldn't matter until after the child was born. No court would recognize it until it was a living, breathing entity. So I didn't see a finished draft until after he was born.

ROBIN: Did you use the same attorney?

NEE NEE: Same attorney. And then after it was drafted. I got a separate attorney to look it over because at that point, she became their attorney, and I needed one of my own. When my attorney looked at it she said, "This is in no way in your best interest." It was so loosey-goosey that anything could happen. It basically set us up for litigation, I think. There were no hard and fast rules on things. It said things like, "They're going to have a meaningful conversation to make things work."

JAIMIE: It sounds like when you started this with them, you guys were kind of all on board with this loosey-goosey, like you were all pretty idyllic about it in the beginning. What switched for you to make you think, "Wait a second."

NEE NEE: Well, when she finished the draft after he was born, and I read through it, I thought, "Okay, you can't just say that we're all going to agree on everything, that everything's going to just flow. We're talking about three people trying to raise and parent one child. We're all gonna have different opinions and viewpoints." So there were a lot of things in there that needed to have been added or at least discussed.

I try not to live in regret, however I don't think that attorney set us up for success. And she also did not clearly communicate some aspects. She was telling them that they could have the non-bio dad legally adopt the child.

ROBIN: Like second parent adoption?

NEE NEE: Third.

ROBIN: Does that even exist?

NEE NEE: No. What she didn't tell them or myself is that by doing that, it would take away my rights as a mother. And I refuse to let that happen. This is a lawyer who specializes in the LGBTQ arena and is a lesbian herself. My gut feeling is they thought that I would not know any better.

ROBIN: What was the end game? They wanted to take the baby?

NEE NEE: At this point? I would not put it past them. And we are now in family therapy as per the settlement, all of us together. The therapist even said, "That attorney, if she didn't know that, then she doesn't know the law. She should not be practicing as an attorney."

If we had had a good attorney that was forthcoming from the get-go, maybe things would have ended differently.

I was angry for a long time. Then I realized, my kid is going to pick up on this. It doesn't matter how hard I try and mask it in front of him, there's an underlying energy. He can feel it. So every time I look at him or think of him, I shift my energy for him. Because he doesn't need to be around that. I'm the adult. I can figure out ways to manage that.

TOM

> Back in 2007, when Tom began donating sperm to two lesbians, they didn't have any legal agreements in place. They eventually completed the paperwork, but it was after he had already begun donating and banking sperm.

TOM: Some people would send me articles of situations turning out badly and they'd say, "Hey, I found this article that you may want to read."

I'd say, "Thanks for your concern, but I don't really want to read that."

Based on everything that we'd discussed verbally, I didn't really feel like there was anything that gave me great pause. If there was, knowing me, I would have said, "I don't think I can do this."

But the years that they didn't inseminate [after he was already donating], I really wasn't in touch with them all that much. That's when I probably had my biggest reaction of, "Oh, is this what it's going to be like? I'm not gonna hear from them as often as I expected?" I even remember I went to a free legal clinic because I felt a little between a rock and a hard place because I hadn't heard from them.

> Once they got to the stage of hammering out an agreement, Tom wanted to find his own lawyer to make sure that his needs were covered. He quickly realized that the agreement was helpful, but may not cover him in the future.

TOM: I sought out a lawyer, but the girls covered it. I didn't pay for anything. They did originally want me to use their own lawyer, but I said, "No, no, no. I want somebody who is just for me."

I recall asking the lawyer, "Can I put anything in there that I have the right to initiate visitation?"

Me donating wasn't hinging on that request, but I was coming off of a four-year period where I wasn't hearing from them for six to eight months at a time, so I was thinking, "What's going to happen?" I wanted to have something in there saying I actually have the right or the ability to say, "Hey, can I see the kids on this particular weekend? Can I come up?"

And the lawyer was like, "Mmm, it's not about you. I can't put that in there."

But that lawyer, interestingly said "It's great that you are doing the paperwork so you have some kind of contract among the three of you, but you have to understand that if something happens down the line to that relationship, or if God forbid, something happens to the moms, the kids are put with a legal guardian. And if that legal guardian is having financial difficulty, even though you have this agreement that says you are not financially responsible, and you are releasing your rights, anybody can walk into a court of law and say you are the natural father and you owe those kids child support."

And she said the judge behind the table can either honor the agreement or say the agreement means nothing. And I would owe them child support.

But I still signed it.

JANA AND LINDA

Linda used a known donor with her ex to create her family, and to this day, they do not have a legal document in place. We think it's important to highlight their story because there are many arrangements like this that have worked out too.

LINDA: We used a handshake deal, and everyone said don't do that. He wanted a handshake deal. He said, "I'm not signing away all the rights."

ROBIN: That didn't scare you?

LINDA: A little, but he wasn't really living in the country at the time, and he was kind of in and out, and I thought I could win in court if it came down to that. So I just made the calculation that it would be okay.

But I'm glad none of that happened because he just ended up being—I think somebody asked me, "What is your relationship with him like?" And I think he's kind of like our brother. That's what he feels like. That's what my relationship, feels like with him, like brotherly, like a family member too.

JAIMIE: So you took a leap of faith and it worked.

LINDA: Yeah.

BRIAN ESSER

Wills aren't something that are talked about regularly when it comes to LGBTQ legalese. Brian points out that it's critical LGBTQ parents have a will that establishes guardians for their children should something happen to both parents. We thought this bit of advice was so important we saved it for last.

BRIAN: All parents should have a will, not just because of dealing with your property, but because a will is the most effective way for you to establish a legal guardian for your child. And I'm kind of stealing this line, but it's a good one. A colleague of mine once said, "Think about the person who you least want to get your kids in the event that something happened to you. And now assume that is the person who will get your kids if you don't write down who you want." So who do you want to make those decisions? Do you want a court to make those decisions? Or do you want to make the decisions?

So bite the bullet on that one and do it. If you don't want to hire a lawyer to do that, there's some great software out there, web based services, where you can do that. The only thing is, follow the instructions about how you execute the will to a tee because there's some very specific requirements for getting a will admitted to probate. If you don't follow them, your will won't get admitted.

CHAPTER 14

GROWING UP WITH GAY PARENTS

"For me, there were questions like, 'Why is my family different? Why do they have dads and I don't?' At one point, in the first or second grade, we made Father's Day cards, but I made one that said, 'Hey, Dad. Looking forward to meeting you. Hope you can come live with us. Love, Zach.'" - Iowa State Senator Zach Wahls

Rumor has it, a lot of folks spend time wondering, worrying, or even panicking about whether or not being LGBTQ parents will harm their kids. Or at a minimum, make their kids' lives harder. If that sounds familiar, then this chapter is for you.

You're going to hear straight from the kids' mouths how it all shook out. Were they bullied? Was it more difficult to have two moms or two dads? Was it not a big deal at all? Did it affect them? Do they think about it? Do they rarely give it a second thought?

The answer to all those questions is "yes."

Okay, really the answers are not black or white. It's a lot more of a nuanced conversation than can be cleared up by answering those simple questions. The answer depends on the kid. It depends on the parenting. It depends on where they grew up. It depends on a lot of factors.

Queerspawn (slang)
Noun

The kids of LGBTQ parents.

When we interviewed queerspawn kids, it was our chance to get more information about how it felt to grow up with LGBTQ parents. We asked if they missed having a father or a mother, if having LGBTQ parents affected their sexuality in any way. We even asked if they were sick of feeling like a mouthpiece for all queerspawn.

The good news is that, in general, the kids are alright. They tend to be no worse or better off than their peers raised in more traditional households. But really, how our kids are going to turn out is a concern whether we're straight, gay, bi, or trans. The fact of the matter is, all parents have to sit back and wait to hear how it turns out. And it's a nail-biter.

JAIMIE HERE

One day last year, while walking to school with my four-year-old, we ran into a classmate of hers, and we all happily decided to walk together.

The conversation was pleasant enough at first. We had a lovely exchange on poo-poo and pee-pee that lasted a few blocks, and then the classmate dropped the "D" word. "Rose, do you have a *dad*?" She overemphasized the last word for effect. When Rose didn't answer, she asked again and again and again. She was really goading her now. I saw a look on my daughter's face that I had never seen before. Was it shame? Uncertainty? Fear? I don't know the underlying emotion, but it shut her down. This girl knew that Rose didn't have a dad, she was teasing her. Before I had a chance to get into it with this darling angel, her nanny snapped, "You know she doesn't have a dad. Stop it." And just like that it was over. The girls switched to a chat about farting, and all was good in the world again.

No harm done, right? I can't tell you how much I wish I knew the answer to that question.

Rose and I had a chat about the incident later that afternoon. Of course she barely remembered it, but I drilled affirmations about our family into her head as best I could. And maybe she took it all in, maybe she didn't. It's really hard to know with four-year-olds.

The truth is, Anne and I are doing our best to give our children all the love and support they might need on this journey of theirs, but we're not doing it alone. We recently attended the Pride Parade in New York City, and watching my kids ecstatically take in the floats and dancing drag queens made me realize one thing—this queer community that we're a part of is open and loving and colorful and eclectic and accepting and supportive. It's everything I want my children to be. So what if they don't have a parent with a penis? They have the love of a whole community in their back pocket. That's got to be worth something.

We're doing our best to raise our kids with a sense of pride in who they are. They have two parents who love them very much. We're instilling values into their lives that we hold dear, and we can only hope we're doing enough. They're going to hate us for one reason or another eventually. Whether that reason is their lack of a father or not enough trips to McDonald's is yet to be determined. I can only hope for the latter.

Speaking with queerspawn on the podcast always gets me a little conflicted emotionally. I can't wait to hear about their experiences, but I'm also worried about what they might say. It would break me down if I heard one of them say the lack of a dad in their lives had irrevocably damaged them, or that they resent their gay parents for choosing this path.

But the conversations we had with these kids are some of my favorites. I can only dream that my kids turn out as beautiful as them. Knowing that they're out there and thriving in the world serves as a beacon of light to me for my kids and their futures.

ROBIN HERE TOO

When Mary and I talked about having kids, the thing that Mary worried most about, behind global warming and the destruction of our planet, was whether having kids sentenced them to be made fun of through all of junior high and high school. Mary worried that we would ruin their childhoods, which would in turn, ruin them as adults.

I didn't feel anywhere near as pessimistic though.

As someone who grew up being fully embarrassed by my straight parents, I figured this was a non-issue. In junior high, when my dad took me to the movies for our twice a month visits, I'd sit by myself, several rows in front of him, so we weren't seen together. I also made my mom drop me off several blocks away from the school because of the old, rusty Mercury Bobcat she drove.

So I assured Mary that yes, our kids would be embarrassed by us, but it could just as easily be for a plethora of other reasons like the fact that we dress badly or we're older parents with very large fonts on our phones.

I'm not naive enough to think our kids won't experience feeling different. They may miss having a traditional parental setup. They may have feelings about the fact that they have a donor not a dad. But I believe we'll give our kids the tools to handle any bullying or low self-esteem moments that may come their way. I know we'll be there to talk to them, as long as they want to talk to us.

All that said, every time we interviewed a kid from an LGBTQ household on our podcast, I felt myself leaning in just a bit closer and breathing just a bit shallower as they spoke.

Because I have to admit that sometimes, there is a tiny little voice inside my head that says, "I hope my kids will be okay, and I hope their childhood won't be too hard because of me."

HENRY

> Henry is the son of comedian and very vocal mom, Judy Gold. She has a large platform to talk about their family, so he grew up in a very "out" family during a time when there weren't a lot of other kids like him.

HENRY: In elementary school and middle school, I'd say that the only thing, and I wouldn't even call it a negative, but the only complication of growing up with two moms was that up until eighth grade, I was very sensitive. I'd cry about a lot of stuff. I was that kid. I'd be crying in class because someone said something mean to me. And anytime someone said faggot, it was just like—

JUDY: He took it really personally.

HENRY: Yeah. But then I just kind of grew out of that when I got to high school, and everything was fine.

JUDY: He's an amazing voice for this. Don't give me a fucking look! Henry, you have grown up in this family, and you've never, I mean have you ever been ashamed to say, "I have two moms?"

ROBIN: That's a good question.

JAIMIE: That's a tough question to answer in front of your mom.

JUDY: Oh, it's fine.

HENRY: No, I've definitely never been ashamed of my moms. Well, maybe I was ashamed, but not because I have two moms.

ROBIN: Were you ever ashamed because they were gay?

HENRY: No.

JAIMIE: Did people give you a hard time because you had two moms?

HENRY: Nope.

> Henry's donor is anonymous, so he may not be able to meet him. But a sibling tracked Henry down and wanted to meet him.

HENRY: I was getting dropped off at college. It was my freshman year, and I was sitting at the table with my really good friend who I went to high school with. His parents and my parents, we were all just hanging out.

And I got a message on my phone from some kid who grew up in Malibu, same deal—two moms. And he said, "I'm your half-brother."

He had done a lot of investigating, and he also found two other half-sisters. We talked about genetic stuff. But I'm very into sports and he was a really good musician and went to The Berkeley School of Music. I just didn't really—if I went to high school with him, we probably wouldn't have been friends. He really wanted to meet me and everything, and I would've met him if I felt like we had anything in common.

I was obviously curious, and I talked to him for a few days. But after that, there was really nothing else to talk about. And so I just told him that.

ROBIN: Was your brother interested in his donor at all? Because I'm curious if there's anything different, or if you both feel the same.

HENRY: It's the same. I got messaged by Ben's half-sibling and I showed him a picture and he like laughed and didn't care. But Ben doesn't care much about anything.

SENATOR ZACH WAHLS

> Even though Zach grew up in a fairly progressive town in Iowa, he still felt his different-ness in school. He not only had LGBTQ parents, but one of his moms was disabled.

It was a lot for him to take on, but his parents used the dinner table as a place to talk about values and give the kids tools to handle the situations they were placed in.

ZACH: There were plenty of realizations along the way that we were different from other families. Some of those were because my family was treated differently—there were certain words that were used in school.

There were a lot of different parts of my situation growing up and one of those things—and it was somewhat related to having same-sex parents—was Terry's diagnosis with multiple sclerosis. Terry was sick and in a wheelchair, and that made my parents even more conspicuous. So not only did I have two moms, but one mom is in a wheelchair and that's even more sticking out like a sore thumb. It felt like one thing on top of another, and it's a great example of how intersectionality works. You've got somebody who is both disabled and queer.

I was living in an admittedly progressive college town. And there are plenty of people who think, "Growing up in progressive Iowa City, I'm sure that was fine." And in some ways, absolutely, it was. Administrators at school had my back and that was huge. Teachers had my back, but kids are kids, you know? The words "fag" and "gay" were thrown around as slurs.

ROBIN: Did anyone ever come after you? Was there bullying?

ZACH: Sure. Yeah. But that changed once I got bigger and taller.

ROBIN: How did you or your parents handle the bullying? Was the house really communicative?

ZACH: Well, as a family the conversations we had around the dinner table were really important. Almost every single night from K through 12th grade, we had dinner at our dinner table. I was very fortunate, very privileged in that respect, that we were able to do that. And we would always start before the meal and have a conversation about that month's value.

ROBIN: You had month's values?

ZACH: Yes, the book is called "Teaching Your Children Values."

JAIMIE: I have to buy this book.

ZACH: It's from Richard and Linda Eyre. Basically they had 12 values. One for each month. And April would be about trust, being trustworthy, or honesty. May would be about being frugal or being thrifty. And so we would start each meal by giving an example either from our own lives or something that we had seen somebody else do of that value. Often, I would kind of skip through it on my way to whatever I was eating for dinner that night, but over time, those sunk in.

It would be around those dinner table conversations where we would talk about bullying or my mom Terry would give us the strategies for how you deal with the bully. I think my mom called it fogging, which is where you kind of repeat this phrase over and over, "I feel sorry for you" to the bully.

I'm lucky I never got punched out or anything. It certainly could have been much worse.

ROBIN: So you literally were in high school, and you're saying, "I feel sorry for you."

ZACH: This was elementary school. It changed a little bit going into junior high and high school. In junior high the struggle was much more because the words "fag" and "gay" were used every morning on the bus going to school.

JAIMIE: Did those words touch a nerve in you?

ZACH: They definitely did. Part of it is you're on the bus, and all the cool kids are the ones saying this stuff. Then I had to get off the bus and go have dinner with my gay parents.

ROBIN: I'm sure every time it was a moment of, am I standing up for them? Or do I want to fit in?

ZACH: That's exactly right.

JAIMIE: How do we protect our kids from this? How did your moms protect you? Do you feel like they did a good job helping you through that?

ZACH: Yeah, I mean, I do think they did about as good as you could do. They made a very conscientious decision to move from Central Wisconsin where I was born to Iowa City, which was a larger more progressive community. That was an intentional choice on their part. And I do think that they somewhat underestimated themselves. I think they probably fell into the trap that many other people might, which is to think, "Oh, it's a liberal, progressive college town. It's not a problem here."

It may be okay. It's not like we lived in rural Iowa. But it's not necessarily going to be a walk in the park either. I think that there are unfortunately, a lot of gay parents who just totally delude themselves into thinking their kids will not face any problems. And it sounds like that's not the case for you guys which I'm grateful for. But I think parents need to be conscientious of the fact that it will happen.

> **Zach never missed having a dad though. In part because he believes you can't miss what you never had, but also because his parents put strong male role models in his life.**

ZACH: I like to differentiate between "dad" and "father". There's a reason—and spoiler alert to anyone who hasn't seen *The Empire Strikes Back*—why Luke doesn't say to Darth Vader, "Luke, I'm your dad."

"Dad", in my mind, is much more of that emotional relationship with a male parent. "Father" is more of a biological connection. So it's hard, I don't have a control group. I don't have something to which I can immediately compare my own life to.

But, look, I'll say this, I had great male role models in my life, and my parents worked to make sure of that. They found good men, whether it was uncles or male role models at church or in the Boy Scouts. That was one reason why they were willing to keep me enrolled in the Boy Scouts, even though they had the policy that officially didn't allow them to participate. So there was no shortage of positive male role models for me. One of my best friend's dads growing up taught me how to shave, so I don't really feel like-

ROBIN: You didn't miss it.

ZACH: Well, you can't miss something you don't have. I can't miss owning a Jaguar, you know?

My moms couldn't teach my sister how to use makeup, so she learned it somewhere else. At the end of the day, there are still men in my life who I talk to about various things, just like there are certain things I talk about with my moms.

When we say it takes a village, this is what we're talking about. My experience was good because I had two loving committed parents who cared about me. There are plenty of shitty dads out there.

MAKEDA AND SADIE

> Friends and co-authors, Makeda and Sadie get asked
> a lot about their sexuality because they come from an
> LGBTQ home. They're a little wary about answering, but
> their journey about how they were forced to come out
> as straight or gay because of their nontraditional families
> feels important to talk about.

JAIMIE: I have a question, and I hope it's okay. How do each of you identify?

MAKEDA: Knowing that you both are queer, asking that feels fine.

ROBIN: Does it not feel fine when other people ask you?

SADIE: I guess my question when other people who are not in the community ask is, "Why are you asking? How is that important?"

JAIMIE: Yeah. I just realized this must be a question that's asked of you guys a lot. I'm so sorry if I crossed a line there.

ROBIN: You should be sorry, Jaimie.

MAKEDA: Ha. No, no, no, no. So I identify as queer, but I think what's interesting is that when I was nine years old, I came out to my moms as straight. That's the difference, right? When you grow up with lesbian moms, your whole worldview is shifted, right? So I did feel like I had to come out as straight. Which is really cool when I look back on it. Most young kids don't do that because it's the assumption.

Then when I was actually 16 or 17, I came out again as bisexual. My moms were flabbergasted. They were so surprised. They were smiling, but also they had to pick their jaws up off the floor.

SADIE: My parents were actually quite similar. For me, being asked about my sexuality is a very complicated question because I was asked a lot about my sexuality as I was figuring it out for myself. I was on panels talking to queer perspective parents. I was in newspapers and on TV and on the radio, and everyone wanted to know my sexuality.

JAIMIE: You were like the poster child for queerspawn.

SADIE: Yeah, queer families and upholding queer families. So I liked to turn the question into a joke. I would always say, "Well, I was raised by too many women. I don't need any more in my life." I didn't even think about that line. It just came out.

Then, when I was 16, I had this huge crush on someone who, if

I dated them would make me, not straight. It was really upsetting for me because it felt like it wasn't just homophobia I would face. Personally, it felt like I was letting down my community.

JAIMIE: By not turning out straight.

SADIE: Yeah. Yeah.

MAKEDA: It's sort of like when you're on those panels, in a way you feel like there's this unspoken thing, in order to prove to the homophobic society that we live in that we turned out "all right" then we have to be straight.

SADIE: It wasn't just a concept. I watched people on TV making the argument that gay people were going to raise gay children. There was one media clip where me and my mom were shown getting ready for school, and the next clip was this homophobic dude sitting in an office, with his big heavy binder that proved that gay people -

ROBIN: "There's science in this binder, there's science in here."

SADIE: Yeah, exactly. And hilariously, on the TV clip, the binder was actually empty, and if the angle was just right, you could see the big black hole.

But he was saying it on all of our big Canadian news channels, that we were going to be raised not right. So of course there was a need to make the counterpoint, that we are all alright, and alright means straight.

> Makeda and Sadie edited and wrote a book filled with stories from kids raised in LGBTQ homes. That process allowed them to feel connected to other queerspawn and to realize that so many of their experiences are shared collectively amongst other kids from LGBTQ parents.

MAKEDA: I think that in pulling together "Spawning Generations," Sadie and I were really clear about a couple of things. One of those things was that we wanted to be able to allow the space for queerspawn to tell a more complicated story than we're often able to tell. We wanted to hear about what people struggled with. We talk a lot about not having to airbrush our stories, and our lives, and existing outside of that narrative that is "we turned out alright." And challenging that because most families don't have to contend or wrestle with that societal pressure.

ROBIN: Did writing the book change how you felt about your family?

SADIE: It didn't particularly change my personal relationship to my family. But it reawakened my queerspawn identity in that I felt a new drive to advocate for our community, in terms of queerspawn in queer spaces. Because often times, we don't feel invited or important or queer enough to be in queer spaces.

ROBIN: Your parents are the ones who are queer. You're just the kids.

SADIE: Exactly. So it really re-awakened that drive to put our stories out there, and to have people understand why we're here and why we're important.

MAKEDA: I think that we often don't feel at home in straight spaces. Yet, we feel like the older we get, the more pushed out we are of queer spaces. That can be very hurtful. We really saw this book as an opportunity for us, not only to claim space, but also to connect with each other as well and build community across borders.

ROBIN: I was just thinking that places like the gay and lesbian center should have a group for you guys.

SADIE: There's COLAGE. It's is a national queerspawn network that has chapters in many states. I started going to COLAGE conferences when I was 15 or 16, and it changed my life. It was the first time I was in a room of just queerspawn, and it made me realize how important it was for all of us. For me, it was something that I was missing, to hear my story reflected. And hear other people say, "Yes, I feel you."

I often equate this to my Jewish identity. I'm Jewish. I was raised Jewish. I will never lose that identity. Similarly, I was raised by queer people. I was raised in the community, but some somehow that identity is different. We all know that being queer is more than who you sleep with. It's a community, right? This podcast is part of a community. To me, it feels the same as my Jewish identity. These are the people I was raised around. This is the culture I was raised in. Why suddenly are you taking away that community from me, the only community I've ever known, you know?

MAKEDA: And more and more our communities are articulating the idea of being culturally queer. It's amazing, having edited our book, and seeing parts of our experiences reflected in other people's stories. It was so affirming to realize, "Oh my gosh, across borders, this kind of cultural experience that you had is so similar to what I experienced." That was empowering for both of us.

Not to say that all queerspawn are going to have a similar cultural understanding because there are so many variations of queer culture within queer culture, but just that I think there is something to this idea of being culturally queer.

SADIE: I get to play the queer card because I'm also queer. But for me, actually, the identity I relate to more than being queer is being queerspawn. I've only been queer for 10 years. I've been queerspawn for 26 years.

EMMA T.

> Emma, who is in her early 30s, has a lot of wisdom about growing up as the daughter of two moms. She's processed so much about the experience, and has a really

**great perspective, even about how she went on a quest
to try to find her anonymous donor that didn't work out
how she hoped it would.**

EMMA: This guy turned up in our search, and he was a perfect fit. My parents and I actually met him for brunch. It was very surreal.

I really felt like I needed to do it. I said to my parents, "This has nothing to do with replacing you. This has nothing to do with inadequacy. It has everything to do with my own journey." And they were really good sports. It wasn't easy though.

But I think they were fascinated when we sat at brunch. I felt like we were all enthralled in the same mystery. Once my parents got on board, they must have been as curious as I was. How could you not be curious about that?

Later we did a paternity test, and it was very dramatic. He wasn't the donor, and I was really sad. I was so sad that I was like, "We're done."

Also, what happened was he was a nice guy, and he was a lonely guy. And there was this feeling of, "Oh, this guy wants a family" which I hadn't even considered. So I was sad, mostly for me, but also for him. And I was surprised to be so surprised by my sadness. I didn't know what emotions I would have.

At the time when he met with us he said, "There's this other guy I donated with at the same time, and he also fits all your specifications. Here's a brochure of him. He's a Republican running for such-and-such office. I'm his friend. He doesn't want you to know about this. I know that, so I swiped this for you."

I looked at a picture of him and his family, and he looked a little like me, but the mind plays tricks. Then I had another important revelation, this guy was definitely on a brochure, and he was running for something. He did not want to be found.

I thought, "I don't want to drag anybody through this."

I already got what I needed. I made an effort, and I also found out the same thing I did as a kid, what do I have if I find him, you know?

There's a difference between wanting to know who your donor was versus missing a father figure. Emma talks about the questions she's often asked about whether she misses her dad.

EMMA: Yeah, the dad thing comes up all the time. As a kid it was always, "Do you miss your dad?"

And I just felt like I didn't even have the language to explain. You don't miss a person you didn't know. People are always like, "I love my dad. Don't you miss your dad?"

I said, "I have two moms. There's not a vacancy."

People never understood that. I feel like I still can't explain it.

One topic that we didn't expect was Emma talking about how growing up with two moms made her very aware of body image issues.

EMMA: I do look back and think having two moms who were short, who were constantly dieting—this was the 90s when people were eating SnackWells—who were struggling with their body image, and realize they couldn't hide that. I think they tried to hide it and then they were sad that they didn't hide it better. I think that's a part of same-sex relationships that's not talked about enough is the eating disorder side of sexual shame.

They did talk about it. They talked about how they loved me. They said I was beautiful, but they hated themselves, right? That's the part that was so hard to hide.

JAIMIE: And it was a double whammy because it was two women.

EMMA: Yes, and I thought about this when I've nannied. If I'm looking in the mirror, I don't want to get caught having bad moments in front of kids.

ROBIN: That's virtually impossible to do.

EMMA: It's impossible, so I wouldn't worry about it too much. But I think there's a connection with the sexual shame aspect that comes up in queer relationships and families. But I don't— it's just a hypothesis, and I don't know.

And look everything went well for me, so well that I get to nitpick.

> As was a common thread in all the conversations with queerspawn, Emma experienced kids who used hurtful words. And she dealt with it by speaking her mind and becoming a self-proclaimed ambassador to the LGBTQ community.

EMMA: That was the time when everyone was like, "That's so gay. That's so gay." All over the playground. Kids were constantly saying that.

JAIMIE: Did you take offense to that?

EMMA: I did, and I was after it all the time. I think the most important thing that a kid can get from coming from a same-sex household or a queer household is the ability to be that Ambassador person, and to empathize.

I think in our political climate right now, everybody thinks, "Well, I can't imagine how that evil person is thinking." Well, okay, try. I felt that as a kid, I faced a lot of homophobia, and it was all ignorance. These were children, so they weren't evil, they were genuinely ignorant, but everyone is a child. They're just bigger, and they just grow and keep the same shit going if they don't deal with it.

The most positive, special thing about the queerspawn community is that we have this ability to be in different worlds at the same time, and that can make you an ambassador and make you able to empathize. That's the takeaway.

CHAPTER 15

OUR FAMILIES ARE JUST LIKE YOURS

So friends, it appears we've come to the end of this book. You're probably wondering what you're going to do with all your free time now that you've finished. Well, we have some suggestions for you. You can listen to our podcast for starters. You can also buy all your friends a copy of this book. You can spend some time writing five-star reviews for our ovaries on Goodreads and Amazon. You can write letters (in cursive because that suggests you're *really* serious) to our publisher, imploring them to lock us down with a four-book deal because with more Robin and Jaimie in the world, life seems less dark. Those are just a few ideas.

What have we learned in these couple of hundred pages? Well, first and foremost, it's darn clear that our families are fabulous and filled with love. We think it all stems from how intentional we have to be when we create our families. We have to define a path, survive the ups and downs of the medical process, or navigate the adoption and foster care systems, all while figuring out how to pay for our dream babies. And we also have to somehow remain positive and keep our chins up because it can be a long road to parenting when you're an L, G,

B, T, or Q.

That same thoughtfulness and deliberateness transfers over to our parenting. We carefully work together figuring out what roles we'll each play in our kids' lives. We're so planned that we spend hours debating and deliberating who will be "mom" and who will be "mama." We research, get tips from our friends, and figure out the best way to talk with our kids about their families. We know that it's critical that they understand their story and also have the emotional support they'll need. Especially as they walk out into a world that doesn't always believe they should exist.

We work hard to claim, appreciate and love our differences because it's our differences that make us special. *But,* and this is a very important but, we also recognize that, in so many ways, we're just like every other typical family in the world.

For example, once we find out that a baby is on the way, some of us panic.

DAVID: So I was thinking I have to get out of here. I can't believe I've done this. But just to jump ahead so you don't think I'm an asshole, the moment she was born, all of the worry and anxiety and stress over all the time and the bazillions of dollars—that I don't have, that we spent—all those worries just receded, immediately.

> **We coach our kid's soccer tevams, lead the Girl Scout troops and open up our homes to the kids in the neighborhood.**

EMMA T.: My moms were the lesbians running the Girl Scout Troop. They were so winsome, you couldn't not like them. And all the kids liked them. I had friends with moms who were not as great or dads who were not as great, and those kids flocked to my family. My family was seen as a haven for people. And a lot of my friends who've grown up to be trans or queer point to my family quite directly. These kids have called my mothers, "You did this for me. You modeled it." A lot of people, when they hear my story, wish they had my parents.

We recognize that we're not perfect parents. Sometimes we even complain about what a pain in the butt our kids can be.

STACEYANN: You think about the relationship you have with your kid between birth and say five, six, maybe even into the teenage years, and some of them are shits. And you know if you think about having that relationship with anyone else, if you said to your friend, "Hey, I was with this person, and they were screaming at me, and I was carrying eight grocery bags, and it was snowing and they wouldn't carry one. And I was also carrying their backpack that I told them not to fucking bring because they're not going to use anything in it. And it's raining, and it's late, and we stopped one last stop for something that they absolutely had to have, and then it starts raining harder, and then they say, "Can you pick me up?" If you had that relationship with anyone else, your friend would say, "Get the fuck out. Leave. Don't call back. Block them!" But here you are, it's the only relationship where if the person is abusive you just have to stay. Especially if you're a lesbian, and you paid a lot of money to have them.

We think we've got it all handled, and then we experience that moment where we realize we totally don't.

PATRICIA: I really did think, "I've got skills. I vision. I do affirmations. I'm going to teach my kids to meditate." But real life happens, and I realized my skills needed a major upgrade because I was losing it all the time. Crying all the time. It just was not good, not good at all, and I had to up my game as a parent.

And our kids aren't exactly who we thought they would be.

STACEYANN: This is where it becomes quite, run of the mill. You don't really anticipate specific problems with your kid.

I didn't think that I would have a rule keeper in my house. I imagined raising a rebel who was going to do everything and anything. And instead she's like, "Mommy, you're not supposed to be driving in this lane." I'm a lesbian immigrant, I can drive in this lane. It's reparations. But she's such a rule keeper. The whole birthday party will be dead in a second because she's like, "Listen. This one had a turn. This one had a turn and now it's this one's turn." I'm like, "Jesus Christ."

But we work hard to clean up our messes.

PATRICIA: It's very difficult, and that's why parenting evolves us. Parenting brings out the best and the worst of us. I thought I was going to be a Mary Poppins mom because I didn't have that, and I didn't want my kids to have the chaos that I grew up with or the fighting, the screaming and the yelling. But I realize now, that's just life. It's chaotic.

KELLEN: And chaotic is good too. It's the only place you can grow. If everything is nice and fluffy, you're not going to learn anything.

PATRICIA: You just try to do better.

And we have come to understand that our families are basically, at the heart of things, typical.

EMMA BROCKES: The thing I always come back to is that the insane period was the period of decision making. That's always the case with everything, whether it's a job or emigrating or whatever. Making the decision feels so horrifying and the minute you've done it, it continues to be really hard, but it's hard in an ordinary way. I feel like it's just deeply ordinary. Like being resentful and jealous of each other and competing for the kids' attention. The dynamic is not that much different from any other family.

So the most important lesson we learned is that we're all the same. We're all just parents, loving our children, supporting them, cleaning up our messes when we make them and teaching our kids to be the best people they can be.

And it's critical that we share our family stories with the world, showing off all our love and intentionality. That's why we wrote this book—to highlight LGBTQ families for all the world to see. Because the more we share ourselves, the more we normalize our families to the world, the less hatred will be directed toward us. And less hatred means a more loving world. Who doesn't want a more loving world for our kids?

In an interview with actress and comedian, Judy Gold, she said the reason she talks openly about her family on stage is because she's proud of them. But she also said that she talks about them because she wants to educate that one person who's never known a gay person and might have negative thoughts about LGBTQ families. She hopes that in seeing her, in hearing about her family, it will normalize us to that one person.

Because once they understand us, they can then love us. And once they love us, they will support us. And then we will all be equal.

Not better, not worse, just equal.

GLOSSARY OF TERMS

Anonymous Donor (AKA Closed Donor)

Noun

> A person who donates sperm, generally to a sperm bank. The personal records of the donor are sealed, and the purchaser of the sperm agrees in writing that their children will not be able to determine the identity of the sperm donor when they are older.

Disclosure

Noun

> The act of talking to your child about how they were made and preparing them to handle their differences in a world that is predominantly heterosexual and cisgender.

Egg Donor

Noun

> A person who donates her/their eggs so they can be used by another individual or couple to make a family by in vitro fertilization (IVF). Similar to sperm donors, egg donors can be anonymous or open.

Gestational Carrier

Noun

> A person who has someone else's fertilized egg

implanted in her/their womb. The objective is to carry and give birth to a child for another person or couple. A Gestational Carrier is also referred to as a "surrogate" in this book. Surrogacy is not currently legal in all states.

Home Study
Noun

A required process for anyone adopting in the US whereby a case worker visits your home to meet you and check out your readiness to parent. They'll interview you and write report about your day-to-day habits, parenting philosophies, the state of your home, and reasons for wanting to adopt. Before the home study, you will panic, complain that you have to do a home study and clean your house to a level that it's never been cleaned before. Then you will bite your fingernails until the report arrives.

Intrauterine Insemination (IUI)
Noun

This procedure happens at a doctor's office. They separate the semen from the seminal fluid (it's called washing). Around the time of ovulation, they put that sperm inside the uterus, and if you remember from your 10th grade health class, the uterus is next to the fallopian tubes. This increases the odds of conception over ICI.

In Vitro Fertilization (IVF)
Noun

A medical procedure whereby an egg is fertilized by sperm outside the body. The fertilized egg is then implanted in the womb.

Known Donor
Noun

> A person who you know and who is willing to donate sperm to make a baby for your LGBTQ family. How much this person will be involved in the child's life, and how much legal protection you want to set up around that relationship, is something you should clarify, preferably in writing, with the donor.

LGBTQ Drafting
Verb

> The act of getting all your information from LGBTQ friends who have successfully forged a path before you. This applies to, but is not limited to, having babies, legal advice, and places to travel that are LGBTQ friendly.

Open Donor
Noun

> A person who donates sperm and who agrees in writing that when the child reaches age 18, the child has the right to learn who their donor was. The agreement may also allow one or more contacts between the child and the donor, and these agreements often vary from sperm bank to sperm bank.

Queerspawn (slang)
Noun

> The kids of LGBTQ parents.

Second Parent Adoption
Noun

> A legal procedure that lets a same-sex or transgender parent adopt a child their partner is the biological or adopted parent of, without terminating the first parent's parental rights.

Superman Phenomenon
Noun

> When prospective parents get so intoxicated by the idea of choosing the perfect donor, they eliminate donors for minor health history infractions or slightly quirky personality traits.

Turkey Baster Method (AKA Intracervical Insemination, or ICI)
Noun

> The not at all scientific name for when a syringe of some kind is used to inject sperm (either from a sperm bank or collected just before injection) into the vagina as close to the cervix as possible, in order to get pregnant. It's got about the same chances of success as straight sex.

GUEST APPEARANCES

Aimee & Myriam: Chapters 2,3,4,7, and 12

Beth & Jen: Chapters 2,5,6, and 11

Brian Esser: Chapters 5,8,9, and 12

Camilla: Chapters 5,9, and 13

Sheila: Chapter 5

Cassandra: Chapter 5

Crystal & Kelly: Chapters 2 and 5

Dani & Mike: Chapter 12

David: Chapters 1,2,3,4,14, and15

David Beach: Chapters 1,5, and 11

Emma Brockes: Chapters 1,3,4,7,8, and 10

Emma T.: Chapters 3,9,10,11,12,14, and 15

Gary & Tony: Chapters 1,2,3,7,8,9, and 13

Henry: Chapter 14

Jana & Linda: Chapters 3,4,8,10,11, and 13

Jessica & Holly: Chapters 5 and 8

Judy Gold: Chapters 3,8, and 13

Julia Scotti: Chapters 6 and 9

Karen & Tobi: Chapters 2 and 3

Kelly: Chapter 3

Kim Bergman: Chapters 3 and 7

Lara & Joanne: Chapter 6

Lisa & Jennifer: Chapters 1 and 10

Lisa the Therapist: Chapters 9 and 11

Liz: Chapters 8,9, and 10

Makeda & Sadie: Chapters 3,10, and 14

Mark & Greg: Chapters 1,3,4,6,8, and 9

Michele the Doula: Chapters 2,5, 8, and 12

Molly: Chapter 7

Nate: Chapter 3

Nee Nee: Chapters 4 and 13

Patricia & Kellen: Chapters 1,4,11, and 15

Rae & Margie: Chapters 1,3,8,10,11, and 13

Romaine: Chapters 3 and 12

Sam & Laura (The Abbys): Chapters 1,3,4, and 7

Sara & Hilary: Chapters 2,3,4, and 15

Stacyann Chin: Chapters 2,3,8,9,10, and 15

The Two Barons: Chapters 2 and 7

Tiffany & Carissa: Chapters 3 and 12

Tiq: Chapters 1,6,9, and 13

Tom Copolla: Chapters 1,3,4, 9,10, and 13

Zach Wahls: Chapters 9 and 14

IF THESE OVARIES COULD TALK PODCAST

If These Ovaries Could Talk episodes available at the time of printing.

Two Wombs, One Baby
Ashleigh and Bliss made medical history when they became the first two women to both carry the same child. Confused? Take a listen.

Rosie O'Donnell
Rosie O'Donnell gives an unfiltered interview about what it was like to be a trailblazer as an LGBTQ parent during a time when few Hollywood stars were out, her struggles with personal relationships as well as with her children, and what it's like to be the target of Donald Trump's wrath.

You Gotta Believe in Mother Mary
Mary Keane welcomed LOADS of kids to her family through foster care. She also made it her life's work, when she became a dedicated director with an organization called You Gotta Believe whose motto is, "It's never too late for family." And Jaimie and Robin learn they're not worthy of someone as amazing as Mary!

Disconnected: Phases in Parenting
Does being in a longterm relationship mean you will grow apart? Robin and Jaimie discuss navigating the disconnect that can happen between partners after kids are in the picture.

Two Moms Pregnant (Sarah Kate Ellis and Kristen Henderson)
Sarah Kate Ellis, CEO of GLAAD and Kristen Henderson, from Antigone Rising join us to talk about having a baby at the exact same time, why representation in media matters, and that time Kristen's water broke.

Your Legal Questions Answered
Tony the lawyer answers listener legal questions. We talk frozen embryos having legal standing, if you get maternity/paternity leave when you're an LGBT or a Q, the fact that a birth certificate doesn't prove parentage, and so much more legal junk.

When You Can't Do it at Home
How do you approach your future "Baby Daddy"? Britt and Liss do it while tipsy at their wedding. Next steps? Explore LGBTQ fertility options in a state where the sperm donor has parental rights if you make the baby at home.

Evangelical Gay Christians in The Bible Belt
Brian Copeland is a self-described preacher's wife. He talks about the struggles they went through as a gay family who wanted a Christian education for their kids, and the importance of helping people understand our LGBTQ families.

Homo-steading and Pigs & Chickens
Madhu and Jes are your typical lesbians who met through Buddhism, live outside the city with chickens named after famous lesbians and have a son named Nio.

Daddy and Daddy featuring Seth Rudetsky

Seth Rudetsky joins with his husband James to talk about adopting a sibling's child, foster care, being the non-bio parent and when parenting gets rough in high school.

From Mom to Dad
Nick lived as a woman. Birthed four babies. Met Katherine. Fell in love. Transitioned. Now they're just another beautiful family with 5 kids and a minivan.

One Dad and Two Kids
Matt is a single gay dad by choice of twins. He thought he was a unicorn, but it turns out there are loads of other SGDBCOT out there. His advice? Get help, and put your kids on a schedule. It works for him.

Live with David Beach
Adoption, waiting till you're 40 to have a kid, being the mom in a two-dad house, and a made-up child named Benjamin. These are all topics that come up in our live show at WNYC's prestigious Greene Space.

Phases of Parenting
Whether your kid is in a good or bad stage, it doesn't matter because soon they'll be in a new one. Listen to our special guest talk about all the phases of parenting, from birth to tween and everything in between. Ophira Eisenberg joins to talk about making her baby!

I'm a Surrogate
The idea of carrying someone else's baby may seem foreign to some, but Kelly always knew she wanted to be a surrogate. She carried two sets of twins and a singleton for 3 LGBTQ families!

Finding a Surrogate
Having a baby with a surrogate can be an overwhelming process, you need doctors, a lawyer, maybe an egg donor and oh yeah,

the surrogate. Kim from Growing Generations stops by to break down the process. And she also talks about getting sperm on the black market!

Foster Care and Loss
Jess and Holly opened their home to a sweet foster kiddo. Almost two years later, they were ready to adopt, but she was sent back to the birth mom (in a rehab) because of a clerical error. But they still believe in foster care.

Foster Care and LGBTQs
Let's dispel the myth that LGBTQ folks aren't welcome to foster. Sheila from the Graham foster care agency swings by to talk about fostering as a path to parenthood.

Shrinks and Family Planning
Picking a donor, choosing a surrogate or talking to your kids about where they come from can be stressful. Lisa Schuman drops by to talk about why it's important to get some professional help on that journey.

Adventures in Transgender Fertility
Lara and Joanne decided they didn't need IVF or frozen sperm to make a baby. Instead, their plan was to do it, the old-fashioned way. That involved Lara stepping down off hormones and a lot of emotional baggage neither one expected.

Sperm Donation in the UK
When Nate found out there was a shortage of sperm in the UK he jumped in to do his part. But he learned it required navigating a complicated system, for little money.

Money and Molly
It costs a lot for an LGBTQ family to make a baby. But how do you save for that? We brought in our financial advisor friend, Molly, to teach us. Also, there's the bonus story of how she

married her Maid of Honor.

A Tale of Two Barons

Research shows a baby boom is coming for millennial LGBTQ families. Is that because millennials don't have any preconceived concerns around creating a family? We brought in a young gay couple to educate us on what that generation is thinking about when it comes to family planning.

Judy Gold is a Great Mom

Comic, writer, actress, and self-described loudmouth, Judy Gold joins with her son Henry. They talk about her ground-breaking second parent adoption, her work to change all the forms that say "mother" and "father" & what it's like to be raised by two moms.

A Queer Vision

Writer, speaker, activist, model, Tiq Milan joins us to talk about losing the lesbian community when he transitioned, his dear sweet auntie who asked if he and his wife were going to use his sperm to make a baby and the importance of visibility.

Romaine Talks Smack

Romaine, of DNR Show fame, joins to talk about her daughter who came out as bi at 11, choosing an anonymous donor and beating the pants off ITOCT for the People's Choice Podcast Awards. We also check in with Tiffany and Carissa on their fertility journey.

Race and Donor Choice

Tiffany and Carissa, fans of ITOCT, reached out because they wanted to hear an episode about interracial couples having babies. So naturally, we invited them on to tell their story. Then turned it into a recurring segment so we can all follow their journey to parenthood.

New Family Gone Wrong
Nee Nee set out to create a nontraditional family with her friend and his husband. It seemed like a great idea to raise a child with a good friend. But then the baby was born, legal talks broke down and now the family feels like it went through a divorce. The good news? Nee Nee's resilient, and she's a mom to a delightful little boy. Also, we introduce our new recurring segment, Tiffany and Carissa Make a Baby.

Live with Staceyann Chin
Poet, activist and powerhouse, Staceyann Chin joins to talk about how our kids are emotional abusers, the importance of telling our LGBTQ family stories, and how maybe, someday, she's going to get a wife.

Queerspawn
Makeda and Sadie talk about the pressure to present a perfect looking family when growing up with LGBTQ parents as well as their book, "Spawning Generations: Rants and Reflections on Growing Up with LGBTQ+ Parents."

The Stepmom
Beth and Jen talk about navigating the first sleepover around Jen's daughter, thinking about having a baby and that time a psychic told Jen she was going to have a baby from the desert.

Why Don't I Have a Dad
Liz's son shares the same donor as Robin's daughter. They're family, sort of. Liz joins to talk about donor families and that time her son asked why he didn't have a dad.

Filling the Hole
Julia Scotti, stand-up comic from America's Got Talent, stops by to talk about family and the moment an ex-wife helped Julia realize that she was a woman.

When Your Husband is a Fertility Doctor
Mark and Greg talk about where a fertility doctor goes to make a baby, why a surrogate is more than a vessel and their website "gayparentstobe.com" and how it helps LGBTQ families get started.

Don't be Scared of the Social Worker
Camilla Brooks talks about adopting a baby from China, when to talk to your kids about their nontraditional family and why the person performing your home study isn't judging you, mostly.

LGBTQ Love and the Lord
Aimee & Myriam were both searching for a partner and a place to worship God that felt like home, which is not easy when you are part of the LGBTQ world. The good news - they found both.

A Kid Like Leo
Dani and Mike were supportive of their 7-year-old son's choice to wear dresses and bend the rules of gender. But his seemingly progressive school was not. The result? A pair of cops on the family doorstep at one in the morning and a lawsuit against the DOE.

Doulas, Boobs, and Raising a Biracial Baby
How do you breastfeed a baby you didn't give birth to? What IS a doula? How do you ask a question that's not offensive about a family made up of different races? Michele, from For Your Birth, tackles these questions and more.

Angels (Crystal and Kelly)
Two moms take in seven foster kids in one year. But that's nothing compared to dealing with childhood cancer. This episode contains potentially sensitive content.

Making A Baby on Her Own
Author Emma Brockes hit 37 and wanted a baby, full stop. So she set on a journey to become a single mother by choice, which turned out to be almost as hard as describing her relationship with her partner, who is also a single mom by choice. They live in the same building, but on different floors, and it all works.

Burning Questions Answered
Are Robin and Jaimie naked while they answer your questions? Spoiler alert, Robin's got all her clothes on. But what about Jaimie? Listen to find out.

They Met at the Disco
Anthony and Gary weren't sure they wanted kids, until they donated sperm to a lesbian couple. But surrogacy felt out of reach until an elderly woman in their rent-controlled building left them money in her will. Did they choose the baby or an apartment renovation?

Bravo Helped Us Make a Baby
Sam and Laura talk about their time on Bravo TV's hit show "The Newlyweds" and how the network made them see a sex therapist, sex hypnotist and gave them a vagina birthday cake. Oh yeah, and how they helped to make their baby.

Needles and Babies
Daniel is a fertility expert in the field of acupuncture, but don't get him wrong, it ain't all about the needles. Listen to how acupuncture can up your rates of success with IVF by 30%.

Motherhood, Mindfulness, and Mother's Day
Patricia and Kellen share the story about that fateful red heart that brought them together, their uncertain path to parenthood and what it's like to parent from a place of mindfulness. The takeaway quote? Don't neuter the other parent!

When You Have a Hard Kid

Jaimie and Robin talk candidly about what it's like to be a parent when one child is easy and the other one is… let's just say makes life more challenging. And what if you only gave birth to one of the kids? It's a recipe for twice the guilt. Tune in for this honest and frank chat.

Could Same Sex Couples Make Babies Without Donors

Rachel Lehmann-Haupt talks to us about science that's being tested where an egg or sperm could be created from the cells of a same-sex partner. Eliminating the need for a donor. This technology could change the face of fertility for LGBT families. But how do we feel about it?

Legalese and LGBT's (Brian Esser)

Our first lawyer, Brian Esser dispels some common misconceptions about LGBT families. The biggest one? Now that we have gay marriage, we 'on't need second parent adoption. He also shares about how he and his husband adopted their two sons. This episode is chock-full-o-info!

The Surrogacy Struggle (David)

David shares his staggering journey to create a family with his partner using a gestational carrier. Strap in and guard your wallet. This episode is expensive!

C-Sections, Epidurals, and Destroyed Nipples

After years of unexplained infertility, co-host Jaimie finally got pregnant. One would think that would mean she was due an easy birth. But one would be wrong for thinking that. From birth to busted boobs. Hear how her second child made his way into the world.

When It All Goes Wrong in Delivery (Sara and Hilary)

Sara and Hilary easily get pregnant and have a smooth pregnancy. But their story takes a horrific turn when the baby is stillborn. How do they recover when the most unimaginable happens? Do they try again?

Laughing at Cancer (Lisa and Jennifer)

Set to move forward on making a baby, Lisa and Jennifer are dealt a blow when Lisa gets cancer. Then her father dies. Then she gets cancer again. Do they move forward? Does this change the fact that they want children?

Gay Man Gets Lesbian Pregnant (Tom)

Tom decides to donate sperm to his lesbian friends and moves forward before he's signed any legal documents. His confidence in how it's all going to shake out is rattled, but all's well that ends well as he's active in the children's lives today, and they even call him dad.

Baby Making Lesbian-Style (Karen and Tobi)

Tobi was everything Karen said she didn't want, yet this hilarious couple find each other then make their way straight into the world of baby making, lesbian-style. The key learning in this episode? Don't forget the genetic testing!

Viral Sensation, Zach Wahls Talks About His Two Moms and His Bid for Senate

You might remember Zach Wahls as the college student who spoke to congress about his two moms in support of gay marriage. Now he's running for Senate in Iowa, and he's got lots to say about going viral, bullying and his 2 moms.

The Lesbians Who Paved the Way (Rae and Margie)

What was it like to be pioneers in the world of lesbian fertility in the early 80s? How did they navigate birthing classes as two women? The suburbs of Connecticut? Their daughter's Brownie troop? Rae and Marie share what it was like to pave the way for the LGBTQ families of today.

Emma Has Two Moms

Emma's two moms used "Artificial Insemination" to make her back in the 80s. She talks about what it was like to be the queer family ambassador on the playground and her experiences trying to find her anonymous sperm donor.

Five Parents Two Kids the new Modern Family (Jana and Linda)

Jana & Linda are the new, modern, nontraditional family. Their family consists of two kids with five parents. And somehow it all works.

Bogota or Bust for a Baby (Robin and Mary)

Robin & Mary go to extreme lengths in an attempt to have their second child from the same donor. Including a tiny little trip to Bogota, Columbia for an insemination. But did it work?

Jaimie and Anne

Our co-host Jaimie and her wife Anne experience unexpected infertility and nearly break the bank trying to make their second kid. When Jaimie can't find anyone talking about what it is like for a lesbian with infertility issues, she asks Robin to help her create a podcast.

JAIMIE KELTON

JAIMIE KELTON is an award-winning actor, voiceover artist, producer, and podcast host based in New York City. She has over 17 years of experience performing on stages in New York City, in Regional Theaters, and on National Tours. She is a Helen Hayes Award winner recognized for excellence in professional theater and a SOVAS Award winner for her portrayal of Bo Peep on The Syfy Network's, *Happy!* Her voice can also be heard in Disney's hit cartoon, *The Octonauts* (Tweak, Pinto, Twinkle the Sea Star), Amazon's *Bug Diaries* (Scarlet Lily Beetle, Ant Leader), and *Fairy Tale Forest* (Gaby). Jaimie co-hosts the popular People's Choice award-winning podcast *If These Ovaries Could Talk*, where she chats with guests about non-traditional families making babies when making babies doesn't come naturally. She lives with her wife, two children, and a tiny dog named Roxie in Manhattan.

ROBIN HOPKINS

ROBIN HOPKINS is an award-winning actor, writer, producer, and podcast host. She began her career as a stand-up comic in New York City, performing regularly at Caroline's, Comic Strip Live, Gotham Comedy Club, and Stand-Up New York. Her acting credits include *Boardwalk Empire*, *Louie*, *Hindsight*, and *Mi America*. In the writing world, she is a frequent contributor to both *HuffPost* and *Medium*. Her television writing credits include VH1's *Big Morning Buzz Live* and *Divas*, MTV's *Teen Mom Reunion Special* and *O Music Awards*, and a pilot, *Age Against the Machine*. Robin is also an accomplished playwright. Her one-woman show *In Search of Tulla Berman* debuted to sold-out crowds in San Francisco with subsequent runs in Winnipeg, Canada, the Pelican Theatre in New York City, and the Ars Nova Theatre. Robin's play *Love, Punky* went on to have a reading at Ars Nova and a run at the Midtown International Theatre Festival. Robin is the co-host of the popular People's Choice award-winning podcast *If These Ovaries Could Talk* where she chats weekly with LGBTQ families, highlighting, normalizing, and lifting them up for all the world to see.

CONNECT WITH IF THESE OVARIES COULD TALK

Winner of best LGBTQ Podcast – **The People's Choice Podcast Awards**

"This podcast is bold, refreshing, and relevant to so many of us, as it brings this community of strong women together. They've started the podcast we never knew we needed the most."– **AfterEllen.com**

"If ever there were two lesbians you'd want to hang out with, it's definitely Jaimie Kelton and Robin Hopkins." – **Gay Parent Magazine**

"Unique, and quirky, and eclectic, and ultimately so fun. The epitome of these hyper-niche podcasts, and a quality podcast to boot..." – **Discover Pods**

"While queer parenting remains relatively common in real life, nontraditional families' stories are rare in pop culture. Thankfully, now LGBTQ families can turn to a new podcast called *If These Ovaries Could Talk.*" – **The Daily Dot**

"*If These Ovaries Could Talk*, a fun and informative new podcast by two lesbian moms, shares stories of baby making and other aspects of raising and caring for our families. Meet them and have a listen!" – **Mombian**

"Typically when I think of fertility issues, I think of them in hetero terms, so this podcast is a refreshing switch up. In it, two lesbian hosts, Robin Hopkins and Jaimie Kelton, talk about the challenges and experiences of gay families having babies and invite guests to discuss their non-traditional families." – **Brooklyn Based**

IF THESE OVARIES COULD TALK PODCAST with hosts Jaimie Kelton and Robin Hopkins is available on all podcasting platforms.

WEB: ovariestalk.com

INSTAGRAM: @ovaries_talk

TWITTER: @ovariestalk

FACEBOOK: facebook.com/iftheseovariescouldtalk

PATREON: patreon.com/ovariestalk